IN SAVAGE ISLES

AND SETTLED LANDS

MALAYSIA, AUSTRALASIA, AND POLYNESIA
1888—1891

BY

B. F. S. BADEN-POWELL

LIEUT. SCOTS GUARDS,

F.R.G.S., ETC.

*WITH NUMEROUS ILLUSTRATIONS FROM
SKETCHES BY THE AUTHOR*

LONDON
RICHARD BENTLEY AND SON
Publishers in Ordinary to Her Majesty the Queen
1892

NEW GUINEA NATIVES.

Frontispiece.

PREFACE

———◦◦———

THIS book contains merely a short account of my impressions during a journey of some 50,000 miles, and extending over three years.

A full account of all the countries visited would fill several volumes, and would form a work of a very different nature to the jottings contained herein, limited as far as possible to my own personal doings and observations.

There is much, very much, both interesting and amusing that occurred during my sojourn in Queensland as A.D.C. to the Governor. But as such experiences would hardly be in keeping with a book of travel, I have not included more than the briefest descriptions of Australian life and society.

My best thanks are due to the Rajah of Sarawak, and many others who have kindly looked through the manuscript.

B. B.-P.

Guards' Club, S.W.

CONTENTS

CHAPTER   PAGE

   I. THROUGH THE OLD WORLD -   •   •   •   1

  II. CEYLON AND INDIA -   •   •   •   •   32

 III. SOUTHERN COLONIES OF AUSTRALIA -   •   •   51

  IV. QUEENSLAND -   •   •   •   •   •   85

   V. PAPUA AND ITS PEOPLE   •   •   •   129

  VI. NEW GUINÉA WARFARE   •   •   •   175

 VII. MALAYSIA -   •   •   •   •   210

VIII. BORNEO   •   •   •   •   •   243

  IX. NEW ZEALAND   •   •   •   •   287

   X. THE TONGA OR FRIENDLY ISLES   •   •   314

  XI. THE NAVIGATORS   •   •   •   ·   345

 XII. THE SANDWICH ISLANDS   •   •   ·   378

XIII. HOME THROUGH THE STATES   •   ·   392

     MILEAGE OF THE JOURNEY -   •   ·   431

     INDEX   •   •   •   •   433

LIST OF ILLUSTRATIONS

	PAGE
A NEW GUINEA LAKATOI - - - -	*Cover*
NEW GUINEA NATIVES - - - -	*Frontispiece*
MAP OF THE WORLD, SHOWING ROUTE FOLLOWED BY THE	
AUTHOR - - - - - *To face page*	1
ADEN BY SUNRISE - - - - - -	30
A NATURAL MADONNA - - - - -	72
PLAN OF SHEARING SHED - - - - -	75
BOTTLE-TREE AND GRASS-TREES - - - -	96
MAP OF EASTERN AUSTRALIA AND NEW GUINEA *To face page*	97
SECTION OF SUGAR-MILL - - - - -	104
A QUEENSLAND BLACK - - - -	116
WOOMERA AND BOOMERANGS - - - -	119
THE BARRON FALLS - - - *To face page*	124
A CUSCUS - - - - - - -	139
VIEW FROM SAMARAI - - - *To face page*	140
MAP OF THE EAST END OF NEW GUINEA - - -	151
CATAMARAN - - - - - - -	153
A NATIVE DRILL - - - - - -	160
THE LAST CHARGE AT HUHUNA - - *To face page*	177
SPEAR-HEADS - - - - - -	188
GREAT BLACK COCKATOO - - - - -	194
A MAN-CATCHER - - - - - -	200
NEW GUINEA TREE-HOUSE - - - *To face page*	201
MOTUMOTU DANCE - - - - - -	205
JAVANESE CARRIER - - - - - -	213

	PAGE
JAVANESE BRIDGES -	227
CHINESE AT DINNER	234
TRAVELLER'S TREE -	237
RAJAH BROOKE'S HOUSE	251
DYAK DANCERS	255
MAP OF NORTH-WEST SARAWAK	256
DYAK SUSPENSION BRIDGE -	262
PROBOSCIS MONKEY	276
MONKEY'S SKULL	278
'MIAS' AT HOME	To face page 279
SANTUBONG -	To face page 282
NEW ZEALAND FLAX	293
GEYSER	3c9
MAP OF TONGA	315
A TONGAN ISLAND -	317
TONGAN NATIVES	318
WOODEN GONG	340
KING GEORGE OF TONGA	342
APIA	346
CONSTRUCTION OF SAMOAN BOAT	347
SAMOAN CLUB	348
THE KING'S GUARDS	355
THE CEREMONY OF KING'S CAVA	To face page 358
AN APPRECIATIVE AUDIENCE	365
LADIES ON HORSEBACK	383
HILL IN OAHU	386
THE LICK OBSERVATORY	408
THE CASTLE GATE -	416
SNOW-SCREENS	418

IN SAVAGE ISLES AND SETTLED LANDS

CHAPTER I.

THROUGH THE OLD WORLD.

THE time for departure has arrived! Feelings of excitement creep over one in spite of one's self. Sensations of pleasure and sorrow rise together. Pleasure at the prospect of all the many agreeable experiences one is likely to undergo during a journey which may last some years, and sorrow at the farewells to one's relations and friends, people with whom one has lived and associated all one's life, and people whom perhaps one may never hope to see again!

Then there's the baggage, and that inevitable apprehension that one has forgotten to pack something of importance, and that brings thoughts of letters unwritten, and directions which should have been left with reference to various belongings and affairs.

However, it is soon over. 'Good-byes' are said; final directions regarding health and the wearing of flannel, etc., are received as they should be by a dutiful son, and one is rattled off in a hansom to the station.   Here one is jostled about among the excited crowd of travellers and their leave-takers, bundled into a carriage, and finally the train moves out of the station and the journey is fairly commenced.   With a sigh of relief, and a reckless, devil-may-care feeling about the 'things left undone,' one settles one's self down to reflect.

Thus I found myself on the evening of February 3, 1888, starting on a journey to Australia *viâ* Constantinople and Suez, and in due time I was safely on board the night-boat for Rotterdam.

Waking early next morning, a peculiar bubbling and scraping noise was going on.   As I sat up in my bunk I began to come to the conclusion that we must be slowly but surely sinking!   I therefore thought it well to arise and dress myself, and on going on deck was surprised to see that the steamer was ploughing her way through fields of broken ice. But she stuck to it manfully till we got to Rotterdam, where, however, the passengers had to be landed at a point some way down the river.

I always liked Holland and the Dutch people; at least, I like the latter, and they make the best of a bad bargain with the former.   The cleanliness and the thrift of these peasants is wonderful to behold, their marvellous economy in utilizing every inch of ground for cultivation, and their delightfully quaint customs and tastes.   How absolutely antithetical

is this half-submerged country with its dense population of old-fashioned folk to the vast wastes and the
shrewd colonists of the Australias which I was about
to visit! But we must be getting on, so, bidding
adieu to the picturesque old red-brick houses, the
canals and their barges, the women and young girls
all wearing the same peculiar costume, and the dear
dogs so cheerfully drawing their little carts, we flit
onwards on our journey.

Then we get to Cologne, that Regent Circus of
the Continent, and without stopping to look at the
tourist-worn cathedral, or to invest in the genuine
water of the place, we continue the tour up the
banks of the Rhine.

It is needless to describe the well-known river, with
its headlands and castles and vineyards, nor shall I
stop to discuss any of the towns we pass through,
one of which, Darmstadt, with its savouring of
second-class royalty, was very well known to me
some years ago. Curious Old Nürnberg is passed ;
one is pulled about by Custom-house officials at
the frontier of Austria, and in a few hours more we
are landed in Vienna.

Speaking roughly, in the centre of Vienna is the
old cathedral of St. Stephen, with its high tiled roof,
and its spire 450 feet high. Round about the
cathedral lies the old town, with its narrow crooked
streets and interesting shops. This is encircled
by the 'Ring' on three sides, and the river on the
fourth. The Ring, which occupies the site of old

fortifications, is, I think, the finest street I know, with its wide boulevards and numerous handsome buildings situated around it. Outside this extends the large new town.

Vienna, like most inland places in these climes, can be very hot in summer and very cold in winter. But as in St. Petersburg you see men going about in the thickest overcoats on a hot summer's day, so here in Vienna in the depth of winter, with snow actually falling, you see men going without coats, women even without hats. Yet it is intensely cold, the streets are covered with frozen snow ; and gaily-caparisoned, bell-bedecked horses dash along drawing their noiseless sledges.

In the old town are some good curiosity shops, and old watches are a great speciality. General Keith Fraser showed me one he got here, which on pressing a knob emitted the patriotic strains of ' Rule, Britannia!'

I went one night to a ball at the British Embassy, where Sir Augustus and Lady Paget were dispensing hospitality to the élite of the place. The society of Vienna is said to be more exclusive than that of any other place in the world. No parvenu can hope to enter the charmed upper circles, and strangers are looked upon with suspicion unless specially introduced. I felt lucky in thus getting an opportunity of a peep at the highest of the high. With gorgeous uniforms (though not so handsome as they were formerly) and orders, from the Golden Fleece down-

wards, old generals who served, and suffered too, in
the war of 1866, as well as young princelings in
their teens, vied in the dance. The Crown Prince
Rudolph, who shortly afterwards met with his tragic
death, was there. So was Count Kalnoky and many
other well-known characters.

Different people have different modes of living,
but to the untravelled habitué of a London ball-
room (or rather supper-room) it might appear strange
to find no champagne at such a ball ; and to see the
dowagers and débutantes, the royalties and nobles,
all eagerly imbibing the foaming beer, is enough
indeed to make him raise his eyeglass.

There is something more than mere chance in the
way in which one often comes across friends. At
this ball I happened to meet the only Austrian I
ever knew, and as I had only seen him in London,
and did not even know he was in Vienna, I little
expected to meet him within a few days of my
arriving in his country.

I went down one morning to the old palace to
see what was to me an interesting ceremony—the
changing of the guard. Although performed with
great pomp, it is hardly so imposing a spectacle as
we exhibit every day at St. James's. The Austrian
uniforms of plain dark blue and soft caps, however
serviceable, do not add much lustre to such a
manœuvre.

The troops, when at home in their splendid
barracks, were busily employed digging shelter

trenches in the snow; capital practice when drill is out of the question, and plenty of ground available for the purpose without disturbing the gravel of the barrack square.

War prophets are usually wrong, and General Keith Fraser, at that time our military attaché in Vienna, was telling me how all the best authorities then declared that war with Russia was absolutely inevitable, and so soon as the snow cleared away operations would commence. The snow has long since disappeared, so has the idea of a Russo-Austrian war; but, like the snow, it will doubtless return in its due season.

I then went on to Buda Pesth. This town, or rather Pesth, is a well-built city, with handsome edifices and embankments on the Danube. It is low and flat, but Buda, on the opposite side of the river, lies on a high ridge. The latter is picturesquely situated, with its citadel, palace, and cathedral rising in the centre. The two towns are connected by a magnificent suspension bridge, built by an English engineer.

One soon realizes that one is in Hungary. The peasants, in their embroidered jackets with silver buttons, are speaking an unknown jargon, quite unlike any other European language; and as you go along the streets, that excellent, well-timed music, now well known to Londoners, resounds from every café or hotel, where the swarthy performers are content with a few kreutzers dropped in the plate.

We leave again to rattle off by the comfortable, well-warmed Constantinople express, and dash through Hungary. The country is now all covered with snow, but I have been here under an almost tropical sun, to wander among the vineyards and maize-fields, and see the rows of æsthetic-looking sunflowers grown for their oil.

Night comes on, and we pass the town of Temesvar, brilliantly illuminated by electricity, at that time the only town in Europe so lit.

As we get more into the mountainous parts the cold increases; the frost formed on the *inside* of the window falls off like powder, and remains as such on the cushions without melting.

Once again we are alongside the 'blue' Danube, and enter Roumania, passing the picturesque Iron Gate near Orsova, and undergoing the usual frontier examination by soldier-like officials. One feels that one is beginning to get beyond the pale of what we consider civilization, when a big man enters the carriage enveloped in an elaborately-worked sheep-skin coat and tall fur hat. But he would have been a more interesting companion had he not snored like a Carpathian bear.

At last Bucharest is reached, and an unusual spectacle meets the eye on emerging from the station. Numbers of small two-horsed sledges with jangling bells dashing wildly about are the only vehicles, and in such a conveyance one takes one's seat. It is as good as a ride on a switchback to be driven along the narrow streets at a furious pace, whisking round corners, zigzagging in and out of the other rapid-going traffic, suddenly pulling up to avoid dashing into some other equipage, and then charging forward again with a yell from the driver and an ear-breaking crack of the whip. Sometimes two or three other sledges abreast are met coming along full tilt. A sudden and disastrous collision seems inevitable. Then all shriek out wildly, your driver pulls over sharp to one side, the sledge scoots along broadside on, and the others fly past within an inch of one. But the roads, instead of being, as might be supposed, of hard, frozen ice (as the country roads are), are deep masses of dirty powdered snow. It is a marvel how the horses get through it without stumbling.

Bucharest is not an imposing town. It is nothing more than an amalgamation of villages, consisting chiefly of small houses, mostly detached, with a very countrified air about them, and narrow, crooked lanes running in and out amongst the houses. Yet this is said to cover as great an area of ground as Paris!

The sightworthy objects are few and far between. The royal palace is nothing very out-of-the-way from an architectural point of view. The museum is, or was, new, and contained but few curiosities, except some stones found in Roumania with Latin inscriptions. And, by the way, the Roumanians look upon themselves as the modern representatives and descendants of the ancient Romans. On the bank-notes is a watered head of Cæsar, and the language is very near akin to Latin.

Sir F. Lascelles, our Minister, seemed quite contented with his lot, though owning that what is to be seen in this capital is 'absolutely nothing.' I had a letter of introduction to a native of the place, and he showed me all he could, but frankly said : 'I am ashamed of my town.' I was on the whole not very sorry to leave what I have heard described as 'the gayest town in Europe' after twenty-four hours, and to be sped along in a comfortable Pullman train in an hour and a half to the banks of the Danube at Giurgevo.

There is often much delay here in crossing the big river. In summer-time steamboats quickly convey people across, but when the ice begins floating down and accumulating in large packs boat traffic must cease, and the voyager must either 'wait till the ice floats by,' or till the river becomes compactly frozen over. The latter state was completely established when I was there, and all the passengers transferred themselves from the most civilized railway-train into the most primitive little sledges, two in each, with a couple of shaggy ponies and ferocious-looking, big-bearded drivers.

The cold was intense, and not only all the trees about, but everything, from the rug of the 'carriage' and the manes of the horses to the beard and eyelashes of the coachman, was thickly decked with white hoar-frost. An icy mist hung over all, so that no extensive view was to be had.

The sledges started off one by one in procession along the road, and after a couple of miles drove down on to the frozen Danube. Surrounded by mist, one could see nothing but the ice around—in parts smooth as glass, in others rough and snow-covered, with an occasional glimpse of other sledges in front.

Following the not well-defined track, we passed several low swampy islands, and some large frozen-in vessels, and it was often difficult to say whether we were on snow-covered ice or land. The tracks on the low-lying banks of the islands had become worn into curious undulations, in such a way that when driving along one could easily imagine, especially with the eyes shut, that one was in a boat in a seaway.

After about a quarter of an hour we got across the river, and arrived at the railway-station of Rustchuk. Numerous earthworks, more or less destroyed, reminded one of the importance this place had been during the Russo-Turkish War in 1877, but the town itself appeared uninteresting, all thickly enveloped in hard snow. We were now in Bulgaria, with its rough, innocent-looking, semi-Turkish, semi-Russian peasants. Russian is the universal language here, which seems curious, considering how small is the connection of this country with Russia.

The railway journey through Bulgaria is not very

interesting—at all events, for the first part of the
route, where wide, open, undulating country is
passed, with occasionally numbers of oak-trees still
covered with brown dead leaves, which are said not
to fall off till the spring. Little picturesque villages
are seen nestling in the valleys, and distant glimpses
of the Balkans gained.

This railway had lately been, and not for the first
time, entirely snowed up for some weeks. These
snow-drifts do not occur in the large defiles, but in
places where there are long cuttings not more than
six to ten feet deep. These had become entirely full
of snow, which had been dug out with immense
labour, and now was to be seen piled up at the
sides. Near Shumla the character of the country
becomes more mountainous, and the snow is less.
Very peculiar-looking hills rise on all sides, sloping
up to near the tops, but crowned with an abrupt cliff
of bright ruddy-yellow rock, looking like castle walls.
Then we gradually get through the mountains, and
pass through miles of swamp, the railway almost
level with the water, and reeds growing up all
around, in some places so high as to cut out all
view from the carriage windows. Passing along the
edges of large lakes, the train starts up thousands
of wild-fowl, which fly around till the air is quite
darkened by them, and on we go, mile after mile,
with more and more duck rising from the water. I
expect a sportsman might find many a worse hunting-
ground than the neighbourhood of Gubedjie, and I

longed to get out and stop there for a time. After
skirting another large lake, which has the appearance of an arm of the sea, but is really cut off from it
by a low bank of land, we arrive at Varna, that port
on the Black Sea so well known to our army in
1854. It is situated on the north side of the bay,
on some small hills rising from the water's edge, but
does not look an inviting town, being merely a
collection of small houses with a few mosques.
The cemetery, with its numerous graves of English
soldiers, is the chief object of interest.

A boat takes us off to the steamer, which lies at
anchor some way from the shore, and the journey
on the Black Sea is commenced. It is curious to
find that all the stewards on board are Italian, just
as in the sleeping-car train all the attendants were
French. Starting in the evening, the steamer is
well in the Bosphorus by next morning, and the
passengers all crowd on deck to see the succession
of grand scenes.

The Bosphorus is like a huge river running (and
with a powerful stream) between high hills abruptly
rising out of the water on both sides. Numbers of
birds of all sorts fly about, but especially noticeable
are the flocks of a certain small petrel, which continually fly rapidly along close above the water, in
a hurried, impatient way, which gave rise to the
idea of their being the 'souls of the departed.'

Numerous fishing boats are dotted about ; and on
shore many fine-looking houses rise one above

another, becoming more plentiful as Constantinople
is approached.

Descriptions have often been written of the grand
sight presented by Constantinople and the Golden
Horn when viewed from the Bosphorus. I am not
quite sure that I was not just a little disappointed.
One generally *is* so when one expects a grand sight.
But to see the numerous white mosques with domes
and minarets, and masses of houses interspersed
with dark cypress-trees, rising in a gentle slope from
the water's edge, cannot fail to please the eye.

Around the entrance to the Golden Horn is a
mass of shipping of all sorts, from large steamers to
the native ' caïques.'

On landing at Galata one has to go through a
most amusing Custom-house examination ; at least,
it amused me, being in no particular hurry and a
happy state of mind, though doubtless very vexing
to anyone pressed for time or out of sorts. Large
packages are easily passed over by the officials, but
it is the small articles that arouse their curiosity.
A box of lozenges with sealed paper cover was an
object of great suspicion, and had to be torn open.
My small camera could not be passed merely on
my word that it was a photographic apparatus only.
Of course, to open it meant spoiling all my best
photographs of the Bosphorus, but the gentleman
insisted on seeing the interior. A happy thought
struck me. Instead of turning the knob and
straightway opening the back, I asked to be supplied

with a screw-driver, in order, as I explained, to take out all the small screws round the edge, and so open the apparatus. But after some hesitation he came to the conclusion that *that* would take too long ; so it was passed forthwith. Then, one would have thought that these officials must be well acquainted with the British tourist, and, as a consequence, with a Bradshaw's Guide. Yet, to my surprise, they eagerly annexed this great work and passed it in to be examined by a literary expert, after which it was duly returned to me.

One has often read of the different parts of Constantinople, but it is difficult for a stranger to get a clear idea of it. Pera contains the hotels and European quarter ; Galata is the shipping part ; while Stamboul is the purely Turkish town, and Scutari a pleasant suburb.

In Pera there are one or two tolerable though narrow streets, but Stamboul is chiefly a mass of irregular, crooked, dirty, badly paved, and often steep lanes.

The mosque of St. Sophia is, of course, one of the first sights to see. Outside it is merely a vast pile of domes of various sizes, with minarets rising from among them. But the inside is truly stupendous, the immense dome rising up 200 feet above the floor. All around are great columns of various stones, flags, ostrich eggs, and lamps hanging from long chains, prayer-carpets spread over the floor, and many large Arabic devices.

Close by is the lofty marble gate of the old palace, which is hence called the Sublime Porte.

Other mosques abound through the city, many of great interest, some being nearly as large as St. Sophia. There are as many mosques in Constantinople as there are days in the year.

At certain hours of the day ' muezzins ' will appear at the little galleries high up on the slender minarets, and, in a loud singing voice, call the faithful to prayer.

Then there are numerous other sights. The tombs of the Sultans; the museum of the Janissaries, a kind of local Madame Tussaud's; the cemeteries, with their curious turbaned and be-fezzed tombstones—all have to be visited. Rides must be taken round the huge old city walls, with their massive gate-towers, and money has to be spent in the Oriental bazaars.

The far-famed dogs of Constantinople, to be seen by the dozen in every street, and who won't get out of your way, are fat, sleepy animals with thick reddish hair, very unlike the half-starved mangy curs who slink away from you in Cairo and other Eastern places.

I felt that it was but my duty whilst here to have a real Turkish bath. However, I was much disappointed, for, although I went to what was recommended as the best, I thought it was not half so comfortable, not half so *Oriental*, as those I had been to in England. The place was like a succession of lofty

cellars, with numerous creeping things on the walls,
and here one was pulled about by some cheeky boys ;
even the sitting out afterwards, to drink Turkish
coffee and vainly suck away at the hubble-bubble,
was by no means my idea of Oriental luxuriousness.

The British Embassy is a fine palatial building,
pleasantly situated on the rising ground of Pera.
Sir W. White (also gone, alas !) entertained us to a
curiously international luncheon, where the general
conversation was carried on alternately in English,
French, and German.

There is a very good club for—I was going to
say *Europeans*, but should say for *foreigners;* in
fact, I believe there are two, though I only went
to the Cercle d'Orient.

Plenty of gaiety seems to go on. We went to
an amusing bal masqué in the Théâtre Française,
which might have been in Paris or anywhere. At
night the ladies are mostly conveyed in sedan chairs
—not a bad idea for getting about the narrow, dirty
streets.

On leaving Constantinople the steamer at once
enters the Sea of Marmora, and after some ten hours'
steam gets into the Dardanelles. This channel is
not so picturesque as the Bosphorus, the shores
being for the most part low open downs. Among
the distant hills to the south is pointed out the site
of Troy, conjuring up visions quite out of keeping
with the surroundings. After some hours the town
of Dardanelles, on the Asiatic side, is reached. It

is situated just at the narrowest part of the straits, less than a mile wide, known as the Hellespont, where Xerxes, and later Alexander, crossed their armies by a bridge of boats.

On either side numerous forts are to be seen, both ancient and modern, the latter being well armed with heavy guns.

We soon get out into the Ægean Sea, and passing Besika Bay and numerous islands, arrive at Mitylene. The town is very picturesque. A fine old castle crowns a small hill on the peninsula which forms the harbour, and splendid wooded hills rise abruptly all round, with houses dotted about them.

As the shades of evening fall the steamer gets under way, and by early next morning arrives at Smyrna.

The Bay of Smyrna is certainly grandly picturesque—a large sheet of water surrounded by great rugged mountains towering up into the storm-clouds. The town is situated on a flat piece of land almost level with the water, but immediately behind it rises a hill, Mount Pagus, surmounted by the ruins of an old castle, the view from which, of the bay in front and the plains of Magnesia stretching out behind, well repays a visit—as a guide-book would say. The quays form fine wide esplanades, but the back-streets are narrow and dirty and thoroughly Eastern, though the houses generally have an Italian look, being painted yellow or pink, with green Venetian

2

shutters and tiled roofs. The population is very mixed—Jews, Armenians, Turks, and Greeks lounging about with Englishmen and Frenchmen. The bazaars are most tempting, being full of quaint curios and antiquities. Luckily, Smyrna is not yet infested with sightseers, and so one goes about rather as an object of curiosity. I had no less than three self-appointed guides in my retinue, each one trying his best to explain everything. I made a great bargain with one 'vendor of curios,' after which one of my guides did me the compliment to say, 'You are yet young! but you have your eyes open!'

Again boarding the steamer, we then make for Greece, and land at the Piræus, the port of Athens. It is a small town situated on the bay, with several fortifications on the hills around. In twenty minutes the train runs up to Athens over a flat open plain.

The country has a very tropical look, considering that it is in Europe, almost the only large plants being cacti and aloes. The general appearance of Athens is well known—the modern town lying in the valley, with the Acropolis rising grandly on one side and Mount Lycabettus on the other, and the many fine ruined temples around.

The tour has to be made of the temple of Theseus, with its fairly perfect though discoloured marble columns; the theatre of Dionysius, with its marble seats of the pattern so well known in Alma Tadema's pictures, with the name, or rather title, of the would-be occupant clearly carved on each; the ugly arch of Hadrian; and the imposing though few remains of the temple of Jupiter Olympus.

But first the Acropolis must be visited. The Propylæa, with its grand portico and flight of steps, all of white marble, is penetrated, remains of temples and numerous columns passed by, and the open space on top, covered with the débris of fine buildings, reached; and now the Parthenon stands boldly before us against the sky, wrecked and dilapidated, not so much by time as by an explosion in comparatively modern times, when the Turks used the place as a fort. Portions of the frieze have come to England as the Elgin marbles, and masses of material removed as 'relics.' Close by is the Erechtheum, a smaller temple, with its caryatides.

But the whole place is in a more ruined state than I expected. I quite agree with the American who, when asked his opinion of the Acropolis, replied: 'Very fine, but it's a pity it's so out of repair.' None of the ruins of Athens are so grand and imposing as those of ancient Egypt.

The modern town presents no great peculiarities, though the dresses of the King's Guards, with their starched kilts or petticoats and short jackets, have a very comical yet fascinating appearance.

The Ægean Sea, thickly studded with islands, would hardly be the place where one would expect to encounter a heavy sea. But it is surprising how suddenly a very nasty sea *can* rise and make the steamer look very silly. We had a bad time of it till we passed Cape Sidaro, in Crete, but then got into the glorious sunshine of Africa.

* * * * *

On first arriving at Alexandria from Europe, one is always struck by the heat, the glare, and the tropical appearance of the place, and one marvels at the energy displayed by the natives as they shout and struggle with one another in their anxiety to assist in some way or other the fresh - arriving traveller; great is the contrast between them and the sleepy Turks! The brilliant sun shows up the white buildings against the deep-blue sky, contrasting with the dark-foliaged trees and trimmed date-palms; while away to either side stretch the yellow sand - hills, with their windmills and dilapidated forts.

Parts of Alexandria are, of course, thoroughly characteristic of the East, though the streets are generally wide and straight. The houses are mostly square and flat-roofed, with plastered, and often windowless walls, decorated with blue or yellow distemper. The crowded streets are thronged with representatives of all nationalities; sailors from various parts of the world sit outside the many Greek or Italian wineshops; while the Egyptian donkey, with his boy and fat pommelled saddle, is ever ready to convey you where you will.

The European quarter, round about the Place

Mahomet Ali, is rising phœnix-like from the ruins caused in 1882. Here are many fine houses, several good hotels, and two clubs.

What seems remarkable is not the remains, but the absence of remains, of the old city, once so prosperous, which stood upon this site. Pompey's pillar and a few walls and other half-buried ruins are practically all that is to be seen of that ancient metropolis, said to have contained over half a million inhabitants, and to have been one of the most magnificent cities of antiquity.

From Alexandria to Cairo (130 miles) the train passes through the prolific Delta of the Nile, that extraordinary country made and rendered fertile by the alluvial deposits brought from afar by the great river.

Here may be seen plantations of cotton and sugar, fields of dourrah and maize, groves of date-palms and bananas, and other cultivation. Ancient remains without number have been discovered in almost all parts of the Delta.

Out of England, I don't know any place more interesting, or offering more variety, than Cairo and its neighbourhood. Nearly everything in the way of the comforts of civilization can be got, while one is surrounded by all the curiosities of Orientalism.

One can go to the European theatre, or see howling dervishes; one can do one's shopping in well-supplied shops, or go and bargain in the picturesque bazaars; good quail or snipe shooting is to be got, or one can shoot pelicans, flamingoes, and other odd birds ; one can play polo, or ride on a camel. As regards antiquities, they are innumerable. Mahommedan mosques and tombs or extensive Roman remains may be compared with the obelisks, tombs, and pyramids of the ancient Egyptians. Then society of all kinds, with its festivities, visits to recent British battle-fields, trips on the Nile, visits to the ostrich-farm, and to the Boulac Museum, all help to fill the time, to say nothing of cricket and tennis, drives on the Gezireh, or losing money at the roulette-tables. Such is Cairo, now becoming almost an English watering-place.

The Egyptian police are very ready with their sticks, and it is a most ludicrous sight to see some man in a crowd dragged out by the police to an open spot, thrown down so as to lie on his front, and whilst one 'bobby' holds him, well belaboured by another with the stick, the man, of course, shrieking like a drunken Irishwoman ; but once the chastisement ceases, he is almost as eager as ever to join the jabbering crowd in their attempts to extort 'backsheesh' (for such seems to be the ultimate object of most crowds in Egypt), or whatever may be their aim.

But the police are very attentive to their duty. I once discovered a donkey with a very bad sore back. I called the attention of the police to it. The donkey-boy was promptly 'run in '; and when I appeared

at the police-station to give evidence, he was brought
before me heavily manacled in chains, and I was
asked by the superintendent what I would like to
award the culprit. 'Courbash' (flogging with a
leather thong) they said was forbidden, so I signed
my name to a document in Arabic condemning the
unhappy wretch to durance vile until the following
day.

The Pyramids, so grandly imposing to look upon,
and so mysterious in their origin, are undoubtedly
among the most wonderful objects to be seen. The
ascent of the Great Pyramid is easy enough to anyone of sound physique and possessing a good 'head,'
though I saw a young and gallant officer get so
giddy at the summit that he had to be bodily carried
down by the Arabs. It is very safe to bet a man
that he will not mount to the top without the aid of
natives. Not that it is so difficult for him to accomplish by himself, but, try as he may, he will always
be quickly followed by half a dozen agile Arabs, who
will surely overtake him, and insist, despite all
remonstrances, on helping him up.

Not many would care to visit more than once the
interior of the Pyramid, with its stifling atmosphere
and smell of bats. I should require a considerable
recompense before I followed the example of an
uncle of mine (Piazzi Smyth), and took up my
quarters there.

Most people consider the Sphinx disappointing.
Many representations of it—as, for instance, on the

Egyptian stamps—make it appear almost as large as the great Pyramids; but although it is a truly enormous head, it looks very insignificant beside these other colossal erections.

Round about the Pyramids, which are of all sizes, are innumerable ancient tombs with paintings on their walls as fresh as if done yesterday.

The Serapeum at Sakkara is another wonderful sight, with its huge sarcophagi beautifully cut out of single blocks of hard stone.

At Heliopolis, whence originally came 'Cleopatra's needle,' except for one obelisk, there is nothing of great interest, though further afield many more marvels are visitable.

Dogs, wretched, barking, half-starved curs, hang about everywhere, but especially in the suburbs. Cowardly enough in the day time when you come across one, they are comparatively bold when prowling around in large packs at night. I had an exciting adventure one evening when returning home alone by moonlight. I had to cross a wide, open sandy tract, and when near the middle of it I heard, and presently perceived, a large troop of yelping curs coming straight towards me. I felt somewhat apprehensive, not having even a stick with which to defend myself. Nearer and nearer they came, as if to surround me. I quickened my pace, but that only encouraged them. I stopped and made insulting remarks, but the only result was that they barked the more in defiance. They closed in, and I

imagined myself shortly being rent in pieces, and
bits of tattered clothes being all that could be found
of me next morning! All around was nothing but
sand, without even a blade of grass to be of any
avail. I was just about to surrender myself to their
jaws, when I thought I saw a stone, and determined
to do what little revengeful damage I could by fling-
ing it into the thick of them. I stepped forward
and stooped to pick it up. It was only a dead leaf!
But, to my utter astonishment, as if delivered by a
miracle, I saw that all the dogs immediately turned
and fled in all directions, with their tails between
their legs! I pursued my way, and when, after a
bit, they rallied and returned to the charge, I quietly
stooped down and hurled a pinch of sand at my
persecutors with most telling effect. They had
evidently stood (!) fire before this.

Visitors in Egypt are tormented with flies and
also with children, both of them being more per-
sistent here than elsewhere. The flies are ill-
mannered, and the children are ever begging for
'backsheesh.' None of the awe-inspiring temples
can be visited without one's running the gauntlet of
a crowd of boys selling scarabees and curios. I am
told that most of these (the curios, not the boys)
are of Birmingham manufacture; but I doubt it. I
hope better work would be turned out there. Very
often, however, genuine articles are got among the
worthless imitations.

Having visited all the sights about Cairo, and

wearying of Shepheard's veranda, and of the itinerant conjurer or snake-charmer; of the tinkle of the drink-seller's brass cups, and of the trilling shriek of the ubiquitous kites; and having seen enough of the gaudy syces running before the carriages of the officials, and of the heavily-laden, slow-progressing camels bearing their goods to market, we may start on an expedition up the Nile.

The railway will take us as far as Assiut, passing between the river and the canals; and after a short stay to inspect the cave-tombs in the neighbouring hills, we may continue the journey by boat. The Nile scenery becomes slightly monotonous as we pass mile after mile of steep mud-banks, with ' shadoofs ' (buckets suspended from the end of a pivoted pole) being worked by a couple of men at regular intervals; above this, green cultivation, with occasional date-palms; and distant rocky mountains of a peculiar pinkish colour in the background. Then we pass numerous villages and towns, with their many pigeon-towers and thousands of pigeons kept to fertilize the ground. Many other birds are seen too—pelicans flying over at great height in long strings, sacred ibis feeding in the fields, and vultures of several varieties. Then we see rafts formed entirely of pottery being floated down stream, and natives swimming the river on bunches of reeds.

The first old Egyptian temple we get to is at

Denderah, near Keneh, where we are duly impressed with the enormous columns and the fresh appearance of the carvings which cover every available part of the walls.   But on getting to Luxor we find still larger and more imposing columns, though the buildings are less complete. We then visit Medinet Aboo, the Colossi, and the site of Thebes, with its interestings tombs.   Esneh, Edfu, and other temples are passed, and so we arrive at Assouan and the first cataract, where the Nile dashes through innumerable small channels among rocks and boulders.

At the other end of this cataract is the beautiful island and temple of Philæ, after which the river narrows and the banks become rocky.   Still further up the Nile, beyond Korosko, is the huge cave-temple of Aboo Simbul.

But I am drifting away into a sort of dreamland, for my experiences of the Upper Nile occurred when I was in the Camel Corps, and years before the journey I am properly describing.   However, these dreams rise before me and drift onward.   I see visions of sandy plains bordering the river, brilliant orange on the left bank, and muddy gray on the right.*   I see curiously-shaped rocky hills rising in the purple distance, fringes of date-palms

---

* An ingenious theory has been suggested that this extraordinary river, running on its course through thousands of years, has been affected by the rotation of the earth, and moved westwards inch by inch.

along the river-banks, with the low mud-walls of native houses. Korosko, Derr, and Wady Halfa, not much more than so many collections of huts, are passed, and the second cataract is surmounted. We get up to the region where nuggers—large, clumsily though strongly built boats, with oblong-shaped sails—take the place of the lateen-rigged dahabiyehs. Creeking 'sakiyehs,' turned by oxen, supersede the shadoofs for irrigation. The people are darker, and become intermixed with the true coal-black negroes. Fuzzy-haired desert tribesmen, with their camels, are met, though we see but little sign of life in the desert; a very occasional gazelle, but more often a number of sand-grouse coming down to the river for a drink in the evening. At certain seasons the ever-changeful chameleon is to be seen in every tree; while crocodiles lie basking on the mud-banks, though I expect that our expeditions up the Nile have done much to drive them away. Nothing worthy of the name of a town is reached until we get to Dongola. But it is no good going further—we must awake again—for changes rapidly take place in these roughly-built towns, and by now, doubtless, there is much alteration in this land, which is, to all intents and purposes, at present quite a *terra incognita.* So let us return to Cairo.

In going by rail from Cairo to Ismailia or Suez, one passes through the battle-field of Tel-el-Kebir, though there is not much to be seen except the half-

demolished parapets and ditches extending across
the open desert.

Suez is much like any other Egyptian town—
mud-walls, lattice windows, mosques, and donkeys.
There are bazaars, of course, but little of special interest to anyone who knows Egypt.

On leaving Suez by steamer to proceed down
the Red Sea, a beautiful sight is presented by the
rocky hills in the distance standing up against the
clear blue sky, of a peculiar and fantastic-looking
pinkish colour, veiled by an apparent mist, although
the country is the dryest of the dry.

But even these are soon left behind, and, with the
exception perhaps of a few islets, no other land is
seen till the Bab-el-Mandeb (Gate of Tears) is
reached. Through this narrow channel a strong
current flows from the Indian Ocean, for the Red
Sea, situate in the midst of the rainless district, is
ever evaporating in the hot sun, unreplenished by
rivers or streams from the parched deserts which
border it.

Passing the little British possession, Perim Island,
the key to the Red Sea and Suez Canal, there is
quite an excitement among the passengers on board,
as glasses of all sorts and sizes are produced with
which to gaze in rapture on the signalman's house,
as if it were an object of far more interest than the
Great Pyramid itself. I know Perim belongs to
England, but I can't find out whether it forms part
of Asia or Africa.

When Aden is reached, and a few hours may be spent ashore to go and look at the old tanks, it is quite a relief after the heat of the Red Sea.

One voyage on a large ocean steamer is very like another. Reading and sleeping generally occupy most of the time. Chess, deck-quoits, and cards fill up a few more hours, and the inevitable Calcutta sweep on the run of the day adds a little excitement,

ADEN BY SUNRISE.

and forms a grand topic for starting conversation. Then theatricals, fancy-dress balls and athletic sports are got up when there are sufficient energetic passengers. It is quite surprising what very effective dresses can be made out of materials at hand. A couple of sheets and a few coloured silk handkerchiefs may be made into most becoming garments for ladies, or even men.

Then some time during the voyage it is usual to

have a fire drill, when all the ship's crew turn out
and go to their appointed stations, man the pumps,
and get the boats ready for lowering. This is a
most wise proceeding; but meanwhile all the passengers look on at the performance, and, moreover,
generally get very much in the way. I always
wanted to know what they would do in the event
of real alarm. Are they then to crowd about and
look on and get in the way? They ought at least
to be told what is expected of them.

CHAPTER II.

CEYLON AND INDIA.

On coming to anchor in the harbour of Colombo, the ship is surrounded by a number of outrigged canoes ; not 'outrigged' like a racing eight, but having a wooden beam fixed so as to float, say, six feet from the side of the boat, which is long, narrow, and high out of the water. It requires some courage on the part of the newcomer to trust himself in such an unfamiliar vessel ; but confidence is soon restored, and one may look around and admire the beauties of the harbour. There is a fascination about the place as viewed from the anchorage which makes one look forward eagerly to a time on land after the week or two spent at sea. The dark shade under the large trees or verandas of the houses, contrasting with the glaring sunshine, is very attractive ; and then, on landing, strange sights meet the eye on every hand : the curious-looking Singalese men, with their straight black hair done up in a knot behind, and combs to keep it in place, their peculiar costume of a small jacket and a 'comboy,' or piece of gaudy-patterned print stuff enveloping the legs; the little miniature bullock-carts, drawn by an animal not much bigger than a large dog; and the lightly built 'jinrickshas' trailed along by running men.

But before we get more absorbed in the infatuation of the place, let me tell a little tale for the benefit of those who intend going on by the boat, which has but called in here for a few hours. A fellow-passenger of mine, anxious to have as long a time as possible in this glorious land, remained on shore till just the time for the starting of his steamer, the *Carthage.* He then took a boat, and in due time found himself alongside the gangway of the big ship. Safely on deck, he looked around and noticed many new faces among the passengers, whom he supposed were coming on from Ceylon. But next he imagined he must have got among the second saloon people, as he found the cabin arrangements so unfamiliar. Going from end to end of the ship, he began to suspect something was amiss, and finally had to ask awkwardly if he was on board his ship, whereupon, to his intense mortification, he was pointed out the *Carthage* some distance off, just at that moment starting on her voyage. Darting to the side, he jumped into the first boat, and begged the men to row for dear life to catch up the great mail-boat. But too late! The *Carthage* was already past the pier-head, ploughing her way to Australia, with all my friend's earthly belongings lying about in disorder in his cabin!

As it turned out, it was a freak of destiny, for I believe he is settled in Colombo to this day.

The Grand Oriental Hotel, said to be the finest hotel in the East, is a splendid cool building, with huge galleried dining-hall and roomy verandas. There are punkahs always going, any number of native waiters ready to supply one with cooling drinks, and what gladdens the heart even more, the charges are very moderate.

Colombo seems to combine all that one can want. A good tropical climate—never cold, and yet never unbearably hot (at least, so say those that live there, though it certainly strikes hot on first arriving from Europe)—comfortable hotels, pretty scenery, yet a good town where everything can be bought; and then, in a very few hours, you can go up into the hills and get a climate as cold as England, or go off and have some of the best of sport in large or small game.

Close beside the hotel are numerous Indian jewellers' shops. Here, in addition to ivory goods and Indian ware, the newcomer is tempted with brilliant unset gems. You hear stories of people obtaining rubies and sapphires, and selling them in London for double what they gave in Colombo. It may be, but I expect the sellers generally know their value, and such successes are few and far between. Anyhow, some very pretty stones are to be bought, whether really valuable or not.

Ceylon is one of the great strongholds of

Buddhism, and in Colombo several interesting temples may be visited. The priests are dressed in yellow vestments, have their heads clean-shaven all over, and invariably carry palm-leaf fans.

Galle Face, a large open green by the sea, is a great resort for all classes of Colombo society. Here the band plays periodically, cricket matches are played, and even football, too, under the roasting sun! Close by are the suitably-built barracks for the English garrison.

Numerous drives can be taken in the neighbourhood, the cinnamon gardens being an especial attraction; and I believe the correct thing to do is to call on the exile Arabi, ex-Pasha, and condole with him on his lot. But I didn't.

Mount Lavinia, chiefly consisting of a hotel perched on a small hill overlooking the sea, is one of the first places to visit outside Colombo. It is a lovely spot, a good hotel, and it is said to be cooler and more airy than Colombo.

By going further along the same line of rail, a small village, Caltura, is reached, very prettily situated amongst masses of green foliage, and bordering on a lake, or inlet of the sea. The village itself is mostly scattered along the very good highroad, the houses dotted about amongst luxuriant palms, jack-fruit, and many other kinds of trees. There is a very interesting Buddhist temple here, with its yellow-robed, shaven-headed, palm-leaf-fan-carrying priests. Outside, it is nothing

much to look at—it might be a Methodist chapel—
but inside gloriously decorated with painted figures
of the usual extraordinary Buddhist type.   The
priest in charge graphically gave me a full explanation of all these in Singalese, or some such language,
while I showed the extreme interest I felt in all he
told me by gravely nodding my head whenever he
appeared to expect such acknowledgment.   Finally,
he pulled aside a great curtain to admit me into the
sanctum sanctorum, a smallish room containing three
huge figures of Buddha.   I had the profanity to
click off my secret camera at these, and it rather
excited the priest's curiosity to see me fumbling
with something which gave an occasional click.   I
think he suspected that I was about to shoot myself.
But after all I got no results; the place was altogether in too much of a 'dim religious light' for
photography.   Tables stood in front of the figures,
on which floral offerings and monetary gifts were
placed.

Near the other end of the pretty village is a
wonderful tree-arch.   A large stem rises on one
side of the road and bends across it, and then seems
to join in with another tree, though probably it has
really only dropped a root on the other side.   This
tree is covered with moss and ferns and creepers,
making it look quite like an artificial and tastefully
decorated triumphal arch.

This is one of the few places in Ceylon—indeed, I
believe out of Malaysia—where that luscious fruit,

the mangosteen, grows. It is 'esteemed one of the most delicious and wholesome of all known fruits,' and is about the size of a small apple, with a brown casing, which breaks open rather like that of a horse-chestnut. The edible inside consists of three or four delicate white pieces, not unlike the sections of an orange in consistency, but not so fibrous, and with a sweet, delicate flavour.

The local 'fly' consists of a hackery, or small two-wheeled cart, with roof of palm-leaf matting, drawn by a diminutive bullock, who trots along in fine style. The 'rest-house,' or hotel, is a comfortable little bungalow of three bedrooms and a diningroom, with a small garden containing turkeys, peacocks, and a tame porcupine.

One passes in the street numerous gem-polishers, sitting in front of their houses, hard at work with their emery wheels, cutting and polishing the sapphires, rubies, and other less valuable stones (especially the last-named) which are found near here and sent to Colombo for sale. I thought perhaps in this home of jewels they would not know their true value, but I found they *did* very fully.

Quitting the busy streets, we find good roads running through the most lovely tropical woods, and past occasional paddy - fields, with the bright green rice springing up through the mud and water, which has been well mixed by the plodding oxen trampling knee-deep in the slush. And as we get further away from the haunts of man, we may see some monkeys; and what a grand sight to watch them boldly jumping from tree to tree, fearlessly plunging headlong from some high branch into the thickets beneath, and nimbly climbing along at a rapid pace from one bush to another.

Then there is some good sport to be got about here, if only one knows exactly where to go. Numerous snipe of various sorts haunt the paddy-fields, and a great variety of prettily coloured pigeons fly about the trees, while there are larger birds, of the pheasant tribe, in the woods, although I did not succeed in getting any of the latter.

In the evening one can have great fun with the flying foxes, which come over in hundreds, and are a great pest to the fruit-grower. These beasts look, when flying, very much like large rooks, but in reality they are simply overgrown bats, often measuring as much as four feet or more from tip to tip of wing.

Being anxious to get a young monkey, and as in this neighbourhood are to be found the ' low country wanderoos,' which are said to be the cleanest and most affectionate of monkeys, I determined one day on a kidnapping expedition to the bush. After an early start, and a drive of some miles in a hackery, we arrived at the shooting-ground, and were joined by several villagers from the neighbourhood. We entered the bush, a smart young lad first, to show the way (and clear away the snakes, I thought), then myself, and then the various servants, guides, ' beaters,' and villagers, who would insist on jabbering and making enough noise to frighten everything away from the district. We soon came upon a troop of monkeys, and followed them some distance, they very calmly hopping from tree to tree, and clambering about the branches, evidently anxious to keep their distance from us, and yet appearing calm and not hurried, so that we were able to get up to them, and follow below till a chance of a shot occurred. It seems downright cruelty to shoot these poor but noble animals. But if you wish to get a tame one, the only chance is to cruelly murder the mother as she carries her little one clinging to her. In my first shot I was unfortunate enough to kill both, one single shot having entered the baby's head. But later on I succeeded in getting a small friend, who accompanied me to Australia—a most affectionate little fellow, but a very bad sailor.

Caltura is celebrated for its basket-work. Most beautifully worked grass-woven boxes with lids may be got here, sometimes made to fit into one another so as to form a 'nest' of ten or twelve.

Going back to Colombo, I then started on a journey up into the hills of the interior.

The railway journey from Colombo to Kandy, and on to Nuwara Eliya, is certainly one of the most interesting in the world. The scenery is magnificent and varied, and the engineering wonderful. The first part of the journey is through low-lying country intersected with rivers and swamps, and covered for the most part with dense tropical vegetation and wet paddyfields, with occasional clumps of bamboo. Gradually one ascends the mountains and obtains glorious views into the huge valleys below, with their most extraordinary-looking terraces of paddy. Numerous queer-shaped hills, fine waterfalls, cliffs, and grand trees are seen on all sides. Rising above the vegetation around it stands the majestic Talipot palm, whose fan-shaped leaves, sometimes sixteen feet across, are used not only as umbrellas, but as tents, by the natives. Strips of the leaves are utilized for writing upon, the letters being merely scratched on with a style, and remaining indelibly impressed for all time ; at least, some very ancient writings exist done in this manner. The flower rises like an enormous plume from the top of the tree, forming about the biggest thing known in the floral line.

By night the place is illuminated by fire-flies, often backed by the distant glow of large forest fires.

After about seventy miles, Kandy, the old native capital of Ceylon, is reached. It is a picturesque place, close to a lake around which rise thickly-wooded hills.

Here is another very interesting old Buddhist temple, surrounded by a moat full of fish and turtles. The walls are decorated with most wonderful paintings illustrative of the various kinds of hells, each offence, according to the Buddhist religion, having its own particular punishment awarded. *The* thing

most worth seeing in Kandy is the tooth of the
veritable Buddha. But this is something far too
good for the ordinary tourist to gaze upon, so he
must be contented with looking upon the bell of
gold set with precious stones, under which, he is
informed, there are five others equally beautiful, and
on raising the innermost of them this valuable relic
is exposed to view. Judging by the many portraits
and statues that I have seen of Buddha, I always
did imagine that he must have been a rather peculiar-
looking man ; but I believe this tooth fairly took by
surprise the few Europeans who had the supreme
privilege of inspecting it at the time of the visit of
the Prince of Wales, for I am told that no ordinary
mortal could have got the thing inside his mouth.

There are various other temples to be seen ; also
a celebrated Bo-tree, a few thousand years old, in
the old cemetery ; and some lovely walks may be
taken among the collection of tropical plants to be
found on the sides of the hill above, and in the
grounds of The Lodge, the residence of the
Governor.

But if you are anxious to see tropical plants in all
their glory, a trip must be made to Peredinia, not
many miles off, where are some of the finest
botanical gardens in the world, with some very
grand specimens of large trees.

We must now go still further up the line, and
on to Nuwara Eliya (pronounced more like ' new-
raylia '), which is the sanatorium of Ceylon.

We pass through some wonderful country—
mountainous, though not as a rule rugged, and
covered for the most part with tea and coffee
plantations. It seems curious that these two
beverages, so closely associated in our minds,
should be derived from plants growing under such
similar circumstances that they are often found
together.

The coffee - planter of Ceylon, however, has
almost ceased to exist, and many would have been
utterly ruined by the disease which ravaged all the
coffee plants some years ago had it not been found
that the ground grew excellent tea, which has now
almost entirely superseded the coffee.

The plantations are a curious sight. Miles and
miles of forest have been cleared and burnt; but all
the larger trees are either left standing, gaunt and
dead, or lie like skeletons on a battle-field over the
country. But, one thinks, how grand the scenery
must have been before, when these giants stood
fully clothed in verdure, with creepers and undergrowth around! In amongst this scene of wreckage
grow the coffee plants—shrubs, perhaps, ten feet
high, with leaves at the top like a crinkly laurel,
and little green and red, cherry-like berries close to
the stem. The tea, on the other hand, seldom
grows more than five or six feet high, and is more
bushy. It requires more care in growing than
coffee. Only the buds and younger leaves are
picked for tea. The difference between green and

black tea is not in the plant from which they come, but that the latter, after being picked, is kept exposed to the air for some time before it is roasted.

The railway is a marvellous work of engineering. In some places it is so steep that the train only travels at an average rate of eight miles an hour for the forty odd miles. The line not only zigzags about in the most extraordinary manner, but in one place goes right round in a loop by passing through a tunnel, then curving round outside the hill, and finally passing over itself again higher up.

There is some fine mountain scenery in the distance, including occasional glimpses of Adam's Peak, the conical hill whence Buddha stepped to heaven.

Having got as far as this line can take one, a coach journey of about four miles has to be made along a mountainous road winding about even more than the railway does, and Nuwara Eliya is reached. We are now about 6,000 feet above the sea, and the air strikes very cold. All the vegetation looks quite homely, gorse and heather being plentiful. There is no town to speak of, but two or three small hotels of bungalow-like build, and several private 'villas,' including the Governor's house, which, as Sir Arthur Gordon himself described it, is very like an English parsonage. There is also a racecourse, where great goings on occur at the proper season.

From here one can make the ascent of Mount

Pedurutallagalla, the highest point in Ceylon, after a five-mile ride through a dense forest, *said* to be infested with wild elephants, cheetah, and elk. I dare say they were there, but I did not see any of them. It is a wild and splendid view from the summit, which is 8,295 feet above the sea.

In the evening, when the sun goes down, one is quite glad to get in front of a good old homely fire—a change indeed from the furnace-like heat of Colombo.

* * * * *

My trip in India was but a very short one, and was confined to a visit to one or two places in the Madras Presidency.

I left Colombo by British-India steamboat for Tuticorin. The greater part of the deck was thickly packed with coolie emigrants—1,400 they say were on board—and all this weighty top hamper seemed as if it must make the vessel top-heavy; and Heaven help us if we got into difficulties! However, as it turned out, we had a very calm and peaceable journey, lasting some seventeen hours. Our destination was hardly what we in England would call a good harbour. A low, flat shore covered with palm-trees, some sand-banks, and a few houses, were all we could discern from the steamer when she anchored a mile or so from land. We were conveyed ashore in a small steam-launch, well loaded with natives, and in due time I found myself ensconced in the hotel of the place, which consisted of three rooms and a balcony, but where, nevertheless, I was very comfortably housed.

Tuticorin is a quiet little place. There is a small club, and a sufficient number of Europeans to make a select circle of society, so that tennis parties, rides, etc., are indulged in as in other places. The manager of the bank very kindly took me round and launched me into the vortex of local gaieties. There is, of course, a native bazaar, which is of interest to the new-comer, who sees for the first time the native Indian in his element. One of the great peculiarities is to see the men going about with their faces painted in various ways to denote their religious caste. Some have bands of white or red, or both. Many wear a white spot just above the nose, and some even mark their bodies with white stripes.

The district around Tuticorin presents no great feature of interest; the country is all flat, but there is a great profusion of Palmyra palms. These have straight, thick stems, and close-lying, nearly circular, leaves. It is one of the most useful of trees, all parts of it being of value to the natives. Toddy is got in abundance from the sap of the shoots, and from this 'jaggery,' or sugar, is extracted. It supplies an edible fruit; the leaves are useful for thatching and many other purposes; and the hard, dark wood of the stem is most valuable for building and other purposes.

Many of the curious banyan-trees, with their many

stems and roots hanging from the branches, also abound.

From Tuticorin a railway runs north. It is interesting to see that here twenty-four hour time is used for all the time-tables. It certainly seems an excellent plan, and saves much confusion, especially when planning out a long and complicated journey.

The country travelled through is mostly flat and open, covered either with cultivation or coarse grass, with a good many small trees. Now and again we pass over a large, dry watercourse, while in the distance to the westward hills rear themselves before the setting sun.

All along beside the railway runs a hedge of aloes planted closely together, many of these plants blossoming, the flowers being raised on great stems fifteen or twenty feet high. When the flower dies, so does the whole plant. On many of the trees are to be seen the curious hanging nests of the weaver-bird. In shape they are somewhat similar to a chemist's retort, the entrance being at the bottom of the depending funnel, so that snakes and other would-be intruders are unable to find the way in.

A long journey by train in India, especially during the hot season, is not the most agreeable of modes of travel. Fine dust gets over everything, and makes one feel very dirty and grimy. The carriages, which are not over large or comfortable on this narrow-gauge line, become like an oven towards mid-day, and it is a great relief to get to one of the well-kept little station restaurants, where one receives the best attention, and is able to get a good wash and a comfortable meal. What strikes a stranger most in Southern India is the great regard paid by all the servants and other natives to one's comfort. Although travelling quite as a private individual, I was received everywhere, not only with cringing salaams, etc., but with real civility. Everything was done as well as one could expect, except, by the way, for one thing which I disliked—the drinks were so warm. In most hot countries the Europeans insist on mineral waters, etc., being kept cool under damp cloths, or in goulahs, etc., but in this district of India I never got a cool drink.

Madura is the first important station up the line, and here is a very fine old Hindu temple. It is said to be one of the finest in India, but it did not impress me. The building covers about twenty acres, and is crowded with natives lying about everywhere. Here they keep four 'white' elephants, one of which is supposed to be trained to pick up any coin you may like to throw to him—and so he does after a fashion, though I hardly considered I had got my money's worth out of the experiment. There are also the remains of an old palace here, in which are a great number of large columns.

Continuing our journey by rail through flat country, mostly cultivated with cotton, we get to Trichinopoly.

The most conspicuous feature about the place is the rock of Trichinopoly, which rises up abruptly out of the plain to some 500 feet. On the top are the remains of a fort and a number of native houses, the result being suggestive of the Acropolis at Athens. The town below is well laid out with broad streets, and crowded with natives. The military cantonments extend for miles outside the town, and as there are plenty of fine trees—palms, banyans, jack-fruit, etc.—it all appears shady and cool.

Trichinopoly is a great place for jewellery, and it is in the wearing of this that Indian natives differ greatly from those of other parts of the world. Nowhere else have I seen such a profusion of jewellery. The women's ears are sometimes pierced to such a size that one could get two or three fingers through the hole, and I should be sorry to say how much weight of silver and gold is sometimes carried by them.

I went out to dine one night with the magistrate, but I took good care not to walk there, for during the afternoon I had seen on his drive the undoubted recent track of a large cobra! I was quite ready to agree with him that the brute was probably gone, and was not likely to return that way, but still I preferred to take a gharry.

Tanjore was the next place I visited, ' in all ages one of the chief political and literary centres of the South of India,' as the guide-book has it. Here is a large palace, partly used as a court-house, with two courts, presided over respectively by an English and a native magistrate.

The great temple of Tanjore is always considered the finest specimen of the Dravidian style of architecture. One enters under the Gopuras or gate pyramids, and finds one's self in a large court, where is the shrine of the bull Nandi. Under a roof supported by columns is a huge stone statue of the bull, which the natives solemnly declare ' is still growing,' as it is natural to suppose that it could not have been originally cut out of one piece of stone of that enormous size. It is, therefore, kept carefully oiled, in order to encourage the growth! Further on in the court is the temple proper, or Vimana. It is some eighty feet square at the base, and rises perpendicularly to two stories high ; above this is the pyramidal roof, covered with elaborate sculpture, and rising to a height of 190 feet.

Tanjore is also known for its beautiful metal-work —usually elaborately-embossed plates of copper and brass, with silver let in.

Having thus had a glimpse at India, and seen sufficient to make me long to stay on and see more of the country, I returned to Ceylon, and there joined the P. and O. boat bound for Australia.

This voyage of some 4,000 miles without a sight of any land is somewhat monotonous, but the monotony is broken by the festivities incident on crossing the line, for on this journey we duly came across the boat, or shell, or whatever it is, containing Neptune and all his crew.   Unfortunately, I did not see the mysterious vessel in which he navigates his kingdom, but I saw the sovereign of the seas after he had boarded us, and watched with interest the ceremony of shaving and bathing some of the unfortunate younger members of the crew.

CHAPTER III.

SOUTHERN COLONIES OF AUSTRALIA.

I.—WESTERN AUSTRALIA.

THE first point of Australia which outward-bound
steamers make for is Cape Leeuwin, the south-west
corner of the continent. It is always supposed that
on rounding this cape a change of weather will be
experienced, and that one will have a very rough
time of it during this operation. But my experience
was different, for we had it calm all the way, and
more calm after rounding the Leeuwin. The only
sight of land one gets, however, is a low line of
darkness, with several rocky islets a long way
from the shore; and all the coast between this
and King George's Sound is low, rocky, and
uninteresting.

We are now within the expansive limits of
Western Australia, which, of all the Australian
colonies, is the most extensive (1,060,000 square
miles), and has the smallest population (50,000).

These are remarkable figures. They mean that
the colony is nearly twelve times as big as the
United Kingdom, with a population only about

one thousandth as great, or nearly as much as that of Anglesey. And, moreover, of this population, Perth, the capital, and Freemantle, its port, take over one-third.

It seems all the more curious that this great territory should support so few inhabitants, considering that it is the nearest colony to England, and contains the first port at which most of the large steamers from Europe call. This port is King George's Sound—a name well known to all who take an interest in the British Empire, though its reputation rests almost entirely on the fact that it is a good harbour, and therefore requires defending.

Now, the defence of this place and of Thursday Island, the extreme opposite point of Australia, has probably been more discussed than any other scheme of defence in recent years. Committee after committee, and expert after expert, have at different times proceeded to inspect the place, and issue a voluminous report on the subject. Not that any great difficulties are presented ; quite the contrary. But probably by this means much expense may be saved, for if a committee is engaged in drawing up a report on the subject, no one can find fault with the powers that be.

King George's Sound looks as if made for defence. The outer harbour, or sound proper, is formed by some islands, admirably suited as sites for fortifications, and a flat promontory which juts out from the shore, ending in a low rounded hill. Then the inner harbour is separated from the outer by a peninsula consisting of a turtle-backed island connected by a sandy neck. On any of these forts could easily be constructed.

The steamers anchor in the inner harbour, on the north side of which is situated the town of Albany.

This place, possibly destined some day to be one of great importance, is at present nothing more than a small village ; and yet the large Australian liners have to call in and waste several hours here simply to coal. This must be, however, a great blessing to the good people of Perth (not half the size of its namesake in Scotland). The country round is rocky and undulating, covered with heather and rough grass, and has quite a Scotch look. The usual thing for ladies to do here is to gather wild-flowers, which grow in great profusion and variety on the slopes ; but there seems to be little else to be done in Albany. It is, however, a thoroughly typical Australian township, and is therefore interesting to anyone newly arrived from Europe.

One of the great peculiarities of Australian scenery is the similarity, not only in the trees, grass, and general appearance, but in the towns and buildings all through the country. From one end to the other of this great continent the ordinary aspect is the same. Go out for a walk round Albany, and you could not tell you were not in the neighbourhood of Cape York. There may be a difference in temperature, of course, and a botanist might detect a difference in the varieties of many of the plants, but in general appearance all are the same.

So also with the houses; those you see in the South are just the same as those in the far North— one-storied wooden houses, the walls consisting of a framework covered with overlapping 'weather-boards,' generally painted white or brown, with corrugated iron roof. The house may be classed by its veranda : only the meanest hovels have none at all ; the ordinary cottage always has its roof extended to the front and supported on pillars. When the domicile gets a bit more pretentious, the veranda extends round the sides. Each house, as a rule, stands in its own grounds, though these are often not even fenced in, and are seldom cultivated. Flower-gardens are few and far between ; and kitchen-gardens hardly exist. One is surprised at this, for when a man settles down on his own property (which is the usual thing out here), and is not as a rule over-burdened with work, one would have thought he would have set to work to make it nice and homely, and spend his spare time in the garden ; but he doesn't.

The village, as we should call it, though Australians would designate it 'township,' consists, like every other in Australia, of a wide street bordered by a number of such houses.

The streets in these small towns always look of great width ; and the inhabitants will generally point out with pride their broad streets, and delight to think what a splendid town it will some day make (for they always suppose the village will soon grow into a city). But when the place *does* increase and becomes a town, it is surprising how the streets diminish in width, or rather in appearance, as the houses on either side rise up. Probably the Strand (in London) would look a splendid thoroughfare if the traffic were removed, and small one-storied cottages put in place of the existing houses.

Albany does not boast many fine buildings. There is a barn-like post-office, and a Custom-house. Then, of course, there are several 'hotels,' as they call public-houses in this country, without which no town would be complete. There is also a very small and rather picturesque-looking church, and that is about all that is to be seen in the way of edifices.

But here also one first becomes acquainted with the Australian native—I do not mean *black*, but the bony, lanky, long-bearded individual, full of brag and whisky, in a wideawake hat, a loose shirt and moleskin trousers. He may be seen riding a horse of somewhat the same description—that is to say, lanky, large-boned, and shaggy, and with a tendency to try to get the best of you—leisurely cantering down hill with loose and rotten-looking reins, the horse, with mangy mane (for a variety of horse-mange is very prevalent throughout Australia), looking as if at every step it must fall. Or you may see such a man, gun in hand, followed by a couple of coarse-looking greyhounds, going out after kangaroo.

When I was at Albany, the only means of getting
to Perth was either by a very rough coach, or
by a wretched little steamer, not at all the sort
of vessel one would choose for making the trip
round that storm-bound coast, either route taking
two days.   But since then a railway has been
opened connecting the two towns.   Not far from
Albany good timber is to be got, especially the
'jarrah,' a species of eucalyptus, which grows to
a great size, and is a most useful wood for building
purposes, being proof against white ants, which
cause so much destruction in tropical Australia.

Under the circumstances one does not, or, at all
events, *I* did not, feel inclined to make a long stay
in Western Australia.   No inducements are held
out to visit Perth, and, as far as I could gather,
there is absolutely nothing else to be seen in this
colony that cannot be better seen elsewhere.

The interior of the colony is comparatively little
known, and many a zealous traveller has had to
turn back, baffled by the everlasting waterless plains
and deserts.   We hear unkind stories of one
exploring party which got on very well for the first
part of their journey, so long as the public-houses
lasted, but after that they found the hardships too
severe to continue the penetration of the great
unknown.

II.—SOUTH AUSTRALIA.

The first land belonging to South Australia that
is sighted by the steamer is Kangaroo Island.

This is a large, uninteresting-looking island, over eighty miles long, consisting of a flat-topped, grass-covered plateau, with cliffs all round, and with only a cloud of smoke here and there from some bush fire to relieve the monotony.   Later on we sight to our left Yorke's Peninsula (not to be confounded with the great Cape York Peninsula on the other side of Australia).   And then, passing through the Gulf of St. Vincent, we get to Largs Bay.   All the country near the coast appears flat and low, but some miles inland it rises abruptly in good-sized hills.

Adelaide is peculiarly situated, being some five miles inland, and though so close to the sea, it can hardly be called a port.   Port Adelaide is a small town close to Largs Bay.   On arriving at the latter, we land at a pier, and get our things passed at the Custom - house, and then take train for Port Adelaide, and thence to the capital itself, which by this route is a journey of some ten miles.

Adelaide is decidedly a fine town, and is built in a regular pattern.   All the streets run at right angles ; exactly in the middle of the city is Victoria Square ; and four other similar squares lie towards the four corners of the town.   King William Street, the principal thoroughfare, runs right through the centre and through Victoria Square.   Most of the principal buildings, which are of fine architectural design, are situated in this street.

Here one first becomes associated with the town

life of Australia, and one is at once struck with the independence and ' well-to-do-ness' of the inhabitants. The streets are full of people, but all are well clothed and contented-looking. Itinerant musicians, discoursing really good music on violins and harps, are common. At night the place is well lighted, and the theatres and all places of entertainment abundantly patronized. Hansom cabs ply in the streets, as well as numerous tramcars. Everything looks English, and it is almost disappointing to find it so familiar ; the crowds are not even wanting for the typical soldiers, as we see many of the permanent artillery dressed just the same as our Royal Artillery, as well as other members of the defence force and volunteers in familiar uniforms. There is, however, one dress that strikes a newcomer as peculiar, and that is that of the Mounted Infantry, consisting of a loose-fitting, khaki-coloured coat, gray breeches, leather gaiters, and a wideawake hat, with one side hooked up. It is a workmanlike if ugly dress, and is almost of the same pattern for Mounted Infantry throughout Australia.

One soon gets to understand the typical Australian. He is good-natured, and ever ready to ask you in to have a drink. Jack is everywhere as good as his master, and the cry is ever, ' Australia for the Australians,' meaning, of course, not for the true Australian aboriginals, but for the English colonists. It would, however, never do to put it that way, for this British-Australian colonist is very jealous, and hates the coming of rivals from England. So those born in Australia become proud of the fact, and like to style themselves 'natives.'

Talking of native-born Australians, I have been told a remarkable fact by doctors, though, being almost impossible to prove, it must perhaps be considered rather as a theory than a fact. It is that the bones of Australian-born children are much weaker than those of other people. The cause is supposed to be that almost all the drinking water is got from rain run into tanks, which is, of course, deficient in lime.

South Australia is a peculiarly named colony. It might just as well be called North Australia, for it extends from top to bottom of the continent. But the northern districts are separated from the southern by a desert, so that the readiest means of communication between the two is by sea, going right round Victoria, New South Wales, and Queensland. Besides, all the most northerly portion of Australia (except the narrow York Peninsula) is in 'South Australia,' while all the most southerly part is in Victoria!

South Australia is the greatest wheat-growing colony, having some 1,800,000 acres under wheat alone.

III.—Victoria.

Victoria is the smallest of the important Australian colonies as regards size, and yet is nearly as big as Great Britain, and it is the most thickly populated.

Port Philip is the large bay or harbour on which Melbourne lies. As we passed in we saw a large wreck on the sands outside, or rather a ship aground, for it appeared but little broken, although it had been there for some years. It seems that when she was being driven ashore they cast out the bow anchors, so that she drifted on to the beach stern first, dragging her anchors. The result is that the seas all break over her bows without doing much harm, although the vessel is so damaged as not to be worth dragging off.

Once inside the 'heads,' one seems to be in an inland sea, for the harbour is some thirty miles across. Williamstown is the port at which the large steamers land their passengers for Melbourne, and one has to go on by rail to get to the city.

Melbourne is undoubtedly a grand town. Though in 1836 it consisted of but thirteen huts, it now possesses some of the finest buildings in the Southern Hemisphere, and has nearly half a million inhabitants.

It supplies all the comforts of any town of its size. There are capital hotels, theatres, and shops, and at least three good clubs. Down the centres of all the principal streets runs a convenient system of cable cars, looking like so many garden seats out for a walk.

The town-hall is a splendid building containing

one of the largest organs in the world; a big cathedral is in course of erection, and some grand new Houses of Parliament are also on the rise.

Government House is an enormous place, well situated on some rising ground to the south of the city, surrounded by extensive grounds. There is a magnificent ball-room, in which I have seen 250 dine without any crowding.

Adjoining the grounds are the Botanical Gardens and a large public park.

I was in Melbourne (for the second time) at the time of the great exhibition in 1888.

The opening ceremony was a grand sight, the huge lofty exhibition building being packed full with spectators, while the platform looked resplendent with all the Governors of the different colonies, and their staffs in full uniform, together with their wives and other ladies.

As for speeches, presentations, and addresses, there was no end to them; but they were not remarkable for any very distinctive or novel features.

Then, of course, other festivities followed—big public dinners in the exhibition and in the town-hall, official lunches, balls at Government House, and big dinners there too.

There is a very fine racecourse at Flemington, where, among many other races, the 'Melbourne Cup,' the 'Derby' of Australia, is annually competed for. The course, like all the principal ones in Australia, is well laid out and nicely kept. They differ in many details from the usual English course. For instance, no one is ever allowed on the actual track except for crossing at certain points. The lines of police sweeping the course, like so many brooms, are therefore quite an unknown sight in Australia. Another institution is the 'totalizator,' now becoming common on European racecourses (indeed, in Russia no other kind of betting is allowed). It seems infinitely the best system of ready-money betting, and, if gambling is to be allowed, it might with advantage be introduced in England. You put down your sovereign at the ticket-office, and get a ticket for the horse you wish to back. All the money so paid in, except, of course, a small percentage, is divided up and paid out to all those who produce tickets on the winning horse. In this way you are sure of getting correct odds, and 'welshing' is an impossibility.

Victoria is the greatest wine-producing colony ; but the native wines somehow do not seem to be properly appreciated by the people, probably only because they are cheap. It is told of a certain Governor of one of the colonies, that, with the most patriotic intentions, he ordered nothing but the wines of the country to be drunk at his table. But, unhappy man ! he was extensively abused for his supposed parsimony.

Victoria is well provided with railways, and many places, such as Ballarat (one of the oldest and largest goldfields in Australia), Castlemaine, Geelong, etc., may be visited, though all these Australian towns greatly lack any special interest. Train may be taken to Sydney, passing Albury, or the journey to Sydney may be continued on the steamer, which calls in at Melbourne for some days.

IV.—New South Wales.

New South Wales is the oldest of the Australian colonies, and the most populous. In 1769 Captain Cook first discovered Botany Bay, near Sydney, which later on received a world-wide reputation as a penal settlement, although, as a matter of fact, the convicts who were landed there only remained a few days, and were very soon removed to a spot in Port Jackson, which is now one of the busiest parts of Sydney.

Everyone ought to know of Sydney Harbour. Sydney people always declare it is the most beautiful in the world, but in reply to the question, 'What others have you seen?' the more usual reply is: 'Oh, Port Philip and Moreton Bay,' or perhaps even 'Suez and Brindisi' may be added. Certainly, as far as beauty goes, while not for a minute wishing to undervalue it, I may say I know many far finer. Sydney Harbour may be very well compared to the Bosphorus, without the picturesqueness and peculiarity of the mosques and Oriental buildings of the latter. But as a *harbour* it is, of course, almost without a rival. Not only is there a very large expanse of water of good depth, but it is intersected by so many promontories jutting out like piers from the shore that the whole thing looks as if made expressly for a big harbour.

The entrance is imposing. It is about a mile wide, and on each side are the 'heads,' remarkably perpendicular cliffs, giving quite the appearance of a gateway through a wall.

Sydney Harbour is properly called Port Jackson, but the former designation is more familiar, and will probably in time supersede the older name.

Sydney lies on the south side, about three or four miles from the entrance. One of the most prominent features on steaming in is Government House, situated on a promontory, on the near side of which is Farm Cove, where the men-o'-war lie, and on the far side is Sydney Cove, where the large liners deposit their passengers. On the other side of the harbour, to our right, is North Shore, a flourishing suburb, and here is Admiralty House and its grounds.

As for Sydney itself, it is a large and prosperous city, more like a large English town than Melbourne is, for the streets are narrower and less regularly laid out.

Government House here is also very different to that in Melbourne. It is like an ordinary English country house built in Tudor style, and, though comfortable enough, is altogether too small for the present requirements of the ever-growing place.

I was once present at a most interesting event in Government House. It was the delivery of a message from Mr. Gladstone to Lord Carrington by the phonograph. Doubtless, in a few years' time this will be considered nothing out-of-the-way, and, indeed, phonographs are common enough even now in America, but I do not suppose that anything of this kind had taken place before in Australia. The apparatus was rigged up and the wax cylinder applied, and in a few minutes Mr. Gladstone's clear voice was distinctly heard by all in the room, delivering an address of congratulation to Lord Carrington! On another occasion the machine was brought up again, and Lord Hopetoun and Lord Kintore spoke messages into it to be forwarded to the other side of the world.

Amongst the many farewell ceremonials to Lord Carrington on giving up the Governorship of New South Wales (1890), in which he had made himself extremely popular, none was more magnificent than the great banquet given in the fine new town-hall. Everyone of note was asked, including all the other Australian Governors, the galleries were crowded with ladies, and I have seldom heard a better set of speeches than those delivered by Lords Carrington, Hopetoun, and Kintore, and Sir Henry Norman.

The Houses of Parliament in Sydney are rather disappointing. The chamber of the Lower House is small, and is arranged more like a music-hall. It had an unenviable notoriety for pugilistic encounters between some of its Radical members.

5

Sir Henry Parkes is, undoubtedly, the most prominent man, not only in New South Wales, but in Australia. He is known as the Grand Old Man of Australia, and is quite as well known in antipodean politics as Gladstone in English and European.

Sir· Alfred Stephen, the Lieutenant-Governor, is another wonderful character. Though eighty-eight years old, he came to dine at Government House, and seemed as hale and hearty as could be. He was Chief Justice in '44!

Sydney has, like all other large towns, extensive suburbs. Here we find familiar names, such as Hyde Park, Victoria Park, and Paddington, alongside Woolloomooloo and other native names. Then, as we get further still from the madding crowd, we come across numerous small watering-places dotted about the harbour, the Parramatta, and Botany Bay.

Further off is the beautiful Hawkesbury River, forming in its lower reaches really an arm, or arms, of the sea. The water lies surrounded by steep hills, suggestive of the Italian lakes. It has recently been bridged by a tremendous work of engineering, and trains now run uninterruptedly from Sydney to Brisbane.

The Blue Mountains are the great holiday resort of New South Wales. After leaving Sydney, the train passes for some hours over the flat country at the back, and then begins a gradual ascent into the mountains, which soon becomes steeper, and a fine view is obtained over the plains. Katoomba, where there is a fine new hotel, is a usual starting-point for seeing the sights. One then has to *do* the neighbourhood in true tourist fashion. There are three classes of sights — the waterfalls, the fern gullies, and the rocky cliffs. There are numbers of specimens of each sort, but they are all very much alike. The country consists of tablelands falling in abrupt precipices to wide forest-clad valleys below, the cliffs winding about in a manner suggestive of the sea coast, with capes and bays. The epithet 'blue' appears to me to apply better to the mist-covered valleys than to the mountains, which latter, in the ordinary sense of the word, can scarcely be said to exist. Over the cliffs in places run the waterfalls, and these water the gullies of tree-ferns below. Certainly a pretty sight, and well arranged with footpaths, notice-boards, and every convenience for excursionists.

On passing right over the Blue Mountains, the railway descends to the more low-lying country on the other side by a most extraordinary zigzag. The train goes down a long incline, winding round the contours of the hills and passing through tunnels and over viaducts, till it stops on a 'safety flat,' and backs down the next incline, and then down a third one.

It is a great piece of engineering, though a novice would have thought the thing could have been done easier by following some less abrupt track.

The Jenolan Caves are one of the great sights of Australia, and well worth a visit. They are near 'nowhere,' though best got at from one of the stations in the Blue Mountains. A great road has been made for miles and miles through the Bush, but I heard many a growl from those interested, who declared that this expensive undertaking had been made in quite the wrong place, for it by no means connected the caves with the *nearest* point of the railway. I would recommend any intending visitors *not* to try stopping the night half-way to the caves, as I did. It is a very pretty and interesting trip, but the ' Half-way House' affords but the very poorest of entertainment. Such luxuries as milk and butter were quite out of the question, and anything more than the very roughest food would require arranging for. The few timber hovels around reminded me more of Russia than Australia, though they were, luckily, *comparatively* clean.

After about thirty miles of road through the Bush, we get out on to the hillside, and the road descends. skirting round the hills, all the way a gradual slope for six or seven miles, with rocky cuttings along one side, and an embankment on the other, with split timber fence. This is a long, monotonous bit, but it is a wonderful specimen of road-making.

The Jenolan Caves, which, by the way, are not called after some native word, but merely after a surveyor of them, J. E. Nolan, used to be known

as the Fish River Caves; but, as the guide-book
says, ' owing to the absence of the Fish River, ten
miles away,' it was decided to re-christen them.
There is a romantic story, strictly untrue, I believe,
that they were originally inhabited by a bush-
ranger, who, when pursued by the police, was always
able to gain one of the many openings of this
extensive warren. The caves are of various kinds.
Close to the hotel are the very imposing large
' halls,' appropriately called the ' Grand Arch ' and
the ' Devil's Coachhouse' (not that I know much
about the latter being 'appropriate,' but the place
certainly is suggestive of Dante).

The more interesting caves are mostly got at
through very small openings, and many of them
have had to be artificially enlarged in order that
they may be easily visited.

Much as one may dislike the regulation tourist
arrangements, there can be no doubt that these
caves are well managed. Locked iron gates prevent
unauthorized persons — that is, those without an
official guide—from entering the caves. This is
a most necessary precaution for two reasons : The
caves are so intricate that a stranger would be most
likely to get lost in them ; and, besides this, the
more inconsiderate tourist could do an immense
amount of injury if he took to breaking the
stalactites in order to get specimens. Then, regular
paths conduct one right through the interesting
parts, with ladders and railings and bridges where

necessary, which, although detracting somewhat from the general idea of the natural formations, still are most convenient if you want to see all that is to be seen in a few days. Some of the caves are illuminated by electric light (the power being derived from a stream close by) ; but this also enables one to see the sights in a manner quite impossible otherwise, and it is, moreover, a great pity that it could not have been introduced many years ago, as it is easy to see that the smoky torches and candles of many hundreds of visitors soon have a bad effect on the beautifully clear crystal formations.

The caves are no mere tunnel, but of all shapes and sizes. Often one appears to be in a chamber with no exit ; but on goes the guide—it may be through some narrow winding crack, down some steep incline, or clambering up a ladder to a hole near the 'ceiling.' The marvel is, not only the beauty of some of the stalactites and stalagmites, but their wonderful variety. In one cave they all appear like so many snowballs, above and below. In others are 'curtains' of stalactite, looking really just as if made of some 'textile fabric,' hanging in folds from above. Then there are others like icicles, clear as glass. The 'broken column' is very curious, consisting of a big stalactite, perhaps eight inches or a foot in diameter, which apparently reached the floor, and so formed a perfect column. But it has been broken, and probably by some

movement of the rocks, the broken end of the
upper part is not exactly over the lower. There
are many stalactites which they call 'mysteries,'
because it seems impossible to account for their
formation ; a mass of crystal is seen sticking out
sometimes even from the side of the cave, and not
only with numerous small crystals hanging downwards, but some actually going straight up or out
sideways. As stalactites are supposed to be formed
by water containing an excess of lime trickling
through the rock, and gradually depositing a coat
of lime, how can we account for these stalactites
growing upwards or sideways ? There are also
many varieties of stalagmites, the result on the floor
of the drippings from above. Some of the larger
ones have the appearance of rough statues, one being
very suggestive of 'the Madonna and Child.' Some
look like cabbage fields, others like the model of a
town with walls and fortifications.

Then one comes across pools of water so clear
that it is almost impossible to see where the surface
of the water begins and ends.

We had a good clamber to see some caves not
generally shown to the tourist, which gave one a
good idea of the difficulties which the earlier explorers must have had, and the advantage of the
artificial openings, ladders. etc.

For some distance we had to get through a
horizontal crack not much over a foot high in places.
This involved lying flat on one's back or face, and

wriggling along as best one could, the ground being covered with a layer of slimy, wet mud. Then we had to climb up a place more like the interior of a good-sized chimney. Part of this had to be accomplished by pressing one's back against one side, and one's feet or knees against the other ; and a nice mess there would have been if one had slipped !

A NATURAL MADONNA.

What with big shelving rocks on a slant, up which one had to flounder in bad imitation of a lizard, clinging on loose boulders which would smother one if they fell, and many other similar modes of progression, I think, on the whole, I shall in future only visit the artificially-improved caves.

On leaving the caves, one may return to civilization by other bush tracks.

New South Wales is a great pastoral country, supporting many times more sheep than any other colony (nearly 50,000,000).

A sheep-station generally consists of a house for the squatter and his family, and several cottages for the various employés. This sort of small village may often be twenty or thirty miles, or even more, from any other habitation. All around it is the sheep-run of open plains or downs. But, of course, care has to be taken to select a suitable kind of grass for the sheep. 'Spear grass,' for instance, is common in many places, and this actually kills numbers of sheep. It is not unlike a small kind of oats, the seeds of which are long and sharp. These seeds catch in the wool of sheep, and, as in the well-known trick with a piece of barley, work their way through the wool. But they are so sharp that they soon penetrate right into the skin of the sheep, and then form bad sores which often kill the animal.

In the shearing season the sheep are collected in flocks, and driven to the shearing shed by mounted shepherds. The shearers are merely birds of passage, going on from station to station ; and much trouble they often give if they are 'unionists,' as then they have everything their own way ; and if the squatter finds fault with any one of them, they have a way of all quietly going off together to another station, leaving the thousands of sheep unshorn. These shearers' unions are becoming much too powerful an organization ; but the squatters have lately been forming *their* union, which, if properly managed, ought to quite nullify any of the bad attempts at reform of the others.

The shearers are paid by the work they do— 4s. a score of fleeces being the usual price. As one good man can shear 130 sheep in a day, it is certainly not bad pay, considering he gets his rations and lodging, too. But then the shearing only lasts a short time.

The shearing sheds are arranged according to the following plan :

A represents the door at which the sheep are first driven in ; they then go into the pens B B, etc.— say, eight or ten sheep in each. At C stand the shearers. Each man pulls out a sheep by the hind-leg from his pen, sits him up, and shears him. When finished, the sheep is pushed out through a small door to the large pens, D, outside the shed, and a fresh sheep is taken from B. A small boy gathers up the fleece (which is all in one piece as if the skin and all were cut off), and carries it off to a sort of counter, E. Here it is examined by an expert, who judges of the quality of the wool, and after tearing off the ' skirtings ' — that is, the edges of short, dirty wool—throws it into one of the stalls, F, according to its classification. Good fleeces fetch about 1s. a lb. ; the ' skirtings ' only about 4d. A good fleece may weigh as much as 10 lb.

The wool thus cut off the sheep is so greasy that if it be twisted and squeezed the oil may be seen running out.

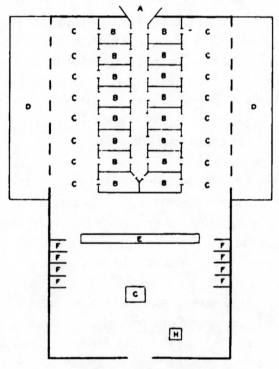

PLAN OF SHEARING SHED.

Then comes the packing. All the wool of one kind, from one of the bins, F, is put into a tall wooden tube, or hollow column, G—say three feet square,—under which fits a box, in which a sack has been spread, with its edges protruding. By means of a huge screw all the wool in the tube is compressed down into the sack, and a piece of canvas, which has been laid on top of the wool, is brought in contact with the top edges of the sack, which are then sewn together, and thus a regular bale of wool is formed. But this is not all, for the bale is then carried to the hydraulic press, H, where it is further squeezed into about half its size, and is then bound with iron hoops.   These bales are later loaded on to waggons, drawn by perhaps ten horses or oxen, and dragged off slowly to the nearest railway-station.

At Ipswich, in Queensland, is a wool factory, where I have seen the further processes of converting the fleece into cloth.

The first process the wool undergoes at the factory is to be well washed by machinery.   It is then spread out to dry ; after that it is usually dyed, and then carded.   This carding is a wonderful process, and should be ' seen to be appreciated.'   Huge rollers, covered with very small wire bristles, are rotated in a series, so nearly touching each other that the bristles on one pick the ' fluff' off the next, and so on.   All the dirt and foreign matter falls to the ground, and the wool becomes so spread out that it leaves the last roller looking just like a big thick cobweb.   It is then divided up and rolled into a string-like form, but without being twisted.   It is removed to another machine to be spun into yarn, and finally put into the looms and woven into cloth. But there are still many processes before the cloth

is complete. It must be washed again (to get rid
of the grease which is necessary in the weaving)
and dyed, if the cloth is to be all one colour. It is
then brushed. The brushes used in this process
are heads of teasels, which plant produces naturally
a more suitable brush than can be made artificially. The minute hooks or 'awns' scrape up the
cloth, and give it the required 'nap.' As a natural
sequence to washing and brushing, it is then *shaved*
by being passed under a large sharp 'razor.'
Finally, the cloth must be pressed, and otherwise
finished up.

Considering the millions of sheep there are in
Australia (over 80,000,000) which require shearing
every year, it is not to be wondered at that inventors
have been busy devising means whereby this may
be accomplished by machinery. There are at
present a number of different machines in the
market, though all more or less similar; and one
of the first brought out, and probably the best
known, is that invented by Mr. Wolseley, the brother
of 'the hero of Cairo.' After these ingenious
machines have been seen in operation, one only
wonders why they are not always used on all
stations. But they are not, and there is one great
reason why. Like so many other great questions
in Australia, the matter is ruled by the working
man. He argues thus: A shearing machine shears
sheep much quicker than a hand-shearer. This
means that if machines were always used less labour

would be required, and therefore fewer men employed. So, he argues, the machine is the enemy of the labouring man, and must be discouraged. In this short-sighted way the Australian workman continually damages himself. He cannot be got to see that it is to the advantage of sheep-farming, and therefore to the advantage of the colony and of himself.

Although not a large sheep-station, being in reality merely an experimental establishment, Mr. Wolseley has a sheep-run at Liddleton, with some 6,000 sheep. Here he has some sheds fitted up with his apparatus. It must be remembered, however, that there are numerous other sheds throughout Australia fitted with them, but I take this as an instance, being, so to speak, the home of the machine.

The apparatus consists of a handle, on the end of which is a sort of many-pronged fork. On the top of this fork or toothed blade is pivoted another, free to oscillate to and fro in a similar manner to an ordinary horse-clipper, so that the wool between the teeth is cut just as it would be by a pair of scissors. A crank behind the pivot moves the blades, and is revolved by means of a flexible cord which runs up a tube suspended from over the operator's head, which cord is revolved by a wheel from the steam-engine or other motor. Though somewhat difficult to describe, the apparatus is very simple, and easy to work. Not only can it be used by comparatively unskilled hands, but one of its great advantages is that it cuts the fleece so closely off the sheep that more wool is got than by ordinary shearing, and without any chance of nicking pieces of skin out, which is so common in ordinary hand-shearing. A sheep after having undergone his toilet by machinery looks positively indecent.

It is supposed that many sheep and cattle are killed by snakes, and there are many instances in which even a horse going along a road has been bitten and killed by the brutes. Generally, if a sheep dies a natural death, the crows soon come down and feed upon the carcase, but sometimes they don't, and then it is supposed that the sheep must have been killed by a snake, and the flesh rendered inedible. But this would open up an interesting question, for I believe it has been proved that the poison of a snake does no harm if taken internally, therefore one would have supposed that the flesh of an animal so killed would not be poisonous. It may, perhaps, be disagreeable to the taste, but I would prefer to leave the matter for others to experiment upon.

Snakes abound everywhere in Australia—black snakes, brown snakes, and death adders, being all most poisonous. It is quite bad enough to come across them at every turn when out shooting in the Bush, but when they take upon themselves to return the visit and squeeze their nasty bodies along into your bedroom, why, they become a nuisance! I had several exciting snake adventures, but as the snake generally got the best of it, I will not relate them. Once, however, I found a snake having a swim in my private bathing-place. I did not bathe that morning, but I pursued the intruder in a canoe, and after a great fight, during which he repeatedly sprang towards me, I succeeded in breaking his back with the paddle.

Another unpleasant, though comparatively harmless, creature is the iguana. This is a big lizard, sometimes attaining a length of perhaps three feet. They are ugly brutes, and often hang about houses to pick up eggs and other delicacies in which they delight. They are said to be very good eating in themselves, but I didn't try. One day I shot one close to the root of a tree; the tree was hollow, and he was just able to struggle into a hole in the tree. But there he remained, with the end of his tail out. I seized this, and pulled all I knew, till suddenly it came off!

My experiences of sport in Australia were of the poorest. I am assured that there *is* some excellent duck-shooting in parts, but I went out again and again to different places highly recommended, and seldom returned with more than two or three head of game. Occasionally a black swan or a pelican added weight to the bag, and 'redbill' are common in some places; while at times one may get snipe, plover, or curlew.

Lyre-birds and cassowary are said to exist in the Bush, but they are rare.

The kangaroo is an animal which one would expect to be very common in Australia. But I had been over a year travelling about the country before I saw any real wild ones. They always keep very much away from civilization. However, I have seen wallaby, a small variety of kangaroo, not far from the Blue Mountains, and it is a very pretty sight to watch them skipping along among the fallen timber. The wonder is that they never trip up, for it looks as if they must catch their toes occasionally in jumping a log, and if they did, they could not help falling flat on their noses.

There are a great many varieties of kangaroo, but the name is usually only applied to the larger species, the wallabies being smaller and commoner. Smaller still is the pademelon, not much bigger than a hare, and excellent eating; and, finally, there are the kangaroo rats and mice. The hunting and shooting of kangaroos is now only to be got in out-of-the-way districts.

One of the funniest-looking animals is the native bear. He has but little resemblance to any other bear, being more like a monkey, and yet is a marsupial. He has great strong claws for gripping on to the trees, large ears, and mild eyes, and looks a typical fool. But all marsupials, as may be seen by the form of their brains, are not so intelligent as other animals. Opossums and native bears offer but

6

poor sport; flying foxes, which do great damage to the fruit-trees, are common enough in some places. Wild horses may be shot occasionally, and there are some red deer in one place.

Gay-coloured parrots are very common throughout Australia, and in New South Wales they are especially numerous. The good old laughing jackass is often to be heard chortling in his glee over a feast of snake or other reptile.

Although I never came across the gentleman, no book about Australia would be complete without a reference to that amphibious, mole-like, egg-laying, duck-billed monstrosity, the platypus. No wonder it was a puzzle to naturalists when first discovered! His sharp hind-claws are connected with a gland, which gave the idea that the beast must be venomous; I believe there is no further proof of it. He is, however, quite wonderful enough without. The animal is very local, and Wolseley's sheep-station is one of the only places I went to where it was said to be common.

Driving through the Australian bush is a curious experience for the 'new chum.' The road generally consists of the merest track among the trees. Occasionally there is some sort of fence on each side; but even then, as often as not, the trees are not cleared between them. But it is marvellous how the horses go, and how the drivers guide them in and out of the standing and fallen logs, over mounds of earth and deep boggy patches. Somehow, the horses drag the coach or buggy through everything, and at a good pace too.

Then a word must be said about riding and buck-jumping. The Australian bushman, who, by the way, very seldom, if ever, wears the boots and breeches so often depicted in illustrations, but is usually attired in moleskin trousers, occasionally donning a pair of gaiters, is by no means a pretty horseman. But there are two reasons why he *ought* to be good. First, he is always in the saddle, though, remember, this only applies to the bushman, and *not* the townsman ; and, secondly, he has any amount of rash pluck.

I saw some buck-jumping competitions ; but the best rider I saw there was an African negro. The horse burst his girths and threw the saddle, but the ‘ nigger ’ vaulted on to his back again and successfully rode him barebacked !

The Australian saddle is peculiar, being very high in the cantle, and with large knee-pads protruding from the sides. Some are even fitted with a handle on the pommel to seize when the horse begins his bucking games.

I bought my experience in due course. A good-looking, if rough, young horse was the object. He was quiet enough for a day or two, but he then took to moving about as I mounted him. Next he developed a taste for standing erect on his hind-legs, and correction affected his temper, which he vented with his heels ; he was not long before he took to his national propensities, and on several occasions I found myself quickly transferred from his back on to my own. It is almost impossible to sit a buck-jumper in an English saddle. Finally, one day he shied at a little barking cur, took to his heels, carried me two or three miles in not many more minutes, and then slipped up rounding a corner. I still possess the marks of that ride, but the horse himself did not remain long in my possession.

CHAPTER IV.

QUEENSLAND.

QUEENSLAND has a very large area (668,000 square miles, or about the size of Austria, Germany, and France put together) ; but all the interior, though supporting vast quantities of sheep and cattle, is very thinly populated, and by far the greater portion of the people live within fifty miles of the coast.

But it is marvellous how rapidly the place is increasing. When, in 1859, it first became a separate colony, the population amounted to 30,000. Now it is nearly half a million.

Near the south - east corner of the colony is Moreton Bay, a large, nearly land-locked, mostly shallow, sheet of water. Into this runs the Brisbane River, which has sufficient depth to allow of the biggest vessels proceeding up it to Brisbane, twenty-five miles distant (by water).

Of Brisbane, although not such a particularly interesting town, I must talk a good deal ; partly because it is less known to the English tourist than the other capitals, but chiefly because it was my headquarters for some years, and therefore I know the place pretty well.

As a whole, it is an extensive and straggling town, occupying a very large area. But the greater part of it is suburbs—miles and miles of new streets with small detached wooden houses (all wooden houses here are built on low piles to protect them from white ants), an occasional row of shops, and any number of ' hotels,' or drink-shops.

The actual city of Brisbane, surrounded on three sides by the winding river, is a well-built town laid out in streets at right angles, those running north and south being called by men's names (William Street, George Street, etc.), and those going east and west by those of the fairer sex (Alice Street, Margaret Street, etc.), the centre and principal one being Queen Street.

Although the population is comparatively small (some 100,000, including suburbs), Brisbane would compare favourably with many of the largest English towns, and is well supplied with public buildings, for there is the Government House, the Houses of Parliament, the Government offices, etc., in addition to the more usual General Post-Office, Museum, Town-Hall, Custom-house, etc., which most towns have. There is a good opera-house, besides two other theatres, and several concert halls; half a dozen banks occupy fine edifices, while several imposing buildings belong to large firms, insurance offices, etc. There are two cathedrals, and many well-designed churches.

And Brisbane, like the giantess in the show, is

still growing. For, even during the time between my first arrival and my final departure, great changes took place, and many a fine new building rose up in place of some small wooden •erection. About forty years ago the place could hardly be called a town.

The Queensland Club is one of the finest in Australia, which is saying a good deal ; and besides this, there is the Union Club, and several smaller places, such as the Johnsonian (a local ' Savage '), Tattersall's, a German club, and others.

Government House is a nice homely little place, but altogether out of keeping with the present requirements of the great colony. It is constructed of stone, with iron-columned verandas (at least, so *I* believe, having lived there some years; but I read in a certain book of travels that it is 'entirely of wood').

Brisbane is frequently visited by several more or less good theatrical companies who tour round the colonies, staying a few weeks at each place ; and then there are the great ' stars ' who occasionally visit the colonies from England, the Continent, and America. Good old Toole kept us well entertained ; and, by the way, an amusing announcement was made in his presence by a well-meaning civic dignitary. Sir Charles and Lady Hallé had just been rendering sweet music to Brisbane audiences, and this worthy referred to them as the ' Halls,' in which style of pronunciation he was duly corrected. In a speech at Toole's public reception he began with, ' We have all heard of Mr. Tool*ay* ' !

In the suburbs many forms of sport are indulged
in. Besides the several race-meetings and pony-
races, there is a hunt club which organizes drag
hunts, and occasionally a dingo hunt. There was
a good deal of chaff about it at one time, when
the pack was getting low. A theatrical company
arrived in Brisbane to play ' Dorothy,' and brought
with them a pack of hounds to go on the stage.
When the company was about to leave, the hunt
club negotiated for, and purchased, the hounds,
which, nevertheless, gave many a good run, and
soon proved themselves to be useful as well as
ornamental. The jumping is almost entirely over
big timber rails, and a clever horse is, therefore,
an absolute *sine quâ non.* Polo also flourishes off
and on, depending chiefly on the presence of a
few good players ; and Toowoomba, Ipswich, and
other places have their polo clubs, so that several
' foreign ' matches can be played. Besides these
there are several good rowing clubs, which hold
regattas and offer prizes for all branches of rowing ;
and there is a sailing club for the numerous centre-
board yachts which navigate the lower reaches of
the river and the bay.

Nor are the Brisbanites behindhand in social
meetings. Dances, both public and private, are
frequently indulged in throughout the season ; and
though, generally speaking, the private houses are
small, and the domestic establishments, to say the
least, compact, yet evening entertainments of all

sorts are continually given, and hosts and hostesses are ever most hospitable.

The Queen's birthday is always a great event in Australia, and the Governor has a hard day's work. It generally starts off with a great school-feast. Some thousands of school-children assemble in the Domain, and have a great day of it. At a given time the Governor arrives upon the scene to deliver an address, and on mounting a platform is received with solemn cheers; but when on one occasion I humbly followed him, arrayed in regimental uniform and wearing a bearskin, roars of laughter from thousands of young throats rose to the skies, and 'the man in the big hat' was voted quite the most comical part of the show.

A review of the troops is the next event of the programme, and a really very fine display they make. But of them I will say more presently.

Then follows a levée at Government House, all the gentlemen unable to raise uniforms having to appear in evening dress.

After this the Governor has to attend in a sort of semi-state the great race-meeting of the year. Escorted by mounted orderlies and a detachment of mounted police, he drives up the centre of the course *à la* Prince at Ascot, and is received by the president and stewards of the Turf Club.

But before the racing is over a return has to be made to Government House, in order to prepare for a big dinner given to all the principal Government officials. It is a great relief to get this day over.

The Queensland defence force consists of three kinds of troops. There is, first, the permanent force, a battery of artillery of about 100 men and half a dozen officers. Then there is the defence force proper, consisting of infantry, mounted infantry, and artillery—a kind of militia who are paid by the day's work, and are called out whenever required. These number nearly 3,000. And, finally, some 1,500 volunteers, very much on the same footing as those at home.

There can be no doubt that these troops, when drawn up on parade, look splendid, and they are also fairly good at manœuvring. But it is questionable whether they possess that great military essential, discipline, to a sufficient extent for them to form a really good army.

A very amusing event took place whilst I was in Brisbane. It sounds, however, rather serious when I say that it was an open mutiny of the Queensland navy, from the commanding-officer downwards! The captain of the gunboat *Gayundah*, the guard-ship of Brisbane, was, for reasons I need not here discuss, dismissed by the Government. But he refused to go, and remained in command of his vessel! One official after another was sent on board to arrest him, but he quietly pointed to his crew, drawn up under arms, and hinted that if pressure were brought to bear, all those on board without his permission might find themselves in an awkward predicament. Under these ominous circumstances the commissioner of police thought best to show *his* strength, and actually ordered down a party of police armed with rifles and supplied with ball ammunition, to line the banks of the river, and, if the occasion demanded, to pepper the steel, bullet-proof gunboat, and so force her, despite her machine guns and armed crew, to surrender!

Crowds lined the river banks, and for some hours the greatest excitement prevailed. However, eventually the matter was peaceably settled, though, needless to say, the hero of the day has since retired from the Queensland navy.

The Queensland police are a very fine body of men. Their dress is peculiar and unbecoming, consisting of a loose jacket, more of the cut of a sailor's jumper, but with tight collar, ordinary dark trousers, and black-cloth helmet. They wear no belt, but keep their staffs tucked into the front of their coats.

This force was put to a severe test during the great dock strikes, when thousands of men turned out to do nothing but live on the money which was freely sent out from England as help for the 'poor unemployed.'

Brisbane is most efficiently protected against hostile invasion, but not so much by artificial fortification as by the natural position.

Moreton Bay is, as I have said, mostly very shallow, and for some miles from land is only a few feet deep at low-water. In order to enable ships to get up the river to Brisbane, a regular canal has been dredged out, and this is carefully marked out with buoys and beacons. With these guides removed, the navigation of the canal would be next to impossible, and could be easily still further obstructed.

The Brisbane River winds about in the most extraordinary way among the hills and undulations on which the town is built. Outside the city there are some pretty reaches, the clumps of bamboo, which have been planted a great deal about the neighbourhood, adding very greatly to the beauty of the place. I always think bamboos in a landscape add just that finish which a spray of maidenhair gives to a bouquet.

Round about Brisbane are several pretty spots. The Enoggera Reservoir, surrounded by wooded hills, is a great resort for picnickers, while Mount Coot-tha, or 'One-Tree Hill' as it is more familiarly called, and White's Hill, enable one to get fine views over the city and surroundings.

On an island in Moreton Bay, called St. Helena, is the principal convict establishment of Queensland. If ever I have to undergo such compulsory retirement, may it be there! Cheerful workshops, with a glorious view across the water, fresh, breezy sea-air, good food and lodging, and, of all things, a ration of tobacco—such are some of the advantages of a sojourn at St. Helena!

But, nevertheless, this institution at one time got
into very bad odour on account of the shocking
tortures which some enterprising member of the
Queensland Parliament discovered were practised
there. He produced in the House of Assembly
(and showed to me) the brutal gag with which he
heard that obstreperous prisoners were suppressed.
The matter was inquired into, but no convict could
be found who had undergone the infliction, and the
instrument of torture was in the end proved to be a
lady's dress-suspender!

Queensland is said (by its inhabitants) to possess
the finest climate in the world. But I was unfortunate in being there during some three years of exceptional weather. First we had droughts—hot sunny
days without a cloud in the sky; all the country
dried up, sheep and cattle dying by the hundreds of
thirst, and people even in Brisbane buying water
by the barrel. Then a year after we had a rainy
season. It used to pour with rain morning, noon,
and night. For some six months we hardly had a
day one could call fine. Floods rose, bridges and
roads were washed away, sheep and cattle drowned,
and once again everyone was discontented. As for
amusements, walking in the wet was miserable;
riding, a labour through the mud; driving, an
impossibility on the half-washed-away roads; and
even the swollen river, bearing along fallen trees
and wreckage with its rapid current, rendered
boating a danger. So indoor amusements were

all that could be indulged in ; but when one day I went into the billiard-room, I found a leak in the roof, and the green cloth a morass! So at all events I believe the Queensland climate *is* the best in one respect, and that is in *variety*.

Brisbane, for a few days in summer, is very hot indeed. Most people, if they possibly can, go away for a month or two. But in winter, although it is never what we would call cold (that is to say, frosts are very rare), yet there are some cruelly biting westerly winds.

There are often terrific hailstorms in Queensland, and if I name the size of the hailstones I am afraid I shall not be believed. I will, nevertheless, state what was printed in the papers (described by a man I knew) on one occasion. The largest hailstone he found was ten and a half inches long by eight inches wide! If you do not believe this, you must be content with the Government meteorologist's account of the same occasion, though he only got a stone described as four inches across. It would be tame after this to say they are frequently so large that they will not go into a tumbler.

Although Queensland can hardly be called a great fruit-growing country—at all events, just yet—still, a great variety of fruits do grow. It is, of course, known in Australia by the nickname of ' Bananaland,' and considerable quantities of bananas are grown, chiefly by Chinese, in the north. Then, oranges are cultivated a good deal, vineyards do fairly well, and many very good pineapples are grown. But, in addition to these warm climate fruits, very excellent strawberries are to be got in Gympie, though, I believe, in very few other places in Queensland. All English fruits can be grown, but a fruit very little known to Englishmen, but which I consider one of the best I know, is the Chinese date-plum or tree-tomato. It is very much like an ordinary tomato to look at outside, though the inside is more like a very fine plum, but with only a few seeds in the centre. Custard apples are another excellent fruit. Granadillas and loquots are also grown.

But, unfortunately, all these fruits are difficult to obtain in Brisbane. There are none of those great fruit-markets such as we have in Europe, and the colonists have to thank that much-abused Chinee for most of what they *do* get.

With vegetables the same may be said. They are scarce and expensive, and it is considered *infra dig.* for any but a Chinaman to grow them for market.

One of the most peculiar trees of Australia is the 'grass-tree.' It consists of a stem about a foot in diameter, and varying from nothing to six or eight feet high, on the top of which is a large tuft of grass. When in flower a spike very like a bull-rush rises from the top. Round the stem is a sort of scaly covering, which loosens and falls off. These trees grow very slowly, and it is supposed that the largest specimens are some hundreds of years old.

Another extraordinary-looking plant is the 'bottle-tree,' of which there are two distinct varieties, both very similar in general appearance, but with entirely different shaped leaves. The chief peculiarity is the extraordinary fat bottle-shaped stem.

The 'bunya-bunya' is another odd tree; it looks like a cross between a fir-tree and a 'monkey puzzle,'

BOTTLE-TREE AND GRASS-TREES.

and has a fruit much esteemed by the natives, though it only appears once in three years.

Australians are very fond of naming places and things after those of any fancied similarity in the old country. It is always confusing, and one is much puzzled on finding the names 'she oak,' 'silky oak,' 'beech,' 'Moreton Bay chestnut,' 'box-tree,' and I don't know how many more, all of

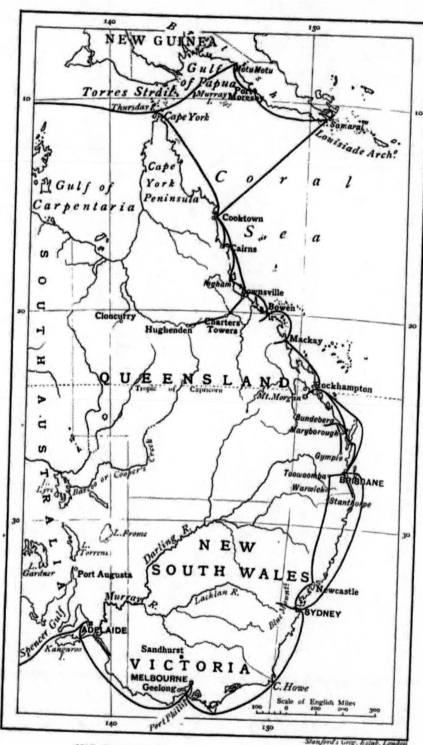

MAP OF EASTERN AUSTRALIA AND NEW GUINEA. *To face page 97.*

which have but the faintest resemblance to the trees of similar name at home. There are, of course, numerous species of eucalypti, each having its peculiar colloquial name. One of them, called the 'ti-tree,' I shall have occasion to refer to later on.

From what I have said it may be imagined that all the towns of Queensland are very like one another, and present no very interesting characteristics. A straight main street with verandaed shops, a town-hall, a post-office, bank, and numerous hotels, summarizes the chief features of all the small towns.

In the south there is Stanthorpe, which, as its name implies, is a small tin-mining place. Warwick, of more pretentious build, is next passed, near to which is Killarney, so named on account of its lakes and mountains, the former being some flat swamps a dozen miles away from the latter. Toowoomba is the principal town of the Darling Downs, which comprise a large area of elevated country, forming one of the chief agricultural and pastoral districts of the colony. They lie some sixty miles inland of Brisbane. Further westwards is Roma, whence come oranges and wine; Dalby, a sheep-grazing centre; and Charleville, the present terminus of the railway. Returning down the line, Grandchester is passed, so rechristened by Sir George Bowen, it having been previously known by the more prosaic name of 'Bigg's Camp'; Ipswich, one of the oldest established towns, near which are the principal coal-mines of Queensland; and Goodna, where is a large

7

lunatic asylum. Marburg is a specimen of one of
the numerous German agricultural settlements, for
emigrants from the Fatherland are plentiful in
Queensland ; there is even a German paper pub-
lished in Brisbane. Southport may be styled the
local Brighton, and Sandgate the local Margate.

Although Queensland has a coast-line of 2,500
miles, she can scarcely be said to possess a single
large port. All the principal towns near the coast are
situated on rivers, most of which are unnavigable
for large ships, so that merchandise from these
has to be carried by lighters to vessels lying in the
bays. It is a curious fact, for there are several
tolerably good small harbours, but for some inexplicable reason the towns on these do not seem to
carry on much trade.

Even down in Moreton Bay there is a fairly good
natural harbour at Bribie Island, which might form
a port for Brisbane if capitalists would take it up,
but they don't.

Going north from Brisbane, we come to Gympie,
one of the great gold-mining centres.

Gold, I may as well explain for the benefit of
those who have not studied the subject, is found
either 'alluvial '—that is, among the sand or 'dirt '
in the bed of a stream—or in reefs, generally of
quartz. In the latter case it is often so intimately
mixed in with the formation of the stone that there
is absolutely no visible trace of the gold. This
may be easily supposed when we know that it pays

to work stone containing only half an ounce of gold
to a ton of quartz—or, roughly, the amount of gold
in a sovereign distributed throughout a piece of
rock twice as big as a man. But if the stone be
pounded up into a fine powder, then the particles of
gold can be extracted. It is by this process that by
far the greater quantity of the precious metal is got.

The mine itself does not present any special
features of interest. One is lowered down the shaft
in a 'cage' suspended from a big pulley by a
steel-wire rope, and hauled up again by a steam-
engine. 'Levels' are passed, suggestive of stations
on the Underground Railway. One can walk along
these good-sized passages, and see 'stopes' and
'winzes,' and various other methods, too long to
explain here (even if I *could*), for following up the
veins and getting out all the gold-bearing stone.

Sometimes a few minute specks of gold are
visible, and occasionally regular little studs and
nuggets are found, but more generally it is pure
white marble-like stone. This ore is then taken to
the batteries above ground. These are in a large
shed, and as one enters it the noise of the stampers
is deafening. All along one side, or sometimes
both sides, of the shed are rows of stampers,
looking like a lot of steam-engine cylinders. Each
consists of a vertical iron rod, at the bottom of
which is a 'shoe,' or hammer, working in a cylinder.
The stamper is alternately lifted and dropped by
cams on a horizontal revolving shaft. The broken

stone is put in the cylinder at the bottom, and the stamper beats down on it, and crushes it to powder. A stream of water running through the cylinder (we will leave out the technical names) carries this away in the form of muddy water, which is flowed over some large slanting plates of copper covered with mercury. The muddy water runs easily off this, and is carried away; but the minute particles of gold, when they come in contact with the mercury, prefer to stay there, and form an amalgam. After a time, then, a mass of mixed gold and mercury is got, which, on being placed in a retort, yields up its gold in a molten mass, which is run off and cast into great ingots.

'No. 1, North Phœnix,' is one of the most successful mines at Gympie. I went down it twice. In the ten years since it was first opened, nearly 200,000 tons of stone have been crushed, yielding over £650,000 worth of gold, and paying no less than £18 per share in dividends.

Fifty miles north of Gympie is Maryborough, one of the principal towns of Queensland. It is older and has a rather more settled look than many of these places. This town is some distance up the river Mary, which, however, is navigable for small steamers coming from the coast. Many of the principal towns of the colony are situated in the same way fifteen or twenty miles up a river.

Not far from Maryborough are the Aldershot smelting works, situated away out in the Bush, where various ores are brought to be treated. These come from all parts of Australia, and contain gold, silver, lead, tin, etc. The different ores are taken and mixed carefully in certain proportions, and put into the furnaces, whence comes the useless 'slag,' and a mass of metal composed of many varieties.

The railway from Maryborough goes on to Bundaberg, and thence inland as far as a very small copper-mining place, Mount Perry. The Governor had a most regal reception when he visited the place. As he stepped from the train the local brass band (and such a band!) played with great solemnity, everyone standing bareheaded, a whole verse of 'God save the Queen.' This done, and hats being redonned, the band suddenly started again, and played a second verse. This was found to be so successful that no less than five verses were played before the address of welcome could be read. This energetic and well-meaning band then mounted a waggonette, and accompanied us all round the town, the big-drum man sitting on the step behind.

About Bundaberg we begin to get into the sugar-growing districts, and in the immediate neighbourhood there are several plantations.

I will now proceed to give a long and intricate discourse on sugar and its extraction, so those who are not interested in the matter had better turn on.

There are many different varieties of sugar-cane, but we need not go into that. Usually the cane, when full-grown, is some eight or ten feet high, and the plantation has the appearance of a very over-grown green corn-field. The cane, which is, say, six feet long, as thick as the handle of a bat, and crowned with a tuft of big grass-like leaves, is cut near the roots in much the same way as corn used to be in the old days of the sickle, and warm work it is for those employed in the operation in the stifling, dusty atmosphere. For this reason black labour is necessary, and hence one of the greatest political questions in Australia. At present Kanakas — *i.e.,* South Sea Islanders —are employed ; and, on the whole, they seem to be most satisfactory. Some outcry has, however, been raised against their employment, chiefly owing to certain abuses which have come to light on the part of those charged with the collection of these men. Vessels leave Queensland for the islands, and recruit natives where they can. They are supposed to engage themselves of their own free will to come to Queensland to work on the plantations for three years, and they are then to be returned to their homes, unless, as is often the case, they wish to remain on. If they are occasionally roughly treated on the ships, they are certainly well looked after in Queensland.

In order to get the cane to the mill—for the plantations extend over miles of country—it is usual to lay down a small narrow-gauge railway. On most estates there are certain lines permanently laid down, on which a small engine can draw a big train into the mills from the various districts ; then from this fixed line rails are laid temporarily on the ground to enable the trucks to be taken to various points about among the cane field, and shifted from day to day. It is usual to draw the trucks on these side-lines by hand or horse-power, though the engine can proceed very well, if slowly, on these loose lines, and even go over the small knolls and depressions which naturally occur on the ground. I wonder, by the way, they don't use these temporary lines more for military purposes. They can be laid at a great rate (a mile or more a day), and a good load (forty tons) can be taken at a time with one engine.

Well, the cane is thus brought to the mill, and there is a neat way of taking it from the trucks to the crushing machinery. The lines pass over an excavated ditch by a series of little bridges, and, by a simple arrangement, when the truck comes on to the bridge it is tilted over, so that its contents are thrown into the pit below ; but at the bottom of this pit (about six feet deep) an endless platform is moving ; that is to say, chains are laid a few feet apart on rollers, and battens the length of a truck fixed across them, the whole forming an endless band, running over and under the rollers. The cane, when upset on to this moving 'platform,' is then carried along, ascending an incline, and is thus taken inside the mill. The crushing is done by three enormous rollers, moved round by steam, and fixed so as to almost touch one another. The cane, being dropped between them, is soon crushed flat, all the juice running into a receptacle below, and the crushed fibre being passed on to be used as fuel for the fire. The juice is pumped out, filtered, and conducted through tubes to cisterns, in which it is puri-

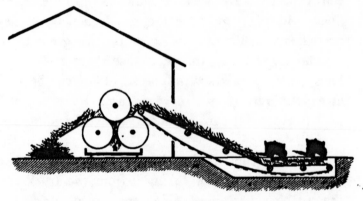

SECTION OF SUGAR-MILL.

fied with lime, etc., and is then put into pans, where it is boiled. As great heat is detrimental to the process, it is boiled in vacuum, going through what is called the 'triple effet.' After this it comes out thick, like so much moist brown sugar, and is conducted into the 'centrifugals,' globular - shaped vessels with perforated sides, fixed on vertical axles, which, when full, are rotated at great speed ; all the moisture is by this means driven out of the sugar through the perforations, and forms molasses, or treacle. In a few minutes nothing but dry white sugar remains in the vessels; this is then taken out and further dried in a big revolving cylinder, and packed in sacks for shipment.

The Kanakas are very funny fellows. I think on the whole they have a good time. Doubtless, once this getting labour from the islands was a species of kidnapping and slavery; but now it is carefully regulated, and the men are taught a great deal when they come to Queensland, for they are generally well looked after by the owners of the plantations and local clergy, and schools and hospitals established for their benefit. It is very comical to hear them being instructed in their 'pigeon' English, which is the only English they understand, and most difficult it is to keep one's serious aspect when one hears the reverend instructor referring to the Creator of all things as 'Him Big-fellow Master.'

Continuing the journey north, we get to Gladstone, where is one of the very few good harbours of Queensland, and on that account it is said to be going to grow. A little further on is Keppel Bay, where the Fitzroy River debouches. Rockhampton, one of the principal towns of Queensland, chiefly known for its meat works and its proximity to the famous Mount Morgan, is situated thirty-five miles up this river. . From here a railway runs some 400 miles inland to tap the 'Hinterland.' We are now just within the tropics.

The preparation of frozen and tinned meats is one

of the industries of Queensland ; and it is a most
interesting sight to go over one of the large works,
such as that at Lake's Creek, near Rockhampton.
The slaughter-house is first visited, situated some little
distance from the other works.   Here the cattle are
driven in from the yards, two at a time being put in a
large loose-box—over this are some boards on which
a man walks, carrying a spear with a chisel-pointed
end ; placing this just above the head of the unsus-
pecting bullock, he drops it, apparently quite lightly,
on to the beast's head, just behind the horns, and
the animal falls dead.   Now and again, though very
seldom, the man, perhaps owing to a sudden movement of the animal, makes a bad shot, and a painful
scene may be witnessed, as the half-stunned bullock
violently struggles, falls, rises again, and makes
frantic endeavours to escape ; it is then impossible
to get another ' shot ' until the beast quiets down
again.   As soon as both animals are killed, doors to
the front are thrown open, chains attached, and the
bodies hauled out and strung up, and in a marvellously short space of time the head is cut off,
the feet removed, the ' innards ' extracted, and the
skin taken off.   Then the carcases are hung on a
trolly and rattled off a hundred yards or so to the
cooling sheds, where they hang for some hours to
' set.'   Next they are quartered, the hind-quarters
being most suitable for freezing ; the fore-quarters
are tinned.

The freezing-rooms are entered by several doors,

to keep the heat out, and are like a series of dark cellars filled with masses of meat hanging up. Though it feels decidedly chilly, it is not unpleasantly cold, and one can hardly believe the thermometer, which is pointing to 10° Fahr. But, doubtless, if one were shut in here for an hour or two, one would have time to realize the lowness of temperature. After a very few minutes, quite enough, however, to inspect the place, one is glad to come out into the warm sun again.

The freezing-engines appear merely as a complicated and inexplicable mass of mechanism ; on parts of this is seen a coating which looks like ice. But being now in the warm sun-laden air, this seems impossible, until, on handling the slimy enamel, you may be convinced that it is actually a coating of pure ice exposed to the air of the tropics !

Then the tinning department has to be visited. First you see the tins being made with some very ingenious machinery. Then the large kitchens, in which the meat is being cooked in numerous huge caldrons. When half cooked, the meat is spread out on tables and cut into small pieces, which are then packed into the tins by hand. Next the tins are put under presses and the meat squeezed in, and the lids put on and soldered down, only a small hole being left in the top. Then the filled tins are put into steam ovens to complete the cooking ; after which the holes are soldered up, the tins cooled under a water jet, and finally painted and labelled.

Mount Morgan, twenty-eight miles from Rockhampton, is one of the mining wonders of the
world, but what seems to me the most surprising
thing about it is the difficulty of getting there.
Considering all the masses of heavy machinery,
and the amount of supplies that have to be taken
daily to supply the community of over two thousand
people, it is extraordinary that they have no better
means of communication for some fifteen miles than
a very bad and difficult road.

It is an ordinary-looking hill, surrounded by
others of very similar appearance, all covered with
gum-trees and undergrowth. Here gold occurs in
a formation hitherto never known to be auriferous,
and though Mount Morgan is generally considered
as a mine, it is in reality but a quarry.

On ascending to the top (most of the way one
can go on a trolly) men are seen excavating the
rock, as in any ordinary quarry. The stone obtained is of several varieties. Here it is a hard
red ironstone, there like white chalk ; in another
place a soft yellow stone, but the more special
variety is stuff like so much cinder, with beautiful
prismatic colours on it. This is, of course, of
volcanic origin, and I believe the idea is that the
whole hill is volcanic, with a core up the centre of
this igneous formation. But gold, oddly enough,
is found in each of the varieties, and all the stone
dug out is sent through the mill. Something like
thirty feet has been cut clear off the top of the hill,

and various shafts and tunnels have been cut into
it to facilitate the removal of the stone, and to test
the extent of the formation.

The crushing mills and apparatus for extracting
the gold are in sheds on the side of the hill, so that
the stone passed in at the top descends, and the
pure gold is got out at the bottom. The gold is
not extracted by the ordinary process which I have
described, but by what is called 'chlorination.' The
first operation is to crush the stone, both hard and
soft being mixed together. It is then reduced to the
finest powder by passing it between large rollers.
This powder is placed in large ovens and baked,
when all the baser metals and other undesirable
foreign matters are melted out. It is next spread
out to cool, and afterwards put into a series of great
wooden vats containing sulphuric acid, water, and
lime impregnated with chlorine, with which the
powder is mixed. After a time the liquid, which has
now absorbed all the gold, is drawn off, looking like
so much green chartreuse. This liquid is then
passed through filters, first of gravel and sand, and
then through fine charcoal, which latter retains all
the gold, and is put into retorts and exposed to
great heat, when the gold melts, and is run into
troughs and formed into solid ingots.

In three years one and a half million pounds' worth
of gold has been got out of the mine, and much
wild speculation has been the result.

Investments in gold-mines are but a form of

gambling. It is, however, amusing, and if you have the money to lose, it is a better form of gambling than most others. As an instance, I bought some shares in a Queensland mine at 4s. each. When I left I sold them, well as I thought, at 5s. A few months after they had risen to £9 a share!

After leaving Rockhampton, the next place of importance is Mackay, situated close to the coast. This is another great sugar-growing locality, but one sugar plantation is very like another, and even the milling machinery, except to a specialist, does not vary greatly.

There is a short line of railway which runs into some of the sugar districts, for Eton, Branscombe, and Homebush are large and important estates. Mr. Davidson, at his comfortable house at Branscombe, has a small but well-found observatory, with a good six-inch refractor telescope.

The most peculiar thing I saw in Mackay was a regularly licensed *lady* cab-driver. (I hope she will excuse my calling her a ' thing.')

On going to Mackay on one occasion with the Governor, I had telegraphed to the hotel for ' rooms for his Excellency, myself, and servant.' On arrival I asked to see the apartments. A good sitting-room and bedroom were reserved for the Governor, but I considered my bedroom rather small, with its two beds crammed in. Moreover, there was someone else's luggage there, and on my inquiring whose it was, the landlady informed me : ' That's the servant's.

This is the room for the aide-de-camp and the servant !' I felt smaller.

Bowen, 100 miles further up the coast, has the unenviable nickname of ' Sleepy Hollow,' and has not much to recommend it beyond a tolerable harbour. They say that Bowen *ought* to have had all the trade that is now done in Townsville, but the latter was ' run ' by energetic men. A railway is in progress, which they hope soon to complete to Charters Towers. This done, doubtless Bowen would wake up a bit.

We then get to Cleveland Bay, whereon is situated Townsville, the chief port of Northern Queensland. But it is a peculiar kind of port, for even the coasting-boats can seldom, if ever, get into the harbour proper (which consists of a wharf-edged creek), while the British-India liners, which call here, and sometimes remain two or three days, have to anchor no less than seven miles from the town ! The people of Townsville are nevertheless very ambitious, and want to make their town the capital of the northern colony, if Queensland is to be divided up.

It was founded originally by one Captain Towns, hence its singular (or dual ?) name.

I will not delay to describe the place, with its town-hall and post-office and fairly good hotel, further than to say that, though the surroundings are bleak and open, dusty and parched, yet the bold rocky hills form a more picturesque background than is usual with Australian suburban scenery.

A long line of railway runs inland, which is of increasing importance. Passing through the Charters Towers goldfield, it runs some 240 miles to Hughenden, and it is proposed to continue the line eventually right across to Normanton and the Gulf of Carpentaria.

Townsville is the headquarters of the diocese of Northern Queensland, where Bishop Stanton, a wonderful preacher, holds his sway.

But it is also the headquarters of the movement for separation, of such momentous interest to all Queenslanders. These northern portions of the colony are so very far from Brisbane, and communication is so bad, that they consider it absurd to be governed from the distant town. Besides, the conditions of these tropical places are not supposed to be understood by Brisbanites.

There is something in all this, and it is very natural to suppose that so huge a colony cannot easily be governed from one centre, or rather from one corner. Some have suggested that the capital should be transferred to a more central place, such as Gladstone; others, notably Sir Samuel Griffith, the present Premier, that there might be a go-between by having small local parliaments, and retaining the chief government, as at present, at Brisbane.

Then Central Queensland also agitates to be

separated. But, without wishing to express any further opinion on the subject, I am convinced that the great reason for pressing this matter with many of its advocates is that they themselves will be bettered if *their* town becomes a capital, and they be made ministers, members, or Government officials.

Charters Towers is a go-ahead mining town some sixty miles inland of Townsville. It has been of very rapid growth, and is already, in point of population, second only to Brisbane among the towns of Queensland.

It covers a large area, and is much spread out, since it is merely a collection of houses nestling around the mines ; so that some of the principal workings are now near the centre of the growing city. On all sides one sees the great pulley-wheels erected on thin wooden towers, denoting the shaft of a mine.

The place has become a regular warren, as from many of the mines bores have been driven into neighbouring claims, and you may go down one shaft, and along underground, and ascend to the surface by another shaft.

The country between Charters Towers and Hughenden, though elevated, is mostly very flat. Mile after mile is passed of land which, when I was there, was covered with long, coarse grass ; but the peculiar Australian climate is very deceptive, and has to account for many contradictory descrip-

8

tions of country given by explorers. This locality, I was assured, is at times, after a season of drought, a bare waterless desert !

Still further inland are rich open plains, supporting large numbers of cattle, and whereon the wallaby and emu can disport themselves almost undisturbed. Without passing any place worthy of the name of a town, we get to Hughenden, nearly 160 miles from Charters Towers. Fancy going from London to Crewe without passing a single village of over 200 inhabitants !

Hughenden itself has not much to boast of. I suppose its entire population is under 1,000, but it is the chief town of a very large district.

Although I won't say that it is a very usual occurrence, on the occasion of a viceregal visit they had a grand ball. There was a splendid band, though I don't know where they raised it, or, rather, where they got the *instruments* from (for I don't suppose any of the performers had ever tried to play before). At the house in which I was staying, the lock of my despatch-box went wrong, and when I asked for a locksmith, the 'butler' tendered his services, for such was his more usual vocation. While at the ball, a gentleman in a very good attempt at evening dress and spotless pair of white gloves, in taking his partner to a chair, stopped to speak to me. I only recognised him when he told me he had mended the lock all right, and, I suppose, having cleared the table and put away the plate,

was now enjoying a little well-earned relaxation.
Quite the belle of the ball was my host's house-
maid ; however, when supper was served she
turned waitress again. Such is society in a Bush
town !

I came across some other odd characters. Lieu-
tenant-Colonel Durnford was one of them. He
showed us with pride his Crimean medal (on a
black and white striped ribbon) with his name upon
it, and told us of the battles he had fought there.
He was a fine-looking man, apparently of some
forty-five summers, and on our expressing surprise
at his looking so youthful for a Crimean veteran, he
explained that he was not full colonel in the Crimea ;
he was *then* only *major-colonel*, and belonged to the
' Third Cavalry' ! What changes do take place in
the ranks and titles of our army !

It was in this district that I first set eyes on some
real wild blacks. The aboriginals of Australia are
an extraordinary people. To look at, they are
quite unlike any other human beings I ever saw.
A thick tangled mass of black hair crowns their
heads ; their features are of the coarsest : very
large broad and flattened noses ; small, sharp,
bead-like eyes and heavy eyebrows ; they generally
have a coarse, tangled bit of beard ; skin very
dark, and limbs extraordinarily attenuated, like
mere bones. But they always carry themselves
very erect.

The aboriginals may-be divided into three classes.

First there are the miserable creatures, dressed in the filthiest of clothes, who prowl about the towns doing little but beg. Then there are the semi-civilized people who roam about the country, who obtain clothes, and also drink, from the white man,

A QUEENSLAND BLACK.

and occasionally make themselves useful on the stations in driving cattle, and suchlike occupations. Then there are the wild blacks, who wander about, stark naked, over the less settled districts, who live entirely on what they can pick up, whether fruits or roots, wallaby or snake, or in an occasional raid on the white man's cattle.

But these last are, in my opinion, by far the most interesting. If not the lowest type of humanity, they would be hard to beat. They show but few signs of human instinct, and in their ways seem to be really more like beasts. From all accounts, they do nothing but wander about looking for food, except for an occasional ' corroboree,' and the only sign of superiority over the beasts appears in the construction of weapons. Their huts are of the rudest description, generally composed of a few slabs of bark piled together, sometimes supported on three or four poles, and often covered with branches. But these are carelessly made, and have no pretensions to being watertight ; in fact, are no more than mere shelters for a night or two. Occasionally they ornament themselves with feathers, paint, etc., but the most usual form of adornment seems to be to cut their skin so as to have scars, as if even their natural covering were too much.

Many of these natives consider themselves at perpetual war with the white men, and it is an undeniable fact that some unscrupulous white men consider themselves always hostile to the black. Doubtless it begins with the aboriginal, who kills some of the squatter's cattle or sheep. Then the white man goes forth to kill, or at all events drive away, the blacks. If any of them are killed, it is very natural for the others to avenge murder and attack the next white man they see. Then they are hunted down by the police, and more of them shot, and so the everlasting war continues. It is a bad state of affairs, but a solution is difficult. I understand that no missionary has ever succeeded in making much headway among them. They are too dense to be educated, and in the few instances in which a black has become apparently civilized, he has invariably gone back after a time to savagery.

We came across a camp one day, and being a large party, the blacks, who otherwise might (*or might not*) have proved hostile, thought it best not to wait, and all ran yelling and cooeying into the bush. They left behind them, however, two old 'gins' (women), who were about the most repulsive specimens of humanity it has ever been my lot to gaze upon. They stood there shuddering and making fearful squeaks, as if vainly trying to scream, and were evidently in the most abject terror, but unable from their feebleness to run away. They wore not a vestige of clothing, neither did they appear ashamed of exposing their graceful (?) forms to the gaze of a stranger. But I will turn from the thoughts of them as from a nightmare—they were too positively disgusting. Lying among the huts were several well-made spears and 'woomeras.' It seems unaccountable that such a low type of man can turn out such good workmanship as is to be seen in their spears and other weapons. And it is 'more curious that they should have such extraordinary apparatus of offence as the boomerang and woomera.

I think there is much often said about the former which is at least exaggeration. To say that a boomerang can be thrown at an object, and will come back to the hand, is absurd. I understand that there are two distinct kinds of boomerang—one for sport or war, which can be thrown straight at an

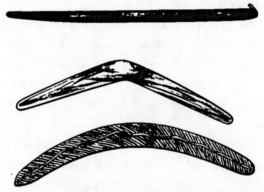

WOOMERA AND BOOMERANGS.

object, and does great execution with its knife-like edge; the other a mere toy, which, when thrown into the air, gyrates around, spinning on its axis, and flies in more or less of a circle, and may fall somewhere near the point at which it was started. Then it has been said that the thrower can at all events state beforehand exactly where it will fall. But I do not believe this. I have often asked a man before he threw the boomerang, and even while it is spinning in the air, but he could never tell me where it would fall. The flight of the boomerang is interesting and fascinating to watch, but it is very erratic.

The woomera is a piece of wood nearly three feet long. At one end a small piece of stick is fastened on like a barb. It is used for throwing a spear, the woomera being laid alongside it with the barb in a notch at the butt of the spear. In throwing, the woomera is retained in the hand, and gives an extra leverage or push to the spear.

One of the few other signs of intelligence in the aboriginal is his message-stick. He cuts certain notches and marks on a stick, which may then be sent off by messenger, and it is said that complicated messages can thus be sent and read by the recipient.

Some fifty miles north of Townsville we come to Hinchinbroke Island, with its grand, rocky crags; and from the mainland opposite flows the Herbert River, whereon are more sugar-plantations. It was at Ingham, some few miles up this river that I saw a large 'corroboree' of blacks. They had all come in to the township to get the blankets which are periodically distributed by the Government. There must have been some hundreds of men, and they had a great day of it on the green. First, they threw boomerangs in the most marvellous way, and then they performed their dance. This was a very peculiar performance, hardly graceful, but still very interesting, and even comic.

One of the most effective figures was when they all crouched down in single file, and, each placing his hands on the sides of the man in front of him, hopped along the ground together, all making a grunt to keep time. It was not at all unlike certain exercises which have lately been introduced into our military gymnastic courses. All these dances partook of the nature of a ballet—that is to say, they depended on the united action of the whole lot — though, beyond that, there was not much similarity to an Alhambra performance.

To the north of Ingham, large areas of thick scrub occur. It is in these that the great cassowary is found. He is unknown on the 'plains of Timbuctoo.'

Further along the coast is Cardwell, on Rockingham Bay. Here numbers of that curious-looking amphibian, the dugong, are caught, and their oil extracted. Then we get to Mourilyan Harbour, a pretty little place, which I expect one day will be of more importance, for now very few vessels call there. The steamer enters through a narrow channel between high cliffs, and an apparently splendid harbour is exposed to view. It is found, however, to be very shallow in most parts, though it is doubtless capable of much improvement. There is at present a small wharf, with a few buildings close to the entrance, and a narrow-gauge railway connects the port with some sugar-plantations about seven miles off. This railway runs through the densest tropical bush, and the construction of it proved most deadly work, no less than thirty-five men dying of fever during the operation! This is about the nearest port to Herberton, a town up in the hills, enjoying a cool and salubrious climate. The Johnstone River runs in a little further up the coast, and in the district drained by this fine stream (which, unlike some Australian rivers, never dries) are some very large sugar estates, aggregating some 6,000 acres. The banks of the river are clothed with splendid tropical verdure, and the densest bush exists in the parts not cleared for cultivation. Alligators are plentiful in the shallows of the river, and aboriginals, untrammelled with the superfluous coverings of modern civilization, may be seen camping on its banks.

Geraldton is the capital of this district, and boasts of a hospital, a bank, a court house, and no less than thirty wooden houses.

The next place of importance we get to is Cairns, a thriving town of several thousand inhabitants, with a fairly good port, and a large inlet which, they say, can be converted into a splendid harbour. It is the centre of a great sugar district, and large quantities of bananas are grown here, chiefly by Chinamen. When the Governor visited the place, a humble-looking Chinee came on board the yacht, and said he wished to present some bananas to his Excellency. With the expectation of seeing him produce a dozen or so, he was asked where they were, whereupon

THE BARRON FALLS.

To face page 123.

he ordered up no less than twenty-five men, each carrying a bunch of some six or eight dozen bananas!

From Cairns runs one of the most extraordinary railways in the world, for it is not only a marvellous piece of engineering, and surrounded by the grandest scenery, but it has cost I don't know how much money, and so far leads to nowhere. It is supposed eventually to get to Herberton, a place of 1,000 inhabitants! I hear it will be a long, long time before it can hope to pay, but the chief difficulties have been overcome. The line runs up the valley of the Barron through a splendid forest of large trees and palms, hung with creepers and lycopodium, presenting a sight far finer than anything else I saw in Australia, and, after going through tunnels and over bridges innumerable, will eventually pass within view of the Barron Falls, which are quite worth going all the way to see.

I was so accustomed to having the marvels of every Australian locality dinned into me, and being very disappointed on seeing them, that when I was told of this wonderful waterfall I did not expect to see much. But I have no hesitation now in saying that those who have not been to the falls and valley of the Barron have not seen the grandest view in Australia. There may be a better, but I never came across it. At this time the journey to the falls was an arduous one, involving a ride of many miles along a narrow track, where, if one had slipped, one would have rolled down perhaps 1,000 feet to the river below! The falls *appear* to come from very near the top of a hill, and dash down in numerous cascades to the river, said to be 2,000 feet below. The river then flows along a narrow valley, with very steep sides thickly clothed in forest. We had an American in our party, and we waited to hear his opinion of the grand sight. He looked at it for some moments, and then said: ' Pity there's no ho-tel up here.'

The only other town of importance on the Queensland coast is Cooktown, a curious little place. It seems, not unlike other Australian towns, to consist chiefly of hotels. It is a bad harbour— very—being merely the mouth of a small river, without much protection from the east, and without any expanse of deep water. However, it has historic interest, for here Captain Cook landed in 1770, and remained some time to repair his vessel, the *Endeavour*. There are some relics of his time preserved in the School of Arts. This is also a great place for blacks, and a few miles out of the town, across the river, hundreds may generally be seen camping. All north of this, which we may style the ' horn of Australia,' the little-explored centre of which has been called the ' Never-never land,' is undoubtedly *the* home of the wild black, driven north by the spread of civilization.

Thursday Island is off the extreme northernmost point of Queensland, and, indeed, of Australia. It is a little to the north-west of Cape York, and is in the centre of a group of islands which serve to enclose the harbour. It is the sort of place no one would care to live in longer than necessary, and as I once had to stay there ten days, I know the place better than most people. There is a Government resident, Mr. Douglas, who appears to be a good man thrown away. He has been in his time Premier of Queensland and High Commissioner of British New Guinea, and is now settled down to look after this wretched, though certainly important, little place.

Practically, all vessels going through Torres Straits, and that means a good many, have to pass within sight of the island. They are always talking of fortifying the place, for it certainly would be a nasty blow to Australia if it were taken possession of by some foreigner, and the Torres Straits thus blocked. But I would not volunteer to form one of the garrison. The island is small, a couple of miles long at the most, and very bare. There is a small town, with one or two stores, the usual hotels, and a bank; there is a Roman Catholic mission station and a doctor, and that is about all. On neighbouring islands are the signalling station (and one blessing is that the place is connected by telegraph with the mainland, so at all events one gets the news) and several pearl-shelling stations. These latter have some interest. The boats go out to the pearl-banks with divers, and return with masses of shell. These are great flat shells about the size of a large plate. I am told that they seldom contain good pearls, these being generally found in a smaller beast having a shell less valuable as mother-of-pearl. But the latter commodity is found to be the most valuable in the long-run, and therefore the divers may keep any pearls they find as a perquisite. I could have bought a lot of pearls there, and might possibly have made a young fortune thereby, but not understanding the technics of the subject, and knowing that persons in these odd corners of the world are not always of that simple truth-loving nature we all so much admire, I thought it best to keep my money in my pocket.

The navigation of the Torres Straits is most intricate and difficult. Numerous small islands and coral reefs exist all around, and the many remains of wrecks to be seen tell their tale of the dangers. It is usual in sailing about these waters to have a man aloft (often the captain himself) on the look-out for the pale-green water which covers the reefs. Often when quietly sailing along one hears the shout of 'Hard a starboard!' and the vessel flies round through a right angle, just avoiding a sunken reef by a few yards.

Shortly before I got to Thursday Island an extraordinary affair occurred there. One day a foreign captain and crew arrived in a boat, saying their ship had been lost on a reef near. The wreck was sold by auction, and was bought by the agent of a shipping firm for £5. The captain and crew then departed by some homeward-bound vessel, and were never heard of again. On examining the wreck, she was found to be a good sound schooner with a cargo of coals, and had nothing the matter with her except two or three artificially-made holes in the bottom! These were soon stopped up, she was floated off, and I saw her lying at anchor as if nothing had been wrong. It was a cheap five pounds' worth!

So much for Queensland in general, though it must be understood that my visits to the places described were made at various intervals of time.

But sorrows cast their shadows over the brightest scenes. Ere I had been six months in Queensland my much-lamented chief, Sir Anthony Musgrave, was no more. A gloom was spread over the whole colony as the telegraph circulated the sad and unexpected news. A grand and befitting funeral took place two days after, which was attended by all the principal officials and leading men, as well as by representatives of various parties and institutions in Queensland. Soon afterwards I started to go home to England, but before I had got half-way received the news that I was to return to my post under the new Governor, General Sir Henry Norman, and with him I remained on for another two years, serving one of the most popular, painstaking, and experienced Governors that Queensland (or probably any colony) has ever known.

Before going into the description of another country I will venture to state briefly my opinion on Australia as a field for the emigrant. It can easily be summarized. The labouring man will find it a paradise ; the professional man will find his profession overstocked ; and the man with money to invest will probably be ruined. Those at work in the colonies naturally dislike to see rivals coming out and taking from their small proceeds, and even if it is to the ultimate advantage of the colony, my personal advice to would-be emigrants, except of the lowest class, is, like *Punch's*—Don't.

CHAPTER V.

PAPUA AND ITS PEOPLE.

NEW GUINEA is the largest island in the world (after Australia), cutting out Borneo by a short head. It is, or, at all events only six or eight years ago was, about the least known part of the world, considering its situation. Many ice-bound countries of comparatively little interest have been explored, so have some places in the far interior of Asia or Africa; but New Guinea, an island the shores of which can be approached without any difficulty, which has vast stores of interest for the naturalist, botanist, and ethnographist, as well as for the geographer and even trader, is still but very imperfectly known.

The history of the annexation of British New Guinea is somewhat remarkable. About one hundred years ago the whole island was annexed by the East India Company. In 1873 Captain Moresby, of the *Basilisk*, hoisted the British flag at several points. But somehow not much notice seems to have been taken of this, for ten years afterwards the Queensland Government suddenly announced

9

their intention to take possession of all that part which had not in the meantime been claimed by the Dutch. The English Government, however, for some inexplicable reason, not only refused to sanction this, but, when the Germans, seeing a chance of obtaining a new colony, stepped in, no objection was apparently raised to their annexing half the country. In September, 1884, Mr. H. H. Romilly formally proclaimed a protectorate over the south-eastern part in the name of the British Government, and two months afterwards Commodore Erskine, in command of the Australian squadron, arrived to hoist the Union Jack and consume much powder in again promulgating the protection. Finally, in September, 1888, another ceremony took place, when the country was finally declared a British possession.

The island used in olden days to be known as 'Papua, or New Guinea.' Thoughtlessly, no doubt, the term 'British New Guinea' was put in the documents of annexation, and so the title remains. But there will ever be confusion between New Guinea, Guinea in Africa, and British Guiana in America ; whereas 'Papua' would have been simple and distinctive.

In Sydney one may read on a brass plate outside one of the principal shipping offices, 'New Guinea Mail Steamers.' But when you come to inquire as to the port whence these boats leave, you are referred to Cooktown or Thursday Island.

On proceeding to these places, you first discover that there is no regular mail; and such a thing as a steamer running regularly to New Guinea is quite unheard of.

The next thing, then, is to find out when the first vessel of any kind is likely to be going, and then to secure your passage while you can.

I was very lucky, for within a week of my arrival at Cooktown I found a small trading vessel, a thirty-ton cutter, about to start for the promised land. She was, it is true, only going to the island of Sudest, a couple of hundred miles or so from New Guinea, and my further means of progress would be uncertain; but that was a mere detail. I took my passage accordingly, but was somewhat surprised to discover that passengers were not supplied with such luxuries as food and drink, and that, as for cooking and attendance, each person would have to look after his own requirements in those respects. Then, with regard to cabins, I found there were none, except the captain's; and passengers were free to sleep wherever they liked, so long as they did not interfere with the efficient working of the vessel. However, by means of a little display of cordiality, I finally made arrangements with the captain by which I might share his cabin, his food, and the use of his servant (a dirty, miserable-looking Malay).

As an early start had to be made, I experienced my first night on board in harbour. The *Mercury* was a dirty, tubby old boat; but she looked strong and business-like. The captain was a plausible, youngish man, and the mate a fine specimen of a Scotchman, whose knowledge of seamanship was mostly acquired, I believe, on some of the gold-fields of Queensland. The remainder of the ship's complement comprised two sailors of sorts and six passengers—miners on the everlasting search for gold. The hold of the vessel had a layer of earth-ballast, and on this these miners camped out. My quarters, though hardly the place I should choose to live in if I had my choice, were somewhat more luxurious—a very small cabin with two bunks; one mine, the other occupied in turn by the captain and the mate.

We started on our voyage in due course, but met with only very light winds, and by evening thought best to anchor under the lee of a small island still in sight of the land we had left. Next day we passed through the Great Barrier reef—that curious coral formation which runs down parallel to the coast of Queensland for 1,200 miles, about twenty to sixty miles from land. It is a very curious sight —long stretches of light-green sea, with white breakers and occasional black rocks, extending as far as the eye can see north and south, yet to the east and west is nothing but open sea. It is supposed that this marks the position of the coast-line in remote ages.

After several attempts to sail through a gap in

the reef, and being carried right back again by the strong current, we finally passed through, and were rolling on the mighty ocean.

But gentle breezes still prevailed, and our progress was slow. It is very monotonous work lolling about the dirty deck of a small vessel like this, under a cruelly hot sun, which seems to bake the whole boat through. I lay there on deck trying to read to while away the weary hours as we slowly rolled to and fro on the great glassy ocean, out of sight of land, nothing but sea and sky to be seen around, no one to talk to except the skipper—a decent enough fellow, but uninteresting—and the miners, who were very dull, and whose sole object in life seemed to be to suck their empty pipes and spit.

We passed several sea-serpents. Although hardly large enough to be worth chronicling in the press—for their length hardly exceeded six feet—they were quite nasty enough to look upon, and are said to be very poisonous. They are of a sandy yellow colour, swim leisurely just below the surface, with the head well out of water, and dive at once on being frightened.

The sight of a shark hovering around in the clear blue water was a great relief to the monotony. He sailed about with a very dignified air, while some half-dozen pilot fish (something like small mackerel, with dark bands across the body) kept so close around him that they looked as if they were a portion of him.

Several other small fish also followed at a respectful distance in rear. Soon we had a line rigged, and a large piece of meat fixed to the hook and lowered overboard. After playing about with the bait for a bit, finally Mr. Shark took his last meal; and a bowline being let down the line and passed over his body, he was hauled on board. Revolver-bullets through his head only had the effect of making him lively, and it was extraordinary to see the manner in which he jumped about, flapping his great tail in all directions, splashing his blood over everything near, knocking down anything movable within reach, and getting fearfully mixed up with his line. However, after a time he got quieter; axes and knives were produced, and soon his tough skin was cut through, and his inside removed and cast overboard as a legacy to his faithful pilots. His jaws were then cut out (and now adorn my room); and after some nice steaks were cut from his sides, his body was committed to the deep. It is remarkable that even a fast-swimming fish cannot be free from parasites; but numerous little black things, the shape of a turtle, with two long tails, were firmly attached to his body. Fresh fish for dinner may be considered a great luxury; but although it was very tender, and looked well, and tasted not at all bad, being very like skate, yet somehow I did not care about eating much of this shark. I suppose I had not a good appetite, for the others seemed to enjoy it immensely.

Day after day passed in much the same fashion. I tried rigging up a small awning to lie under, but the powerful rays of the sun penetrated through it, and the heat was more stifling than ever. Gazing into the blue water, I was anxious to know how far down one could see. I lowered down a lead line of thirteen fathoms (seventy-eight feet, remember), and could see every inch of it! But reference to a physical chart informs us that the sea about here is 2,000 fathoms deep! I noticed at one time in the water innumerable white specks like fine hairs: could these be a species of that mysterious animalcule which natives of the Pacific Islands go forth to hunt for on one particular day of the year?

Onwards we drifted, occasionally cheered by a very slight puff of wind, which soon died away. The captain did great business with his sextant, but I, ever anxious to pick up a hint, was quite unable to elicit from him his object in bringing up this instrument and gazing at the sun through it at various odd times of day, considering he had neither chronometer, tables, nor nautical almanac, and I imagine had but a very poor idea of the simplest mathematics. But having a sextant on board, I suppose he thought it had better not lie idle.

One evening some booby birds flew around and settled on board. They were easily caught with a little patience, and when put on deck were unable to rise off it, and floundered about until thrown overboard, when they flew off quite happily.

After five days of calm the sea began to rise; still, there was very little wind to speak of, and yet our discomfort was augmented by the heavy swell and noise of the flapping sails. And now we began to get anxious about water, for all we had was carried in five casks on deck, of which two were now empty, the water in the third had gone bad, and that in the remaining two had evaporated a great deal.

But next day things looked different; a fresh breeze blew, getting stronger, and knocking up more sea. When night came we saw we were in for a bit of a dusting. Squalls and heavy showers livened us up, and we ripped along under close reefed sails.

On the eighth day out we sighted what we presumed to be the New Guinea coast, consisting of a few rocky islands looming in the haze. After much argument, we came to the conclusion that we must be not very far off Samarai, the port at the east end of the island to which I wanted to go. And now the bad weather favoured me, for the captain, seeing a snug harbour close at hand, determined (on my strong advice) to turn and run in there for the night. But there was nearly a 'slip 'twixt the cup and the lip,' for as we 'gybed' round, our scratch crew made some bungle of it, and let go the main-sheet. The result was that the boom flew over to leeward, and the sail was brought round at right angles with such a tremendous jerk that the backstay was carried away, and we heeled over till I thought we must capsize. The boom and all the lower part of the sail went right under water ; the sea dashed in at the lee scuppers and splashed over the deck. All was hurry and skurry, and every moment I expected to see the mast, unsupported by the stay, go by the board. The main-sheet had run out of the blocks, so that there was no hauling back the boom, and we flew along before the wind. However, after considerable excitement, the ship was brought round, the boom somehow got back, and things put more or less in order, and we settled down to thank our stars that we were so lucky, and had not been left hopelessly drifting about, mastless, in that sea, with very little chance of our having been seen from the shore.

In a few hours more we had run in between the islands and were safely anchored off Samarai by nightfall.

Samarai, formerly known as ' Dinner Island,' but now rechristened by its former native name, is a small island, not much over half a mile across, but admirably suited for its purpose, that is, a Government centre and port of entry. The harbour merely consists of the portion of the sea enclosed by the somewhat extensive group of islands, of which this is one. Nearly half of the island is flat and low ; in fact, this part *was* a swamp, only it has been drained and planted with cocoanuts. The other half rises abruptly to a good height, and on the top of this little hill is the Government bungalow, in a fine airy situation. The Government agent, Mr. Edelfelt, came off to meet us and took me ashore.

We landed at a small lightly-built pier, and passing two or three small stores, walked through the groves of palm-trees by moonlight, and up the path to the house. There were numbers of large land-crabs crawling about, which somehow I didn't like. As we went we got nicely caught in a sharp, heavy downpour of rain, which just soaked us through, and it was but a poor recompense to exhibit for our benefit a magnificent lunar rainbow just afterwards. Finally we got up to the house, a new, well-built, three-roomed bungalow, with kitchens, etc., at the back, and verandas all round. Here Mr. Edelfelt lived with his wife, and endeavoured (without much success) to collect harbour dues and customs from the craft which entered the port. And, by the way, it seems odd under the circumstances that the New Guinea Government should lay heavy duties on nearly all imports. These consist almost entirely of articles for the consumption of the white people. The white people consist almost entirely of missionaries and Government officials. But the missionaries are, or at all events were, exempt from taxation, and the few remaining whites are chiefly storekeepers; and the way it affects them is to make them add an extra charge on to the goods they sell (mostly to officials). Therefore almost all the taxation is derived from the pockets of Government officials! However, it is doubtless arranged with an eye to the future, when the colony may contain a large white community.

I had a restless night, notwithstanding the comforts of a real bed and a firm house, chiefly because some wild beast kept prowling about the veranda. At last I discovered he was safely confined in a

A CUSCUS.

large cage, so felt happier, though still mystified. When dawn broke I discovered the unknown beast to be a fine large cuscus. This animal is a kind of opossum or phalanger. There are several varieties. This was a large white one with brown spots, about the size of a cat, with a beautiful thick coat, a bare, pink, prehensile tail, a head not unlike a large ferret's, and curious light-coloured eyes which seemed to be almost blind in daylight, for, as I now know to my cost, they are nocturnal creatures.

From the veranda of the bungalow splendid views may be had in all directions. The sea runs in amongst numerous islands, thickly covered with vegetation, and many of them rising to a considerable height. To the westwards, within a couple of miles, is the mainland of New Guinea, rising abruptly from the sea in forest-clad hills. Behind them still higher mountains rise into the clouds.

After a sumptuous breakfast of tinned meat and eggs, I went down to the 'town' below. This chiefly consists of two stores, where provisions may be bought by the various small trading vessels which call in. Just now there were a good many miners staying in these 'hotels,' who had come over from Queensland to look for gold. Some small quantities of the precious metal had been found on the island of Sudest; a rush was made for this unknown land, and, as a consequence, for many neighbouring places as well. But, although gold continues to be found there in small quantities, I expect it is very few indeed, out of the hundreds who rushed there, who have come away richer men than when they started. Mr. Kissack owns the principal store, and is one of the leading men on the island. His private residence, to which I had the honour of being invited, is situated near the store, but on a site such as is seldom chosen as the location of a white man's house. It is, like many houses in New Guinea,

VIEW FROM SAMARAI.

To face page 140.

built over the sea. The piles, or rather slender poles, are stuck into the sand some little distance, perhaps twenty or thirty yards, from the beach. On these the house is constructed of poles and sticks, somewhat after the fashion of hurdle-work, and is covered with a carefully-constructed covering of pandanus-leaf on the principle of thatch. The floor, even, is merely made of thin laths put half an inch or so apart, so that one may see the waves playing beneath. It all looks very frail, and I think I should feel rather nervous were I attempting to sleep in the house during a gale ; but I suppose the sea is never very boisterous in this many-mouthed harbour. Such a house, I need hardly add, is delightfully cool and airy, and I was assured, though I can hardly believe it, that it is absolutely free from mosquitoes. A flimsy bridge takes the place of a carriage drive, and connects the mansion with the shore.

The store is built on much the same principle, being also raised, though only a foot or so, above the ground.

Farther along the beach is a heap of coal, this being one of the coaling-stations for the navy, of which we hear so much. Then past the other store is a native village ; but this is entirely deserted, as far as the real inhabitants go, since the Government wisely negotiated for the purchase of the whole island from the natives who formerly made it their home.

The native houses are well built. They are always erected on piles, generally four to six feet above the ground. The usual form, though it varies in some places, is a long shape, with doors at each end, the gable roof rising at the ends and projecting beyond the walls so as to form a sort of veranda or porch at each end. The walls and roof are constructed of a framework of poles covered with a thatch of pandanus-leaves. In order to get up to the door, a flight of steps is represented by a log stuck in the ground in a sloping direction and notched into steps.

The floor consists of a series of split sticks tied across. About the centre is a fireplace, where the floor sticks are arranged rather differently, being stouter and wider apart, and on these a number of stones are laid to act as a hearth.

Then, leaving the native village, as we go still further along the beach, we get to a point where are the old buildings formerly belonging to the mission, which has now also moved to another island. Past the late missionary's house, surrounded by pretty crotons and hibiscus bushes, and the small cemetery, we get on to a path leading back up the hill to the Government bungalow and the flagstaff.

But when we descend to the other side of the island, a vast change occurs in the aspect of the country. Here, after passing some clearings with remains of the cultivation of the natives, we get into denser growth, and finally pass through on to the sea-shore, unsoiled by human contamination, and but seldom visited by white men, for this stretch of beach is shut in at each end by rocky promontories. Here, in a very short space of time, I picked up a great number of the most beautiful shells and bits of coral.

Fresh meat is but seldom obtainable on the island. Occasionally a chicken is killed, and a pig may be got once and away. However, there are plenty of ' yams,' which are very like large tasteless, watery potatoes ; ' pawpaws,' a kind of small melon growing on a tree, an excellent fruit, and said to be, though I did not find it so, a febrifuge ; and the well-known, or rather much-heard-of, ' bread-fruit,' which, when boiled, makes a good vegetable, tasting rather like the *fond* of an artichoke.

One sees a great variety of trees on the island : large bread-fruit-trees, with their big leaves ; queer-looking, straight-stemmed pawpaws; betel-nut palms, bananas, and, on the lower ground, cocoanut and sago palms. There are also a few ' screw pines,' or pandanus-trees, which have great tufts of long reed-like leaves on otherwise bare stems, and are supported at the bottom by their curious aërial roots, from which excellent fibre is got (see tree on left of illustration). The fruit is not unlike a pineapple to look at, but has very little on it that is edible.

Then, many peculiar birds are to be seen. You hear a noise like a steam-engine before you descry a couple of hornbills flying overhead. These birds have a very large beak with corrugations on top, which latter are supposed to be for the purpose of denoting the bird's age. Cockatoos and parrots of various kinds are plentiful, so are black-and-white pigeons. Birds of paradise, those beautiful creatures almost entirely confined to New Guinea, are seldom seen on the island, they being very local; there are a great many different varieties of the bird, all more or less brilliantly plumaged.

But the most interesting objects here are the natives—the first Papuans I had seen—and fine fellows they looked in their simple attire and barbarous ornaments. The head is covered with a thick mop-like mass of woolly hair, often decorated with little white feathers, flowers, or even shells, and with a fan-shaped, long-handled comb jauntily stuck in. Round the upper part of their arms the men wear a band made either of plaited grass or bark, generally blackened, and frequently they stick into this a hibiscus flower or strip of pandanus-leaf. Through the septum of the nose most of them have some ornament, in some cases only a short piece of greenstone, but some having a long piece of bone or shell. All have the lobes of their ears pierced with large holes, in which they stick all kinds of ornaments—coral rings, pieces of bamboo, green leaves rolled in a cylinder, or anything else that takes their fancy. Many of them have round their waists a couple of turns of rattan cane, and all wear a girdle of black string round their loins, sometimes made of human hair, supporting a dried pandanus-leaf, which is passed between the legs. Some also wear necklaces or 'leglets' of white cowry shells.

Sometimes they dye their hair to quite a reddish colour with lime. None of them have much in the way of beards, only some of the older men having a few grizzly hairs.

In height the men are probably well below the average Englishman, though their carriage and symmetry of build would lead one to suppose them much taller.

But many of the otherwise fine-looking fellows are disfigured by skin-disease. It is a kind of ringworm, which extends over the whole body, and is very prevalent throughout New Guinea. Another common disease is elephantiasis, which causes the legs to swell in some cases to an enormous size.

The ladies dress in a most becoming style, their sole garment being a grass petticoat, looking just like that of a ballet-girl, especially so as they generally wear a number of them one over the other. Both men and women are also disfigured, to our ideas, by their teeth being such a bad colour, brought about by the chewing of the betel-nut, which is a constant practice. At first this reddens the teeth, but after the habit has been indulged in for long they become quite black. The nut is wrapped in the leaf of the betel-plant, and then chewed. A small flask of lime is always carried,

10

with a spatula or wooden spoon, which latter is dipped in the powder and sucked. It sounds nasty to take a mouthful of powdered lime, but they seem to like it. These spatulas are often of beautiful design, being made of carved wood or bone elaborately ornamented.

Then the natives are great hands at smoking. The 'baubau,' or pipe, is a large piece of hollow bamboo, generally embellished with quaint patterns. One end is stopped up, and near this end a small hole is made in the side. The tobacco is rolled in a leaf, like a cheroot-shaped cigarette, and is stuck in the small hole. One man then lights it, and putting his lips around the open end of the baubau (for one can hardly say he puts it in his mouth), draws away until the pipe is full of smoke and the cigarette consumed. Then, removing it from his mouth, he places his hand over the open end, and hands it to the next man, who draws a mouthful of smoke from the small hole, and passes it on.

It is a sociable way of smoking the pipe of peace, for it passes round and round the circle, being replenished when exhausted.

Tobacco, in most parts of New Guinea, may almost be said to be the current coin of the realm, for it is a more certain article of barter than anything else; though in some parts beads, hoop-iron, etc., are of great monetary value.

As regards cannibalism, there can be no doubt that it is still frequently practised, especially at those places more removed from missionary influence. I heard some horrible tales about it, but I can't vouch for the truth of them.

The natives are very proud if they have killed a man, and entwine one of his smaller bones as a trophy in a lock of their hair, which then hangs below the mop-like top. Sometimes they attach a small cowry shell in the same way, or tattoo a mark like a sun on their breast, to denote their valour.

It seems unaccountable that, although New Guinea is so close to Australia, and the flora and fauna so similar, besides the fact that the Papuans are such great navigators, yet the people are so entirely unlike the Australian aborigines, and that no signs of Papuans are visible in Australia. As for language, the usual tongue spoken about here is allied to the Malay and Maori, but throughout New Guinea there are many different languages. Indeed, the number of dialects that are to be met with is quite surprising.

After I had been a few days at Samarai, the Government schooner yacht *Hygeia* sailed in, and I left in her for the North. But I must explain the situation.

There was an old and well-known trader named Ancell, who owned and managed a ketch with the inappropriate name *Star of Peace*. For years he had sailed around these coasts collecting copra (the dried inside of the cocoanut, from which the oil is obtained) and curios, paying the natives for all he got in what is called ' trade '—that is, knives, tomahawks, beads, red cloth, etc.

Shortly before I arrived in the country he was in his ship in Chad's Bay, not very far from Samarai. He had anchored close in shore, and had been doing business with the natives. It is said, and I can't help thinking there may be some truth in the statement, that he had celebrated the event in a way which left him not quite so competent to handle the ship as he may have been on other occasions. Any way, it seems that on leaving he ran her on the rocks. Now, his only companions were two more or less native youths. The people of the district, who had presumably assembled from some distance round to effect their bargains, saw in the semi-wrecked ship, with its semi-incompetent captain and semi-compatriotic crew, a chance of getting back not only all they had sold, but also a quantity of 'trade' which they knew must be on board, as well as arms and tools belonging to the old man, which would be of incalculable value to the whole tribe It is easy to imagine how the plot must have thickened, how the bravest heroes were chosen to perform the more important acts, and how they settled the distribution of shares in the plunder. Canoes were launched and manned, and numbers of natives went off to the distressed vessel, while those left behind stood along the shore eagerly watching for the success of the expedition. The ketch was boarded, the crew severely handled, one of them being nearly killed, and then the poor old captain was seized. One man held his hands, another his legs, while a third, taking up the pump-handle, dealt him some terrific blows on the head! The body was taken ashore in triumph, and was buried (not a usual custom) ; the ship was looted, and afterwards burned to the water's edge, and one of the crew was brought back half dead. But two important things were left unheeded, without which the whole of this anecdote might have remained unknown to this day. The one was the blackened remains of the hull, which showed up on the rocks when the tide went down ; and the other was Charlie, the black boy, who had formed one of the crew. Somehow he had managed to escape. He had gone into the Bush, wandered about until he at last crossed the promontory on which this bay is situated, and eventually got to a place called Killerton, where a missionary establishment exists, with a native teacher in charge, who took the lad in, and later on conveyed him across to Samarai.

The *Hygeia*, with the Administrator on board, happened only a few days afterwards to be passing Chad's Bay. Those on board, unaware of the tragedy which had taken place, chanced to notice the blackened remains on the rocks, but, being unable to obtain any information from the natives, had sailed on. Meanwhile, when the news reached Samarai of the boy's account of the murder of the captain and the looting of the ketch, a part-owner of the vessel at once got together a party, and sailed round to ascertain the truth of the story, and see whether anything could be done. They landed in Chad's Bay, but were terrified at being received with discharges from the firearms known to have been stolen from the ill-fated vessel.

H.M.S. *Rapid*, which was in Samarai, thereupon went round to the scene of the disaster, but found the place quite deserted, so proceeded on her way.

Under these circumstances, Sir William (then Dr.) MacGregor, the Administrator of British New Guinea, determined on gathering together all the force he could muster, and making a determined onslaught on these natives, capturing the murderers if possible, and severely punishing the ringleaders of the movement. It was to join this expedition, then, that I left Samarai on November 21, 1888, in the *Hygeia*.

The Administrator and his party had gone round a day or two before to the scene of the murder, and, finding that the natives had retreated into the Bush, camped in the now deserted village, and had sent the yacht back for certain stores, and to obtain any assistance from whites or friendly natives.

Leaving Samarai, we sailed up the China Strait and made for Killerton Island, where a couple of Europeans had been left to gather information.

The captain of the *Hygeia* is an old hand in these waters—one of those sort of men who would

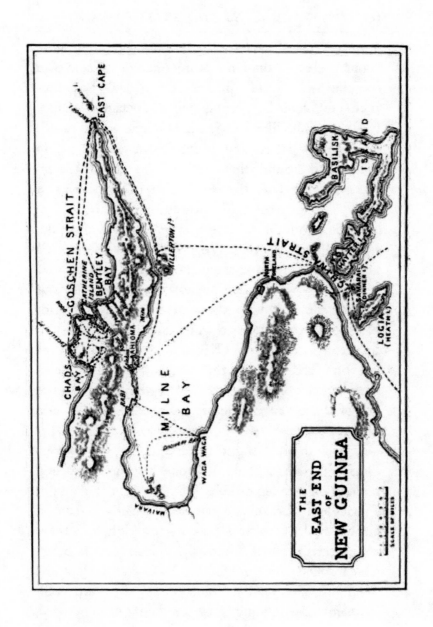

THE
EAST END
OF
NEW GUINEA

SCALE OF MILES

despise a chart, saying that he knew infinitely more about the coast than the semi-amateur officers who compile the charts. I also made the acquaintance of 'Denis,' a young pig of peculiar nature. He acted just like a dog, would come when called, liked being patted and fondled, and would gallop round and round the deck in the most playful manner. He had, like most New Guinea pigs, a hairy coat of skewbald chestnut and white. But later on, when meat was scarce, he died a noble, self-sacrificing death. We could not starve for his sake, and he tasted as well as one could expect.

Towards evening we anchored off Killerton, and a canoe came off with the native teacher on board. He told us that the two white men, Mr. English, a collector, and Charles Kovald, the Administrator's factotum, had gone up the bay, and were to conceal themselves in a village, where they hoped to capture one of the actual murderers. So we remained here till next day.

I had another night disturbed by wild beasts. During the small hours I awoke hearing something moving on the cabin-table. By the fitful moonlight I thought I discerned a big rat. Quietly I reached out for a stick; softly I raised it on high, and then, with a terrific crash, I brought it down on the beast, which rolled over on to the floor, and I slept the sleep of the just. Some days afterwards Sir William was relating how he had got on board, alive, a very rare species of cuscus, about the size of a rat, but he had not seen it the last few days! Neither had I.

Next morning the yacht was surrounded with canoes containing numbers of jabbering, laughing natives. These boats are of three sorts : catamarans, simply formed of three, or sometimes more, logs of light wood, lashed together at the ends with pieces of bark, and on which a couple of men kneel and paddle themselves along. Secondly, the outrigged 'dug-outs,' formed of a single log of wood, very

CATAMARAN.

carefully hollowed out (by fire), and worked into shape so as to have a section like a horseshoe. These have a log fixed so as to float alongside and steady the boat, with often a platform of sticks connecting the canoe with the outrigger. Then, thirdly, there are large dug-out canoes, big enough to be steady without any outrigger, and in one of which I counted no less than eighteen men and boys, all sitting, of course, one behind the other, so that the boat must have been over forty feet long.

Kovald and English came on board during the morning, having failed to get their man, though they had actually seen him, and soon after we sailed off and rounded East Cape. As we glided along before a pleasant breeze, we set lines overboard, baited merely with a piece of rag, and soon had a couple of fine large kingfish for dinner.

Towards evening we got to our destination, Chad's Bay, which is a picturesque spot, backed by bold volcanic hills, rising abruptly beyond the thick belt of cocoa-nuts which lines the shore. As we sailed in we could hear the conch-shell horns resounding weirdly among the hills, blown by the natives to give warning of the approach of a vessel.

Here we found our party, all well, encamped in a native house near the beach which was said to belong to one of the principal murderers. During their stay they had gained much information, and had not been without some excitement. They had learnt that the country was thickly populated, that a great number of people were concerned in the murder, and that they evidently meant fight. The native village close by had somehow been burnt down, though there was much doubt as to how this came about.

Several natives had been seen, and two women captured. The Administrator himself, walking along a track, had suddenly encountered a native in his war-paint, spear in hand, but before he could raise his spear, MacGregor fired off his gun without even aiming, and the startled native fled like a hare. I may here remark that all through our having fire-arms was a great advantage for us, they being practically unknown to the natives. Although the latter were plucky enough, it must have seemed per-fectly diabolical to them to see men with a sort of spear which very suddenly emitted a mass of fire and dense smoke, making a terrific noise, probably louder than anything they had ever heard, and yet able to kill men and birds at a distance far greater than the best spearsman had ever been able to attain! No wonder the poor fellows didn't much care about fighting us!

Sir William is a wonderful man, and quite an instance of the right man in the right place. Strong, hardy, and active, he is also a learned scientist; and often he may be seen sitting beneath a palm-tree, gun in hand, reading Goethe in German, or a French edition of the 'History of the Ottoman Empire.' He is a keen naturalist, and one must be a bit that way inclined to appreciate and enjoy New Guinea; and, above all, he is a clever doctor—a most desirable qualification in this fever-stricken country.

Besides the Administrator, there was Mr. Basil Thomson, his private secretary (son of the late Archbishop of York), and Mr. B. Hely, a young Australian, the local magistrate. The rest of the party consisted of the mate and the crew of the yacht, some Kanaka water-police, and some volunteer miners, which latter, however, were found useless from utter lack of discipline, and were therefore returned to Samarai.

It was a curious scene that evening, now that I think of it sitting comfortably at home. We sat there in the dark, among the palm-trees, with the brilliantly star-lit sky above, on a piece of an old canoe, just outside the native house. Close by was the small camp-fire on which our frugal dinner was cooking. Around in the darkness many strange sounds were to be heard. Dugongs, those ugly great sea-monsters, splashed about in the shallows of the bay. A noise just like a woodman chopping was often heard, and, though there was some doubt as to how it was caused, it was generally supposed to be made by some sort of bird. Then close at hand could be heard the rustle of the small crabs, who have the curious habit of climbing trees at night and stowing themselves away in the cracks of the bark. It would be interesting to know why they should do this.

Dinner over, a great examination of the prisoners was held, for an early start was planned for the morrow. One of the women was an ugly old thing without much interest, and from whom we elicited but little information. But the other was almost nice-looking, and was decently dressed, for, in addition to her grass petticoat, she had a handkerchief over her shoulders. But, oddly enough, the handkerchief was designed as a royal standard, and she looked quite regal as she sat there being cross-examined through the interpreter. It was a long business. Everything had to be translated, both question and answer, by the interpreter, and then it had to be written down. Of course a great deal of the evidence had reference to certain persons and places, and it was rather difficult to get at the exact names and invent a way of spelling them. Among the murderers were Tutinawaii, Yagoagoigoahi, Lailaina, and many others of equally euphonious nomenclature, and when you hear their names jabbered off in a string it is not easy to comprehend them in a moment.

Even the 'pigeon English' of the interpreters is often somewhat difficult to understand, for it is very peculiar. All natives of the Pacific who profess to talk any English make use of this queer jargon. It is a language in itself, and almost requires to be learnt before one can understand all they say. For instance, instead of saying 'A boat like this,' they would say, ' Boat all the same this fellow.' I heard an amusing anecdote with reference to it. A native was ill, and one morning the doctor asked him how he felt. ' Oh,' he replied sadly, ' me very all the same bamboo.' This answer greatly puzzled the inquirer, but finally it was explained this way. Natives very often carry water in a long hollow bamboo. In raising this to drink from one end, one has to be very careful, else all the water suddenly shoots out over one. The poor invalid had found that he had acted like the bamboo in suddenly letting the liquid contained within him shoot out of his mouth !

Next day we started off to explore the villages in the neighbourhood, and see certain houses described by the witnesses, for we had gained much valuable information from them.

It must be remembered that many of these places had probably never been visited by a white man before, so that we knew nothing of the country or its inhabitants.

We marched off, fully armed, in single file, along the well-worn track through the scrub, the men, all having Winchester repeating rifles, carrying fourteen rounds, and some of us having shot-guns and revolvers. We soon came upon several small villages of four or five houses, all deserted, and each of them we proceeded to ransack. The doorways of the houses were all barricaded up with a number of thick sticks and cocoanut-leaf mats, but it did not take us long to break our way in and examine the interiors.

In many of the houses we found spears laid along under the roof. These were about eight or ten feet long, of hard dark wood, and generally barbed. Swords and clubs of hard wood were often found, and shields of softer material, these being about an inch thick, usually two and a half to three feet high, of oval shape, curved somewhat like the old Roman shields, and often painted in red and white patterns. Then, besides earthen cooking pots, fish-spears, good fishing-nets, large coarse nets for catching wild pigs, and stores of yams and other edibles, we came across feather war-plumes, kept in hollow bamboos, just as an English Hussar would keep his plumes in a tin cylindrical case ; netting-needles, made on very much the same principle as those used by our fishermen at home ; drums with iguana or snake-skin tops ; conch-shells, with holes drilled in them for use as horns ; adzes and axes, generally made out of hoop-iron, but also some few of stone ; and various specimens of wearing apparel.

Among the more peculiar articles I found a primitive needle and cotton, consisting of a sharp-pointed bone with an 'eye' made in the top, the cotton being finely-spun grass fibre, and the reel a piece of tortoise-shell. I got also a drill, ingeniously contrived of a stick two feet long, about six inches from the bottom of which a piece of pottery is tied on as a weight ; near the top two strings are fixed, which are tied to the ends of a cross piece of bone, some eight inches long ; the bottom end is slit, and a small piece of flint inserted. To work it, the strings are partially twisted round the upright stick, and the cross-piece pulled downwards, the result being that the instrument is rapidly revolved, and on relieving the pressure from the cross-piece it turns back again, so that the flint is turned very rapidly, and soon drills a hole in any shell, etc., placed under it. I also found a human jaw-bone, ornamented and fitted up so as to form an armlet.

Although we kept a few of the smaller articles, it was impossible to carry off many of the larger

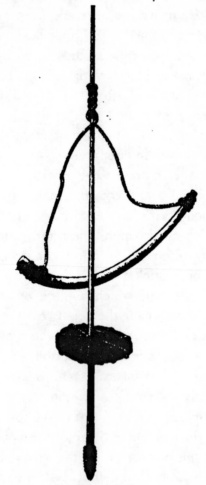

A NATIVE DRILL.

ones, and as they had to be confiscated, they were all smashed up. It seemed a great pity thus to destroy many articles which would have adorned a hall or enriched a museum, but it had to be done.

Then, in almost every house we found remains of the wreck, which told their tale of guilt. Everything must have been divided up most carefully into portions, but in a most useless manner. Here we would find a piece of sail-cloth three or four inches square, there a piece of rope as long as one's finger ; in another place a brass screw, or a block, or bits of copper sheathing.

It was most interesting work examining these huts. One could see in this way many details of their construction, and of the domestic customs of the natives, which would not have been easily observed otherwise.

Most of the houses had something in the way of ornaments hanging over the door. Strings of nautilus-shells were pretty enough, but often there were old blackened human skulls, or pieces of human bone, probably all that remained over from dinner one day. Then we found wooden cages containing live cuscus, doubtless kept for the larder.

In the more important villages there was a primitive parliament-house. This consisted of a certain number of flat slabs of stone placed in a ring in a space in the centre of the village. Often these had an upright stone behind as a back-rest.

The country about here was for the most part flat, and covered with an undergrowth very like an ordinary English covert, with a few big trees. There were always a lot of cocoanut palms about a village, which came in very convenient, for we found this decidedly thirsty work, so at each village we were able to have our nut or two of refreshing milk. There were numbers of crotons about, also dracænas and red hibiscus bushes, but these were found more especially near the houses, where they seemed to be cultivated for ornament. The villages were neatly kept, the ground being paved with pebbles or small stones.

Patches of country were here and there cleared for cultivation, where yams, taro, and bananas were grown. These were generally fenced in with a palisading of poles, probably to keep out the wild pigs.

Across some of the tracks we found a piece of stick lying, or fixed across from bush to bush. These were said to be 'taboos,' that is, they were put there, and a curse laid upon the head of he who should remove them. This would be a simple and excellent method of fortification if the effects were a little more certain, but the only results that I ever saw was that the advance of the cursed was but little delayed, while the curses were returned with genuine British interest on the heads of those who had erected the frail obstructions.

After a halt beside a nice stream of water at lunch-time, we continued our march along the foot of hills. Presently we all stopped on hearing that some natives had been seen. We hoped to be able to catch them by lying still, spread out in ambush; but it only showed our ignorance; for afterwards we got to know that the natives were always watching our every movement, and that they, with their noiseless feet, their agility, and their knowledge of the country, could always keep up close to us without our hardly ever seeing them, while they could hear our boots and rattling equipment for miles off. After a time we went on, following some tracks up a hill, and discovered a camping-ground, where the fire was burning and the dinner cooking. This latter was in an earthen pot, and consisted of a whole bread-fruit, wrapped in big leaves, with enough water to fill up the pot, and looked quite a tempting dish.

Finding pursuit hopeless, we returned. On the way we passed two big wild boars, which galloped wildly by. About six rifles were discharged, but the pigs seemed none the worse, notwithstanding that four at least of the firers declared that they had wounded one of them. We got some pigeons, which are common about here, and also a couple of fine birds of paradise.

We had a hard, tiring march back, and went a long way before getting to a village, but when we *did* get there, we sent a native up the trees, and down fell any number of fine cocoanuts, and what a drink we had! One of the party got outside about three or four, and then suddenly declared himself waterlogged.

' Ginger ' was the most useful man we had. He was a nondescript. His age might have been anything between fifteen and thirty, and he might have been just any nationality, for he was rather dark, yet had reddish hair and not bad features. But he distinctly had black blood in him, and was a native at heart. His English was of the funniest, a pigeon-English entirely his own. But he was an ardent sportsman, very bloodthirsty and very plucky, and he could run up a palm-tree like a monkey.

After my sea-voyage and inexperience in Bush-marching, I felt pretty well done up by the end of the day, and was glad the next day that we devoted our energies to visiting some of the nearer coast villages, also all deserted ; here we found some fine, big war-canoes. These, however, were so slenderly built that, in trying to launch one, we broke it.

Meanwhile the Administrator went over to Tau-puta, on the other side of Chad's Bay, where we heard that a tribe existed who were generally hostile to those we were engaged in pursuing, and that therefore we might be able to get their assistance. He was successful in his mission, and early next morning numbers of canoes full of men were seen coming across the bay. They landed near our camp, and many others came round by shore from Tauputa.

It was a great sight thus to see the entire army of this savage tribe in all its war-paint. There were some 140 men armed with spears (most of them carrying two or three), wooden swords, tomahawks, etc. A few carried shields and paddles. Some carried a sling with one big stone. They were got up in all sorts of wonderful ways. All wore the usual 'costume' of black string and a leaf. Many were decorated with feathers (cockatoo, bird of paradise, or cassowary). Some had their faces blackened or painted, and numerous other kinds of adornment were adopted. But a new difficulty presented itself when we saw all these men ready to join us, and assist in doing battle with the other natives—for how were we to distinguish friend from foe ?

However, a piece of Turkey-red was soon produced, and torn to shreds, and a ·piece of red rag tied round each man's neck, and thus the entire army donned the red uniform, worn for the first time by these far-away loyal subjects of her Majesty. Meanwhile, the jabbering and shouting were deafening, and the control and management of a large body of savages, of whose language not one of us knew a word, was no easy matter. But eventually we got off, and marched in single file along the tracks, the Europeans being distributed along the line so as to control the whole. I found it rather nervous work at first, I must confess, to find myself walking along a narrow Bush path, without a friend near, but with a crowd of jabbering natives before and behind, all armed with spears, and of very

doubtful fidelity. Occasionally, in coming to some
bend or open spot, it seemed quite a relief to catch
a glimpse of a fellow-countryman. After a time,
however, one got more accustomed to it, and the
natives became quieter and less demonstrative. We
entered more deserted villages, and soon found that
our newly-acquired allies were, at all events, most
useful at one function, and that was looting. It did
not take them long to turn everything movable out
of the houses, and annex all that was worth keeping.
We then divided up into three parties, each including two or three white men. The lot I was with
went off across some open country, and a rough
time we had of it. We got to a place which had
apparently originally been one of those large swamps
which exist in these parts, probably covered with
rank grass and bush as high as one's head ; but the
drought had come, it had dried up, got on fire, and
now was nothing more than a plain of ashes. These
ashes were soft, so that, in treading, one's foot sunk
in nearly up to the knee. It was like walking in
deep snow, except that every time on drawing out
one's foot a cloud of black dust rose up and filled
the air. It seemed at times as though we must be
suffocated with the dust made, and we had to halt
occasionally to let it settle somewhat. After a time
we got into the dry bed of a river, and followed it
up towards the hills, presently getting among some
trees. Suddenly we heard someone shouting in the
distance, as if delivering a long speech. The natives

about us at once got very excited, and seemed to say that this shouting was from one of the enemy. When we got a better view, we could see three or four natives standing up on a projecting spur. One of them was waving a red shawl, and yelling out a string of words which I should imagine must have been very unparliamentary. But we came to the conclusion that this might be meant for a flag of truce, and that the enemy wished to make peace with us. Accordingly English and a couple of blacks boldly went off unarmed to parley with them, but found this not so easy. It was quite amusing to watch them. As soon as our men got close up to the cautious natives, they retreated further up the hill, stopping now and again to harangue their pursuers. We followed at a respectful distance ; but seeing after a time that it was hopeless to get up to these men, we despatched a single black with some tobacco as a present, and he soon got up to the gallant ambassadors, and engaged the attention of two of them till we got up. But finding themselves surrounded with armed strangers, these men came to the conclusion that they would rather be at home among their friends, so started off without delay in that direction, and struggled violently when they found that some of our men preferred them to stop with us for a bit. Thus we secured some prisoners ; but unfortunately we had no interpreter with our party, and it was a long time before we could communicate with the others ; however, when eventually we *did* get one, we were unable to elicit much from our prisoners.

Meanwhile, when we had got our parties together again, we found a sad falling off in the numbers of our allies—more than half had deserted, and, doubtless wisely from their point of view, preferred staying and looting the villages to coming on with us to fight.

Our third party, which we met later on, had not met the enemy, but had found the rifle which had belonged to the murdered captain. When we got back to Chad's Bay, we took our prisoners on board the yacht, where was one of the crew of the ill-fated vessel. To our surprise, and almost delight, he at once recognised one of them as the man who had held the captain's hands whilst he was being murdered. This was a great success ; but how it was he allowed us to capture him we never could make out. Perhaps his friends forced him to give himself up !

The next day we determined to do without the assistance of the cumbrous body of allies, and to thoroughly search the country further afield, which would involve camping out for a night or two. We again split up into several parties to examine different places. My detachment, after a long march, came upon the shores of a deep bay, Annie Inlet. Here we descried a canoe with two natives in it coming across from a large island a mile or so off, and making for a point some way along the coast. We

at once started off, keeping ourselves well concealed
in the bushes to head them. But it was not so easy
a matter. To get along the coast we had to cross
several creeks and mangrove swamps, which involved wading up to our middles; and there were
some very awkward places in the thick bush to
struggle through. This so delayed us that we lost
our chance of capturing the men, so we returned.
A wallaby passed close by me on the way, and I
could have had a beautiful shot at two white ducks;
but of course any firing would frighten away the
natives we were so anxious to get, although a little
fresh meat would have been by no means amiss.
Presently we were arrested by a large creek which
we could not cross. Just then some others of our
party appeared on the other side. They soon
managed, however, to discover a catamaran, which
they lashed together, and thus navigated their way
across to us. We then all started on another expedition along the coast in hopes of finding the men
we had seen, Thomson and a native proceeding by
water in their newly-acquired catamaran. But we
were again unsuccessful, although we discovered the
landing-place; so, leaving a party in ambush there,
we returned, passing through a fine little bit of forest
scenery with huge trees and hanging creepers.

It was already getting dark before we had
assembled all our party and got to a suitable camping ground; but there was another detachment,
under Hely, which had gone off into the hills, and

we had agreed that if we did not meet before dark each party should send up a rocket at nine o'clock to acquaint us of the position of the other. Accordingly, we let ours up punctually to the minute, but despite all our eyes eagerly watching from a small hill, no sign was seen of the other rocket. Afterwards we learnt that not only did they send up their rocket, but, although not a couple of miles distant, they also failed to see ours!

We camped in a native house, and made ourselves fairly comfortable, considering the baggage we brought. Mine consisted of a mosquito-net and a towel; though I must confess I did find it a bit cold. But, of course, we had plenty to do, and not many men to do it with, so we carried as little baggage as possible, and I daresay we were all the better for it. I often wondered how a body of regular troops would have fared there, with their heavy clothing and accoutrements, valises, and big boots (we found canvas shoes best); I don't suppose they could have got through half the amount of work that we did. I believe the best costume for a soldier in these parts would be a hat, and a shirt, with a pocket for ammunition, and nothing else except a rifle and a knife!

At night, of course, we always had to have sentries on the alert. Natives could not be relied on, and we soon found that even our coloured water-police had a happy knack of dropping asleep as soon as they were posted, so later on the whole of this

arduous work devolved upon the Europeans. And
a most trying duty it was. Only those who have
undergone it can appreciate what it is, after a long
and tiring day, when you throw yourself down to
rest and sink at once into a deep sleep, to be roused
up and have to stand there for an hour or two
keeping watch, feeling that if once you allow your
heavy eyelids to close it may mean not only your
death, but that of all those slumbering forms around
you.

Then, as you stand there gazing vacantly into the
fire, thinking of far-distant scenes, suddenly you
hear a rustle in the bushes! You turn sharp round
and bring your rifle to the ready. Cautiously and
anxiously you advance towards the spot. Then
with a rush and scurry, that sends your heart with
a jump into your throat, a great wild boar dashes
away into the bush!

Morning broke calm and serene, and soon we
were started on our day's march. After a bit we
entered a deserted village, in the centre of which
was a big tree, and on that tree a small white object.
This soon proved to be a letter from our other party,
saying that here they had camped the night, and had
gone on. Later on we met them, and heard that they
had seen some natives, one of whom had thrown his
spear at them; but they had captured the aggres-
sor, and now had him safely pinioned. Another
long and toilsome march told severely on my feet,
which were getting 'worn out' with blisters; but

there was no chance of healing them by rest. We got down to the coast by Annie Inlet, and came across several big canoes hauled up beside a creek. This was close to a large village, so here we camped for the night. We now learnt some rather startling news from our prisoner. The natives, it seems, had intended attacking us during last night, but were horribly alarmed when they saw a huge fiery serpent rise high into the air, and then burst into thousands of brilliant stars! But it made us all the more cautious this night, and besides clearing away the bush close round, we lit a number of watch-fires, so that the natives might think there was a large party encamped, and not know which part to attack first. It would also give a better light for us to see by if we were attacked.

Meanwhile, Thomson had been doing good service with his catamaran. Seizing the bull by the horns, so to speak, he went off with one native and his gun to the large island at the mouth of the inlet to see if he could not find the men there whom we had seen in a canoe. He dressed himself up in such a way as to look at a distance like a native, and in this way succeeded in getting to the island. To squat down on three small logs and paddle one's self along is no easy matter, but to be alone with a native, and to go off across a mile or so of water to encounter single-handed an unknown quantity of savages, certainly shows great pluck. He got to the island, and there, to his dismay, saw a number of natives awaiting him! But they soon saw through his disguise, and retreated. Here he landed, and found several canoes, which he and his assistant coolly proceeded to launch, in the hope that they would be carried off by the tide, and that by thus cutting off their means of escape we might be able to secure a number of prisoners on the island. But the owners naturally objected to a solitary white man landing thus and stealing their boats, so they came down in a body with their spears. Thomson thereupon got his shot-gun, and fired it at random in their direction, which had the desired effect of frightening them back, which account was afterwards verified by our finding a man who had been wounded by the shot!

The next morning we all overslept ourselves, no one waking till half-past eight. But suddenly someone suggested, Why did not the sentry wake us? It then transpired that one of the Kanaka police had been put on guard towards daybreak, with the result, of course, that he straightway fell asleep! When we went down to the creek, we were horrified to find one of the canoes gone, and other traces, proving that natives had actually been close about us during the night!

We had arranged for the *Hygeia* to come round to Annie Inlet and meet us there, but as she did not turn up, we set to work to patch up some old canoes, which leaked badly, with the idea of going over to the island. However, before we were ready we sighted the ship's boat, so lit a bonfire, consisting of an old thatched shed, to attract her attention, and soon after we were comfortably on board the yacht, which was anchored some way along the coast, in Bentley Bay.

CHAPTER VI.

NEW GUINEA WARFARE.

So far the result of the expedition had been that we had got to the bottom of the whole story. We had learnt who were the ringleaders, and where they lived. We had captured three or four prisoners, and we had driven all the people out of their country and ransacked their houses. We heard rumours to the effect that the people driven to the hills were starving and getting desperate. So we hoped matters would reach a crisis.

The Administrator now sent a boat to some villages along the coast, where a number of natives had been seen—in fact, some had come off to the yacht. The party returned with important news. At one of these places, Huhuna, there was said to be a man who was one of the principal murderers. He had a gun from the wreck, and a full description of him was obtained. Moreover, they learnt that the villagers meant to show fight. So we were to have an exciting time. In the afternoon we prepared to go ashore. Our party in the first boat consisted of the unlucky number of thirteen, of whom seven were Europeans. Another boat was ready in case of emergency, but the ship and the prisoners had also to be guarded.

As we approached the shore, with its white beach backed by cocoanut groves and thick scrubs, we saw numbers of people come out. They were all unarmed. Cautiously we rowed up and landed. The natives, we now saw, were all got up in their war-paint. Did this mean war, or only a great fête? They professed to be very friendly—in fact, *too* much so; but wishing for peace if possible, we got out unarmed. Two women were there to receive us, and the gentle sex are usually considered a sign of peace. But there were only two, and they were young and active; if it was to be real peace, where were the old women and children? We were suspicious, and the Administrator ordered us to quietly get out our guns. I got my shot-gun. The natives crowded round us, jabbering and laughing and shaking hands. Then, when they saw our guns, they pointed at the trees, and asked us to shoot the birds. Thinking it might be useful to demonstrate the power of our weapons, Thomson and I went off to look for some pigeons, followed by the jabbering crowd. We turned up a small track in the bush which led to a village, and as I passed along, I noticed a number of spears lying among the bushes. We spoke to one another about getting too far from the other party, but we agreed that we must show ourselves confident. Our guides encouraged us on by point-

ing to trees still farther off, where were undoubtedly
several pigeons, and we went on through the village
and along a winding path. Curiously enough, we
each had one shot, and each brought down two
pigeons, which, of course, delighted the natives, but
must have impressed them with the power of fire-
arms. We then said we must go back to the others,
who were now separated from us by 300 or 400
yards of thick bush. Just then we heard a loud,
shrill shriek—the war-cry!—then a number of yells
and shouts in all directions. In an instant all the
natives around us disappeared in the most surprising
manner, and immediately after we heard the sharp
reports of the rifles of our party. I firmly believe
our success in the pigeon-shooting saved our lives.
All those men who a moment before had crowded
round us dare not now show themselves!

We at once made along a track taking us in the
direction of the firing, feeling not at all happy, as
our people were probably shooting straight towards
us! As we ran, we had to keep our eyes about us,
and we saw many a head and arm with upraised
spear appear above the bushes, but they ducked
down at once on seeing us. Presently we came
across English wrestling hard with a native who
was yelling at the top of his voice; while Ginger
stood on guard, firing at every head that appeared.
We soon found that this native was the man we
wanted, with the gun in his hand! We soon had
our prisoner handcuffed, and Ginger leading the way,

and I bringing up the rear, we took him on to the beach, where was the rest of the party drawn up round the boat, firing at the natives about them. Many spears lay around, and more came flying towards us; a large stone also fell close to my feet, hurled from a sling. Then a regular charge was made by the natives, but they were soon driven back, and we quickly got into the boat, not wishing to kill any more men. When most of the party were in the boat, another charge was made from the other side, which was met by a ragged volley from our men. This diverted our attention from the prisoner, who at once jumped overboard and ran up the beach. I, being the nearest, ran forward to seize him, but stopped short, on seeing three or four rifles aimed on him, and just in time, for the rifles flashed and banged, a stream of blood shot out from the man's back, and down he fell dead!

We then all got into the boat and put off to the ship, glad to have got away with all safe and sound.

It was a curious retribution. There was no doubt about the man's guilt; and as he was shot dead, handcuffed, there on the beach, doubtless the natives thought it was intended for his execution.

It is difficult to account for the attack we had met with. Was it a regularly-planned and preconceived idea? and did they, therefore, purposely entice some of us away from the others? Or could it have been that they heard our shots at the pigeons, and

THE LAST CHARGE AT HUHUNA.

To face page 118.

imagined that we were fighting the natives with us?
As far as we could gather, the war-cry was raised
before the prisoner was set upon by English, who
only saw him about that time coming forward with
the gun. We afterwards learnt that eight men had
been hit, of whom three were killed and five 'sick,'
as the interpreter called it.

Within a few hours of this affair, a canoe full of
natives came off from another part of the coast,
quite fearlessly, to sell cocoanuts. Moreover, they
had heard all about the fight, and now wanted to
make peace with us! I think it showed great pluck
on their part; but, of course, we treated them well,
and explained that we only shot down their country-
men because they had killed an Englishman, and
that if more white men were killed we should shoot
down more natives.

At night the country, especially the hills at the
back, was illuminated with watch-fires. It is supposed that the natives have elaborate means of
signalling by these fires, and often we saw two or
three together in a row, or one above the other.

We now had a much-needed day of rest to patch
up our tattered garments, and ointment our worn-
out feet. Later on we rowed off in the boat to
another coast village, Kidara, further along. There
we saw numbers of unarmed men on the beach, but
also some at the back carrying their spears, so we
were very cautious; and not wanting to have another
row, but only to make peace, we did not land, but

merely rowed close in, and carried on a long conversation through the interpreters.

Talking about interpreters, it is a remarkable fact
that in a place like New Guinea there should be so
many different languages. Every few miles along
the coast the natives not only speak a different
dialect, but sometimes a totally different language ;
so that often in our intercourse we were only able
to understand what they said by means of two
interpreters. We generally found some local man
who could speak another dialect as well as his own,
and someone else who understood that language
and also English.

For the next few days we did boat work, going
right round Catherine Island and Annie Inlet. We
saw several natives, and got within speaking-distance
of them ; and one we saw we chased and caught.
Another was seen in a canoe, and we gave chase ;
but the man never attempted to avoid us, but
volunteered his assistance, and turned out a very
valuable ally. As a woolly-haired savage he looked
very fine ; but when he had had his hair cut short,
and had put on some dirty old European clothes, he
looked an awful scoundrel. The first request of
these natives generally was to have their hair cut
short ; I suppose they thought it looked more
civilized, and gave an effect which they were unable
to accomplish at home. It is also cleaner.

This inlet is a beautiful coral sea — in most
places so shallow that one could clearly see the

bottom. I know no sight more beautiful than a natural bed of coral. One often sees some delicate pieces of the bleached material under a glass case. But here not only was it in great masses like so many bushes, but it was often of beautiful colours and great variety. Swimming about among the ramifications were some lovely little fish; one kind was especially brilliant, being of a clear, almost transparent, blue.

Occasionally, too, on the sand among the coral, one may see the huge sea-slug, the 'bêche de mer,' or 'trepang,' so much relished in China, and, indeed, in other places now, for making soup. It looks like a big slug, about two feet long, generally black, but sometimes reddish, with numerous legs or fins at the sides. This repulsive-looking object is caught, boiled, dried, and smoked, when it shrivels up considerably. It really makes an excellent substitute for turtle.

One day, in returning to the ship, and while there was a bit of swell on which made the boat somewhat unsteady, we descried a turtle swimming some twenty yards off. Without the slightest hesitation, Sir William seized a rifle from the bottom of the boat, and with quite a snap-shot knocked the top of the head of the beast off. We were rather afraid it would sink; but, with an equal presence of mind, Mr. Ginger was overboard in an instant, clothes and all, and swam to and caught the animal. That evening we enjoyed a great feast, partaking freely of that most delicious though rare dish, turtle liver.

During our search round we came across numerous canoes. The larger ones were always carefully covered with mats, and often kept in special sheds.

Catamarans were always kept in separate logs, apparently so that the light porous wood might thoroughly dry. Only when wanted are they lashed together.

Some of the canoes we made use of, and we soon became great adepts at kneeling in the bottom, and digging our way through the water with the pointed paddles.

We also found lots of splendid fishing - nets. These are carefully made on just the same principle as our own; they are weighted below with shells, and light wood floats are attached above.

Our newly-acquired guide undertook to take us to the house of a gentleman we wanted, rejoicing in the name of Yagoagoigoahi; but finding him 'not at home,' we determined to call again next day. In order to let him know, in case he should be watching us, that the coast was clear, and that we had all gone away, our party assembled in the evening, and went off with much demonstration in the boats to the yacht. But it so happened that half a dozen of us were at that moment silently preparing for a night out on shore on the quiet. Craig (the mate), Charles, and myself, with three black boys, including our new ally, made ourselves comfortable (or, I should say, very uncomfortable) in a native house. Not only was it cold and our beds not of the downiest, but each of us Europeans had to take one-third of the night on watch; and several times I woke with a start, wondering whether the sentry was on the alert, and felt especially anxious about our guide, who might betray us. However, at five o'clock next morning we were up and on the march. Our friend was again away from home, and had evidently not been there. But our guide seemed anxious to take us somewhere, so we blindly followed. The one interpreter we had proved to be quite useless, so we could only carry on conversation with our ally in dumb show. On and on we went, working round to some small hills to the north of us, ever encouraged on by the guide. Soon we found some traces of natives —to wit, some wild mangoes, which had been recently chewed and spat out. Evidently someone had been along the path that morning eating his breakfast. I was wishing we could do the same! At last, after two hours' hard walking, we reached a village on the coast near Cape Ducie with a grove of cocoanuts. The village was deserted, and we were thankful to get a rest and a refreshing drink of cocoanuts, although the guide was evidently bent on going further, and beckoned me to come on. I went on with him along the shore to see what he could mean, and just as I had got some distance from the others, they suddenly began firing and running in one direction. I rushed back to hear that several natives had come up on different sides to attack the village. We at once went in pursuit ; but our attackers were already out of sight, and six spears we picked up were the only traces of them. There was now nothing to do but return, which we did most of the way along the bed of a stream ; and tedious work it was, walking over the slippery rocks and loose stones with wet feet. At last, however, we got back to our place of rendezvous, very exhausted and ready for a good breakfast after four hours' arduous work.

About this time we were beginning to get very short of provisions, and it was determined to send off the *Hygeia* to Samarai for more. She accordingly sailed from Bentley Bay, and the party was left to its own resources.

We worked our way back to Chad's Bay, visiting many villages *en route*, chiefly with the object of collecting provisions. Every house had its store of yams somewhere, generally in a small building by itself. We were also able to get a few bananas from the gardens. These, with cocoanuts, at last became our only food, occasionally supplemented with any birds we could shoot.

A new mode of operations was now proposed. We asked our friends the Tauputans to come to our assistance once again, but this time to go off on their own account and see what they could do.

We had come to the conclusion that those we wanted were thoroughly frightened of us, but might show fight to other natives, and be captured. Accordingly the great army arrived again one morning. Their former successful raid encouraged more to come, and now we had 170 stalwart warriors, all splendidly 'got up' with feathers, shells and paint.

After the usual amount of jabber and excitement they started off into the bush to hunt down the murderers, with one man, whom we had appointed as leader, and to whom we had given an old sword, marching proudly at their head. They had been gone an hour or so, and we had been having a quiet wash in a stream near, when some of them came running back to announce that they had met the enemy, had fought him, but that they had been beaten, adding that two of their men had been killed. At first we could hardly believe this, but soon they all returned, greatly excited, and shortly afterwards brought in a man with two or three severe spear-wounds, one of them in the neck. Nothing could be done for him, and he soon died. The body of the other man had been carried off by the enemy, and we were assured that they were now engaged in cooking him!

All our force was at once mustered and sent off to search for this formidable enemy, and we expected some real fighting this time from the elated victors. We soon saw a native some hundred yards off. He was at once unmercifully potted at by several men, but they all missed, and the native went off like a hare. Then we got to the battle-field, and there we found one wretched man of the enemy badly speared and dying. But no other sign could we find of any more men, so we returned.

The Administrator very properly offered to 'pension' the widows of the men who had been thus killed in fighting for the Government of their country. They were not long in putting forward their claims, and a couple of knives and some tobacco seemed to amply recompense these poor bereaved creatures for the loss of their husbands.

Meanwhile one of the principal murderers, Tutina-waii, had been captured by some friendly natives in Bentley Bay, and he was now brought into camp and kept prisoner. He was a most gentlemanly person, and a man of considerable importance in these parts. He was a great dandy, and wore a very large shell ornament through his nose (which he used to take out at night), and he was very fond of picking up any bits of stuff lying about and making them into some ornament to stick in his hair or ears, etc. He was also most polite and condescending, and when examined freely owned that he had taken a principal part in the murder, and did not appear to regret it in the least. When asked why they had buried the captain, and not eaten him, as was their custom, he replied through the interpreter, 'White man he all the same poison.'

One day we had a stone-slinging competition. Some of the natives did it wonderfully well, making very accurate shots, but the majority were very bad. We also saw a neat piece of spear-throwing. A native dog came hanging about—these are mangy, half-starved, jackal-like brutes—and one of our interpreters, seizing a spear, ran after the dog, and at ten or fifteen yards hurled the spear so that it went right through the poor beast as it galloped away!

Spears are of two kinds—barbed and plain. The barbed spears vary a good deal, some having great thorn-like barbs, standing out perhaps an inch from the shaft, while others have mere notches in the wood. But all barbed spears have, where the barbs end, another sort of barb reversed, so that if a spear goes into a man, not only can it not be withdrawn, but it cannot even be pushed right through.

Komodoah (as his name is officially spelt, though I believe he was so called after a visit of Commodore Erskine to the place) is a great man in these parts. He is Chief of Polotona, and was the capturer of Tutinawaii; so he and his men, who were now with us, had to be rewarded. They accordingly received six tomahawks, two dozen large and two dozen small knives, and twenty-five pounds of tobacco; but above all, with great ceremony, we robed him in a white linen shirt and an old black silk tie. He has probably never taken them off to this day.

On the return of the yacht it seemed as if nothing

more could be gained by stopping where we were, and, as we heard that some of the guilty ones had crossed the hills to the villages in Milne Bay, we accordingly sailed for that side of the peninsula. Moreover, we had received some insulting challenges from one of the tribes there.

SPEAR HEADS.

We stayed a day or two at Killerton Island, and then went on to Rabi. In the evening the native mission teacher, who came along with us from Killerton, held a service. It was a curious sight, there in the moonlight, to see numbers of these wild savages flock to the house from the veranda of which the missionary was to preach. They came and joined in the hymn-singing, and listened to the sermon ; but it did not seem to impress them much, many of them laughing and chattering all the time. Still it was an excuse for a pleasant social gathering ; and such is human society all the world over. We then sailed to Maivara, and later to Wagawaga, and anchored in the nice little harbour at Discovery Bay.

Next we went back across to a bay near Ahioma, where we had learnt that one of the murderers was. This was the place whence we had received a message to say that all the tribe would sit in a circle round Hannewanna, the murderer, and defy us to touch him, for they would all die rather than surrender him.

On December 18 we started off on an excursion to annihilate the tribe and secure their chief. We got together nineteen armed men and several allies, and went off in two boats round the point to the village. As we approached we only saw a few men about, and they professed to be quite friendly. We landed, and these men expressed utter innocence of any desire to fight us. Mr. Hannewanna, they said, had gone to the hills for change of air. But we were cautious. We soon noticed quite a number of armed men in among the trees at the back, and messengers continually walked off to them. So the Administrator asked what the men with arms were doing there, whereupon they dispersed. Soon we noticed them assembling again, so Sir William said, 'If you want peace, let all those men come here and lay down their arms; if not, we will fight.'

Then most of them came and laid down their arms. But there was still evidently something in the air. Then did the Administrator defeat all their little plans, and outwit them with a bold stratagem.

He called together a council of the most important men of the place. Seven old men came forward, and were asked to sit down. Then he said Hannewanna must be caught and brought to him, or it would be war. To this they willingly agreed, and many of them jumped up to go at once after the culprit. But that would not do; there were plenty of young men about who were more active; all the younger men were to go off, taking their arms with them, and bring back Hannewanna, while the old men were to remain as advisers to the Governor. Then some of the aged ones, doubtless fearing the worst, bravely volunteered to lead the expedition against the vile murderer; but they were advised to remain. The other men all went, but, as we expected, none returned. Then the yacht came round, and the councillors were invited to come on board. Some declined, but they soon saw that the invitation partook of the regal character— there was no declining. Our party formed around them, and they were forced into the boat. The remaining natives were clearly told that so soon as Hannewanna was brought in the old gentlemen would be released.

Later on we got hold of another fine tribe, who declared that they would assist us, and bring in Hannewanna. Yakoba was their chief, a man of great influence, for he donned the white man's dress; at least, so far as his battered white helmet went (which he always wore backside foremost). To increase this influence, the Administrator invested him with an order, which was in solid silver, with a representation of her Majesty on the face of it. Its intrinsic value would be about sixpence. The ribbon by which it was suspended from his neck was of green silk, not at all unlike that seen binding the corners of despatches to the Secretary of State. Next day the chief warriors of the tribe came out in a big war-canoe, and paddled several times round the yacht at a great pace, and then with many a yell went off in quest of the fugitive, and eventually they got him.

Meanwhile we went ashore, and visited several more villages; but, as in the Chad's Bay district, they were now all deserted. In one village we had some excitement. A rustling was heard in the thick bushes close by. Cautiously we advanced, and almost surrounded the spot; but the herbage was very thick, and it was difficult to see. At last we made out something like a hairy old man struggling on the ground. Then we closed in, but only to find an old pig with his legs tied.

But another time there was a more serious alarm. We were resting, when a huge butterfly flew past. I believe I am not exaggerating if I say his wings were as big as my two hands. I was anxious to capture this curiosity, and started in pursuit like a schoolboy, cap in hand. The butterfly dodged round some thick bushes, and I ran round after him, to find myself face to face with a native with spear poised as if he was about to throw it! Luckily I had my gun in hand, and immediately brought it up. But it was the affair of an instant. The moment the native saw me thus suddenly run at him, he turned and bolted into the bush.

Nothing more of interest occurred here, and after two or three days we sailed back to Samarai.

The yacht now presented a curious spectacle. The deck was crowded with native fishing-nets and bundles of spears and curios. Below were boxes full of birds, skins, and botanical specimens; on each mast was to be seen a large cuscus (they always lived up there, and only came down at night to feed), while cages hung around containing young hornbills and parrots. One of the last-named fell overboard one day while we were at anchor. A sailor, according to his custom, promptly threw the bird a rope: but it had the desired effect, for he seized the rope in his beak, and soon clambered up and was saved.

Then we had some lovely little flying-squirrels, or flying-phalangers, as they are more properly called, not much bigger than a mouse, but with beautifully-marked fur, and folds of skin which are spread out between the legs when they jump from a height, enabling them to descend à la parachute.

At Samarai we stayed for some time, enjoying our scantily-supplied Christmas festivities, and contrasting them with other Yuletides we had spent. The prisoners and councillors, of whom we now had fourteen all told, we lodged in the old mission-house, all fastened to long chains, so as to prevent their escape.*

One day I went over to the mainland for a shoot. The country is all fine virgin forest, with some very large trees. There was not much to shoot, but I succeeded in getting, amongst other things, a great black cockatoo (Microglossus), which is a remarkable bird, peculiar to New Guinea, and the biggest of the parrot tribe.

Another day I went off to Logia, or Heath Island, so called, by the way, after our old friend Captain Heath, the Portmaster in Brisbane, who was surveying in those parts in the *Rattlesnake* very

* As an instance of the innocence and honesty of Papuan nature, I may here relate that, on another occasion, a prisoner, when released from his chains to do some work, requested to have the chains kept on, because he said he felt so strong an inclination to run away !

many years ago. The people of the island have a bad name, and are supposed to be great cannibals, but I was getting accustomed to this sort of thing, and felt quite safe with a gun and revolver, so went

GREAT BLACK COCKATOO.

off into the bush with two small local boys as retrievers.

The island consists of a steep hill, thickly covered with forest, and with the usual fringe of cocoanuts round the coast, where most of the villages are. We went a long way up the hill, and I shot a few birds of different sorts, and got some lovely views of the harbour. On coming back from my shoot, I saw a huge war-canoe in a shed on the beach, decorated with numerous painted human skulls.

We now started to build a prison near the old mission - house, making a substantial building of heavy cocoanut wood logs, in which the prisoners were afterwards confined. Eventually they were tried for murder before the Chief Justice, were found guilty, and four of them suffered the extreme penalty of the law.

Whilst we were at Samarai a vessel came in loaded with pearl-shell, leaking badly. She was .beached, and all the shell thrown overboard. I had my eye on some of this beautiful and valuable material, supposing it to be thrown away; but I soon found that the man on watch also knew its value, and although then lying in the shallow of the receding tide, it would soon be gathered in again, and shipped to England for ultimate conversion into buttons and collar-studs.

By this time I had got the inevitable New Guinea fever on me, that wretched disease which attacks almost everyone who visits the country, and which takes months, if not years, to get rid of.

On December 30 we sailed in the *Hygeia* for Port Moresby, the capital of British New Guinea, passing South Cape and the island of Su-au, which is the headquarters of the eastern district of the London Missionary Society.

All along this coast is a barrier reef of coral,

which we got inside when nearing Port Moresby, and sailed along in calm water. We sighted a large alligator calmly swimming out to sea, and had a shot at him with a rifle, but whether hit or not, he dived and did not appear again.

We passed Tupuselei, a town built on piles entirely over the sea, and a good distance (perhaps 400 yards) from land, too.

Port Moresby is a very fine harbour, and will doubtless be of much value as the colony grows in importance. The country round here, however, looks very bare and barren as compared to the east end, especially owing to the almost entire absence of cocoanut-trees.

Near the entrance to the harbour, and opposite the most frequented anchorage, is a collection of houses rejoicing in the name of Granville, where are the Government offices, the rest-house, Goldie's store, the lock-up, and one or two other houses, all built of wood with iron roofs. Nearly two miles away from this (by some bad arrangement) is Government House, and a mile further up the harbour is a large mission-station, consisting of several houses for the missionaries, teachers, etc., a church, school, and other buildings. This is situated on rising ground, below which, on the shore of the harbour, are some large native villages.

Thus this small settlement is divided into three distinct communities.

At Granville lives Mr. Anthony Musgrave, the

Government Secretary (nephew of the late Governor of Queensland). He has been here for many years, and makes plenty of work for himself. He has acted as Administrator more than once. Here also is to be found Mr. Chief-Judicial-Officer Winter, who dispenses justice throughout the colony, and several other Government officials.

Mr. Andrew Goldie is another New Guinea ' identity ' (as Australians would put it). He has knocked about these parts for years as a trader and explorer, and has finally settled down in his large store here, in which everything can be obtained, from a waggon to a needle, including many beautiful bird-skins and native curios.

The rest-house is like a small club, where not only meals and a bed can be got, but there is also a well-supplied reading-room. At the back is the Government printing-office, whence the gazettes and such-like official papers are issued for distribution among those who can, and care to, read up the decrees and ordinances.

As for Government House, it can hardly be said to compare favourably with the like establishments of the other Australasian colonies. It is a one-storied building constructed of the usual weather-board walls and galvanized-iron roofing. Though not so large as that at Melbourne, for instance, it is quite roomy enough for its purpose, which is to provide accommodation for the Administrator, and perhaps his private secretary, during the flying visits he makes to the capital ; for Sir William spends most of his time travelling around the coast or exploring inland. These requirements are amply provided for in about seven small rooms.

There were a fine lot of chickens about the garden, and though roast fowl and fresh eggs are great luxuries in this land, the crowings and cacklings of an early morning do not add to the comfort of a fever-stricken patient like I was when there.

The mission is presided over by the Rev. W. G. Lawes, of the London Missionary Society, who is another comparatively very old resident of the place, as he has been here, with his wife and family, for nearly twenty years. There is here a training college for native teachers, though, as a matter of fact, few of them are natives of New Guinea, the majority coming from some of the South Sea Islands, which have been longer under missionary influence. These people, however, odd as it may seem, suffer terribly from fever, and no less than one-half of those sent to New Guinea have died there.

Numerous services are held in the church, and at the Communion service, it may be interesting to note, cocoanut milk takes the place of sacramental wine.

There are two distinctly different tribes of natives located at Port Moresby, who keep very much apart, although their villages almost join. The Motu people inhabit all this coast for many miles, while

the Koitapu belong properly more to the interior.
Both are very different to the east-enders hitherto
described.

All the houses are built actually on the sea-beach,
like so many bathing-machines. At high tide the
water lashes about the bottom of the piles and
carries away all the refuse. The men here wear
no clothing whatever except a thin piece of string.
The women have grass petticoats, while the upper
portions of their bodies are completely covered with
a tattooed pattern.

At this time of year there is great excitement
among the villagers, who are watching for the return
of the 'lakatois' coming back from the west. These
are huge vessels consisting of a number of large
canoes lashed together, generally four to eight, but
one I saw of thirteen, with a deck built over the
whole. Two large sails, of the shape of a crab's
claw, are rigged up, and often smaller ones as well.
These queer vessels load up with pottery, which is
a great industry at Port Moresby, and take it along
the coast to the west, to exchange for sago and
other provisions, the voyage occupying some months.
It is a great sight to see the fleet returning, and the
demonstrations of joy of the wives and mothers
welcoming home the navigators.

When Captain Moresby first discovered the port,
and sailed in in the *Basilisk*, one can imagine the
surprise of the people on seeing an enormous canoe
of unheard-of dimensions, and their method of re-

cording the description was very quaint. Numbers
of reeds were noticed in some of the canoes which
surrounded the vessel, and these the Motuans rapidly
tied together, so as to form a long string, with which
they carefully measured the length of the ship. This
primitive measuring tape was then carefully rolled
up and taken back to the village, to be kept as a
record.

Then they have a capital system of doing such
arithmetic as is necessary in their mercantile transactions. In exchanging so many earthenware pots

A MAN-CATCHER.

for so much sago, the counting would be a difficult
business to their mathematically untrained brains
were it not for the following method : All the pots
are laid out on the beach ; a short bit of stick is
laid in each ; these sticks are then gathered together,
and represent the number of pots. When a deal
is to be made, the material, whatever it may be,
is divided into heaps, each an equivalent to one
pot. The sticks are then laid beside them, and in
this way a fair exchange may be made.

I got here a most peculiar weapon of war. It
consists of a long handle, at the end of which is a

A NEW GUINEA TREE-HOUSE.

To face page 201.

ring of cane ; a sharp spike of hard wood extends
from the end of the handle to near the centre of the
ring. It is used during the pursuit of a vanquished
foe, the ring being placed over the head of the
fugitive, when a sharp pull back causes the victim
to fall backwards, and the spike to enter the base
of his brain.

One day we rode out (for they have horses here)
to see some of the tree houses which are common
in most parts of the country. They are not usually
used for habitation, but as look-out houses, and as
citadels in case of attack by a hostile tribe. A large
ladder connects them with the ground, and they
are often kept stored with arms and stones.

The country about here, which just at this time
had been suffering from severe drought, was like
any English copse-land, with a few of the familiar
Australian gum-trees, but all very brown and
dried up.

There was a good deal of wire fencing near the
town, which gave the place quite a civilized look.
It is to keep in the cattle and horses which have
been imported here. But, nevertheless, in these
dry times the settlers got no milk, and fresh meat,
except chicken and kangaroo, was rare.

Wallaby are common on the grass-lands in this
district. The natives often get them by setting
fire to the long grass, and driving them, on the
principle of a grouse drive, to a point where they
await the game with their spears.

The London Missionary Society's yacht *Harrier* now came into Port Moresby, and, thanks to the missionaries, I got my passage in her. She has a history, for she was originally the Duke of Connaught's yacht, was then purchased for the navy, became a surveying vessel, and finally was sold to her present owners.

There was quite a merry party of missionaries on board the yacht (which, I must own, I hardly expected). We had a tedious journey, nevertheless, for there was a strong tide against us, and as the breezes were of the lightest, we kept drifting back on our course, and next day we were still off Port Moresby.

On the third day, however, we arrived off Motumotu, but had to anchor a mile or more from the shore, which, in the absence of any barrier reef of coral, is bounded by surf. The Rev. J. Chalmers, another well-known New Guinea missionary, came off to us, and then we all went ashore.

Only about a year before this, a Polynesian teacher, together with his child and four friendly natives, were massacred here, and it is a plucky thing for a white missionary to come at once and settle in the district.

The country for some miles inland is flat and swampy, but thickly covered with palm-trees, while at some distance from the coast mountains rise up and stretch away into the interior in those districts never yet explored by civilized man.

The town is not easily reached. We first rowed

to the entrance of a large inlet or lagoon, cut off
from the sea by a long sand-spit.   Then we got into
a river with mangrove-covered banks, on the mud
of which were numerous little crabs each with only
one big claw.   After that we landed, walked across
a bit of country, and again came to some water
where canoes were waiting for us; we crossed a big
river (the Williams River), and were finally landed
on a stretch of sand dividing the river from the
sea, and along this we walked to the mission-house,
where Mr. Chalmers and his wife live.   The natives
came out in hundreds to meet us, and extraordinary
people they were, much more elaborately got up
than the natives at the east end or at Port
Moresby.   Most of the men wore their hair brushed
back, and a circlet of feathers (of cassowary, parrot,
or bird of paradise) placed round the front.   On the
centre of the forehead was placed a circular disc of
white shell, on which was a beautifully-carved open-
work ornament of tortoiseshell.   Most had a large
crescent-shaped piece of pearl shell hanging in front
of the neck.   But one of the most peculiar features
was the manner in which all the men had their
waists drawn in by a large belt of carved bark or
plaited grass.   These must have been four to six
inches wide, and fastened very tight.

The women were dressed in the usual grass
petticoats, but made of very fine grass, and dyed in
colours, while some of the ladies were daubed over
with what looked like very greasy red clay.

The mission-house is a large airy building, mostly constructed after native fashion. It stands by itself facing the sea.

The native village, which might really be designated town, for it is very large and has several regular streets, lies behind this on the river. Here are several 'dubus' or 'elamos,' which are very large houses, and are for a peculiar purpose. All the boys of the place on attaining a certain age have to go and live together. They are kept here in a sort of confinement until they attain a marriageable age, when they are released.

The dubu is raised on large piles twenty feet or so above the ground. One clambers up a regular ladder to it, and in front is a big balcony, on which many men and boys sit about. The interior of the house is fitted with seats all round, and a sort of loft or second floor, for the house has room for about 100 boys. In the centre is a large rudely-carved figure, which is said to be a sort of god, but is apparently not treated with any great reverence, for it is used as a staircase to climb up to the upper story. The boys are mostly busy manufacturing their armlets and other ornaments ready for making their débuts. They also were daubed with red clay.

We visited the great man of the place, a fine old warrior, who was very friendly and hospitable. In these districts, I must mention, bows and arrows are used more than spears, and the old man brought out his bow to show us what he could do. He made some fairly good shooting at cocoanuts in the trees, and finally presented us each with some arrows.

We witnessed a curious dance from the veranda of the mission-house. A number of men appeared in what they call 'masks,' but they were such big

A MOTUMOTU DANCE.

masks that they covered all but the legs of the men! They are somewhat difficult to describe, being in form more like the head of a crocodile than anything else I can think of, and I believe they were supposed to represent that object. But this was covered with elaborate ornamentation in various colours, and from around its edge hung a deep fringe of grass, while from the back of the head stuck up a huge 'tail,' perhaps ten or fifteen feet high, a 'stay' covered with feathers joining the tail to the nose.

The dancers merely stood in a row and moved their feet about in rather a feeble sort of way.

One man, apparently the leader, but without any mask, stood in front and was wonderfully got up. Among other things, he had some pieces of white bone hung all about him, so that they looked like ribs, etc., and gave him the appearance of a living skeleton.

I stayed on shore the night, and in my feverish state was glad of the hospitable treatment I received from Mr. and Mrs. Chalmers, and of the comfort of the mission-house.

On the banks of the river were some of the very large dug-out canoes like those of Port Moresby. They really compare more with our canal-boats in size and shape. The smaller canoes are generally lashed together in pairs, with a platform between, which makes a very good boat for carrying merchandise, and a comfortable one to travel in when lying on the platform.

The Williams River, on which the town is situated, has a good volume of water, and swarms with crocodiles, one of which came after a boat we were in, swimming under water, and occasionally coming up to the surface within a few feet of us.

We sailed again next day from Motumotu in the *Harrier*. We had the usual calm weather, of which I had had so much in these seas; but they were especially unpleasant now, as the ship had lately run on a coral reef, and was found to be leaking badly. The pumps had to be kept going day and night, and what with the noise they made, and thoughts of the possibility of the water gaining, things were not as agreeable as they might have been. Then, to add to the discomfort, we had on board a missionary with his wife and *baby* who had been on a visit to Port Moresby. Fancy taking a poor wretched baby on a visit to New Guinea—that land of fever, where fresh milk is unknown, food of the poorest, and luxuries unheard of!

However, this miserable child did nothing but scream the whole day and night too. I am not complaining—I am only pitying the poor creature in its time of misery.

To crown all, my fever attacked me more or less every day, which is not calculated to add to one's enjoyment of a trip.

However, at last we got to Murray Island all right, where we were to call for a day on our way to Queensland, anchored a couple of miles off, for there is no harbour here, and went ashore in the boat. But oh, that baby! Of course it had to be taken too. The sea was not as calm as it had been, and baby's wraps were forgotten. My best and only rug was of course cheerfully tendered, and gratefully accepted and brought into use, but—the baby was not a good sailor!

Murray Island, which properly belongs to Queensland, is an interesting place. The natives are quite different from Papuans, as well as from Australian aboriginals, and, indeed, I expect, take more after the Samoan and Malay type. The houses are built on the ground, not on piles, and are somewhat like those of the Tongans. A considerable trade is carried on in bêche-de-mer, fishing-grounds being plentiful round the coast. It is a very fertile island, and all the usual tropical plants are grown. Here is a great mission station, it being the missionary headquarters for the western district of New Guinea, and many native teachers receive instruction here. But Mr. Bruce is *the* man of the place. He has a store, and is also a great shipbuilder. I had the honour of staying with him the night, and very jovially he entertained us. He told us some extraordinary yarns, and I found to my surprise that, although he has been secluded on this island for very many years, he knew a great deal more than I did about most things, especially military matters and London Society.

Here I came across Professor Haddon, who was staying on this out-of-the-way island with the object of collecting and reporting on the wonders of the deep, or rather shallows, of this neighbourhood, and a most interesting collection, now in the British Museum, is the result.

When bed-time approached—and it was at no early hour—my host politely expressed a hope that I did not expect to be very luxuriously housed, and on my assuring him that I was quite accustomed to roughing it, he pointed to a cane arm-chair and, wishing me a comfortable night, left me to my privacy.

CHAPTER VII.

MALAYSIA.

Java.

Java is the principal possession of the Dutch East Indies. But the story goes that it ought to be English, for in about 1811 it was occupied by the British, and it is *said* that it would never have been given back to the Dutch except that a despatch from the English Governor was pigeon-holed in London without being read.

Be that as it may, it has become a most lucrative colony for the Dutch. Thirty years ago the revenue for one year, chiefly derived from forced labour, exceeded the expenditure by some £3,000,000.

However, this system of compelling natives to work a certain number of days on Government plantations has gradually decreased, and has now, I believe, practically ceased to exist. But the same may be said of the revenue, for whereas formerly a contribution was paid to the home Government, there is now an actual deficit.

The capital town is Batavia, which is also generally said to be the chief port, but as a matter of fact, Tanjong Priok, which is connected by rail and by canal with Batavia, is the principal port of Java. Directly the steamer enters the harbour one notices something about the vessels and the buildings around that reminds one of Holland, especially as the country here, and for many miles inland, is low and marshy, and is intersected by canals.

But we find a very different type of working-class. The Javanese, a type of Malay, are of a coppery-brown colour, with straight, shiny black hair, done up in a handkerchief tied round the head. They have rather a Mongolian type of countenance, and always wear a 'sarong,' or loin-cloth, of bright-coloured material, even when they have trousers underneath.

Nothing of special interest is to be seen in Tanjong Priok, so, after undergoing examination at the Custom-house, one is glad to take train for Batavia.

The first thing that strikes a stranger, especially if he has come from Australia, is the wonderful luxuriance of the vegetation as seen from the train. Everything looks green and rank; masses of long grass spring up on all sides, and an abundance of trees shut in the view. This low-lying country is very suitable for growing sugar, and a considerable quantity of it is produced in this district. The train, running beside a canal, arrives at the capital after some twenty minutes.

Batavia is divided into three parts, the first arrived at being the business quarter, where are the banks and shipping offices. Here, again, you might quite imagine yourself in Holland, for there are old houses, canals packed with barges, and paved streets with big trees along them.

Close to the station are the old Government offices, guarded by Dutch soldiers armed with pikes !

I found it necessary to apply here for a local passport to enable me to travel about the country, and a lot of bother and delay there was about getting it.

Business over, you can get into the steam-tram, or take a *dos-à-dos*, the local cab (a sort of small dog-cart with a roof, drawn by a pony), and soon find yourself being whisked through the Chinese quarter. And now you might fancy yourself in Pekin, for the streets of Chinese houses, with their big-tiled roofs and carved woodwork, and placards and devices in hieroglyphic - like characters, are thronged with Chinese people.

Numerous half-dressed natives in big straw hats hurry hither and thither at a sort of run-walk, carrying their loads suspended at each end of a bamboo pole over their shoulders.

After another mile comes the European part, where are the hotels, clubs, shops, etc. And if you care to go further you will get to some of the pleasant suburbs where are the private houses of the Europeans.

But to go back to that portion devoted to the Celestial element. So great and important has this community become in Batavia, that Chinese officials have to be appointed to look after it, and the 'Captain of the Chinese' is a great man. He has

A JAVANESE CARRIER.

a large abode with big courtyard in front, like a Chinese edition of Devonshire House. I happened to be in Batavia at the time of the 'Feast of a thousand lanterns,' and had an introduction to Mr. (or Captain?) Khouw Jaouw Kie, who very kindly invited me to a dinner-party at his house on the occasion. It was a most interesting sight. The streets were crowded with people, torches and small fireworks being displayed on all sides. Gongs and rattles, drums and cymbals, dinned the ears till one was nearly deaf. On reaching the Captain's house we found the courtyard packed full of people, evidently enjoying themselves greatly, feasting on fruit and various creature comforts.

We went expecting to dine off bird's-nest soup, roast dog, and such-like heavenly delicacies, but were, in a way, really disappointed to find that our kind host had hired in for the occasion the best French cook to be got in Batavia, and an excellent little dinner he gave us. The other guests, to the number of about a dozen, were mostly Dutch officials. The dinner was served in a somewhat novel, but very pleasant, fashion. Instead of sitting round a table, we sat about as we liked in the spacious veranda, whilst waiters brought us cups of soup and plates of dainty morsels.

Meanwhile some great performances were going on in the court in front. Fantastic processions were perambulating the streets with allegorical figures grouped on platforms carried on men's shoulders; terrible-looking, life-like dragons of enormous dimensions; bands of cymbals and drums, and any number of torches and lanterns of paper or gauze on frames carried on high poles.

As each of the groups came to the Captain's house they entered the gates, and, after displaying them-

selves and receiving two red candles and a ticket,
moved on out of the other gate. But many of the
processionists were acrobats or actors, and these
stopped in front of the house to go through their
various performances illuminated by the torches and
lanterns.

Some of the performances were very solemn and
unintelligible. Three or four men and a woman
would dance about slowly, throwing attitudes, which
chiefly consisted in leaning back as far as possible
and swaying about, all the time singing their parts
in a weird, monotonous strain, keeping their eyes
fixed on the ground, and looking very serious, whilst
an orchestra of cymbals and drums kept time. Yet
some of the characters had a comic appearance,
especially one man who was got up in large black
goggles.

Other performers went through acrobatic feats,
such as may be seen better accomplished nowadays
at any London music-hall, though, doubtless, fifty
years ago they would have greatly surprised an
English audience.

Afterwards we went over the house itself. There
were a number of good large rooms, though each
had more the appearance of a shop or museum than
a living room, and none had any appearance of
comfort. One of the chief peculiarities was the
number of clocks—three or four in every room—
most of them not going, and those that *were* pointed
to various different times. Looking-glass balls were

another great feature, as well as musical boxes, trick cigar-boxes, and various odds and ends of cheap and gaudy European goods. But, after all, why should we laugh at these decorations? Do not we at home often decorate rooms with cheap, trashy Japanese fans and quaint, but common, Chinese ornaments?

In one of the rooms a sort of altar was erected, decorated with flowers, and illuminated by candles and lamps. In the middle were portraits of our host's father and other relations. Such is 'Confucianism.'

We had the honour of an introduction to the lady of the house, looking very glum, in a dress rather suggestive of nocturnal attire, but resplendent with diamonds; and after a most interesting evening we returned to our hotel.

A great change it is to get back to the European quarter of Batavia. The Chinese are only represented in this part by the ubiquitous hawker of stuffs and Chinese curios, who, when not employed in haggling for a good price for some worthless article, is always engaged in twirling in his fingers an instrument looking rather like a small mallet or auctioneer's hammer; but it is really simply a diminutive drum fixed on a stick. A little ball is attached by a piece of string to the centre, so that as the stick is twisted in the fingers, the ball taps alternately each end of the drum, thus producing a rattling noise.

In bargaining in Java one has to be careful not to

get confused among the different coinages. The Chinaman deals in dollars (Chinese, too, not American), the Indian merchant in rupees, while the Dutch charge gulden. One often forgets this, and offers a man two dollars when one means two rupees, and so on.

The European part of Batavia is quite unlike any other town I have seen. All the houses, even including the shops, are surrounded by some sort of 'compound,' or garden, generally containing some fine large trees ; and coleuses, crotons, and other bright shrubs add a great brilliancy to the foliage. There are a lot of good shops, a theatre, a residence for the Governor-General of the Dutch East Indies, as well as a palace where he holds levées and receptions, etc. There are also two good clubs—the Harmonie and the Concordia (military)—fine, cool buildings, where one can get everything one can want. The first-named has been in existence over fifty years.

There is an interesting zoological garden, where may be seen such rarities as the ourang-outan and the proboscis monkey in healthy confinement.

The museum is another interesting place, with a good collection of New Guinea curios and a great assortment of native musical instruments. There is also a library, in which many English books referring to Java may be read.

On certain evenings all the world assembles in the Waterloo Place to hear the military band:

Fashionable carriages drive around with fine-liveried coachmen ; but natives always will wear the handkerchief arrangement round their heads, which detracts somewhat from the appearance of the gold-banded hat worn on top. Cavaliers and equestriennes also grace the scene.

The hotels of Batavia, palatial buildings with pillared verandas and marble steps, are fairly comfortable, though the attendance of the Malay 'boys' (as servants in this part of the world are always called) leaves much to be desired. Most of the bedrooms have no glass windows, but tatties are hung about to keep out the glare and the gaze of the inquisitive public. In the hall or veranda is a table laid out with decanters and glasses, so that one can have a glass of schnapps when one feels so inclined without any charge.

But the whole place is low and damp ; rivers and canals run through the centre of the town, and I, for one, suffered greatly from malarial fever.

The Dutch mode of life is decidedly peculiar, a sight of the costume alone being rather startling to a new-comer. Whilst sitting at your breakfast in the public hall of the hotel, you must not show any surprise if a gentleman in the lightest of pyjama suits comes walking in with a towel over his shoulder on his way to the bath. Meanwhile, the ladies strolling round are costumed in the 'sarong' and 'kabaye,' and nothing else so far as the eye can see. The sarong is, as I have said, a length of native print stuff wrapped around the nether body, and the kabaye is a mere light linen jacket. Below the sarong the lady's dapper feet appear in their natural state, the toes seeking shelter under the elaborately-embroidered toes of high-heeled slippers.

Children go even further; their costume consists simply of one linen garment—a combination of short drawers and sleeveless shirt: cool, I dare say, but peculiar to ideas trained outside Eden. Talking of children, it is curious to notice how very fair most of these young Dutch children are. One would have thought that the climate might have had some effect in darkening their skins, if not hair, especially when we see that their mothers, however Norse in position, are in many instances obviously equatorial in descent.

Nor are the meals much less peculiar than the costumes. One starts the early morning with *café au lait* and eggs. Hunger shortly produces 'rys-tafel,' a truly alarming meal. The basis is one only soup-plate. On this you successively place piles of rice, hot stewed chicken, tropical fried fish, curry of butcher's meat, omelets, and other delicacies, the number ordinarily amounting to ten or twelve—I have known more. Dozens of chutneys and condiments follow, and it is strict etiquette to take and pile up on the same plate portions of everything handed round. One is overwhelmed with all the variety, and internally feels quite content to confine one's attention to two or three, at the most, of the dishes brought round. But it then transpires, to one's stomachic horror, that this great 'rystafel' is only the preliminary to an ordinary course of beef-steak, and after that one is supposed to partake of banana or pineapple fritters.

Dinner in the evening is a rather more ordinary meal, though one has to get into the way of that also.

Fruit is plentiful enough in Java, but does not seem to be much appreciated by the Dutch.

Mangosteens are *the* fruit, got here in great plenty, so much so that we made ourselves quite ill on them. Rambutangs are another nice fruit, looking outside like red Spanish chestnuts, but, on breaking open the prickly husk, the interior has more the appearance of a plover's egg, being of a jelly-like substance. Dukkoes are also very good ; but dorians, though much liked by some people, possess a taste which has to be acquired. I call them disgusting.

On going to bed the new-comer is again some-what puzzled. There before you is a large wooden four-post bedstead with mosquito-net. On it is a hard flat mattress. But there is no idea of any bed-clothes. Then there are the usual pillows at the head, but down the centre of the bed lies a hard round bolster, which is a great puzzle to those who do not know its use. However, after a short experience one greatly appreciates this 'Dutch wife.' With the thermometer hovering around 90°, and a steamy, oppressive atmosphere, one lolls about the bed, finding even the hard mattress hot; and it will soon be found that, in lying on the side, two adjacent parts of your body will always be hot, and you therefore long to separate your legs and arms. By placing the hard bolster between the knees and lying with one arm underneath and the other over it, you find yourself comparatively cool and comfortable.

The bathing arrangements are also peculiar. In one corner of the brick-paved bath-room is a large brick tank about three feet high, full of water. But on the top of this is a wooden grating, as if to prevent your getting in. There is a hole left in the grating, and a tin dipper is the means by which you take up the water and throw it over yourself on to the stone floor. There ought to be a domestic guide to Java. I failed to fathom some of the mysteries.

The principal suburb rejoices in the peculiar name of Mr. (or Meester) Cornelis, and here one can get a glimpse of how a Dutch East Indian lives when at home. The houses are all well built, with large verandas, generally marble floors and columns, and the already noted lovely gardens. Of course all the morning the ladies are in the sarongs and kabayes, and hair in some negligé arrangement; but in the evening, when the sun goes down, best frocks are donned and coiffures made up, and all go forth for a drive or walk, but without hats. Then, later on, the family assembles for dinner in the veranda, where is a table laid out with schnapps and sherry, and here one sits and talks (and I understand it is quite the usual custom) for perhaps half an hour, before proceeding to dinner. Children all dine at table, and often make a great noise. Sometimes in the evening the band plays in the grounds in front of the Concordia Club, and dances are also given by the gallant members.

One day there was a great Malay fair, with innumerable booths and native versions of the familiar fat woman, living skeleton, etc. Theatrical performances and concerts on the most discordant instruments were also to be seen and heard. The scenery in these shows is mostly composed of thin paper or gauze, and appears to represent nothing in particular. The female characters are played by male actors, very much got up, and continually chanting in a high, squeaky voice. Some of the dresses are very elaborate.

The Dutch colonial army is a curiously-organized body of some 35,000 men. Europeans and natives (the army being composed of half and half) stand side by side in the ranks, and in the same uniform, except that the latter as often as not have no boots on. They wear dark-blue tunics and brass-bound dark helmets, which I should have thought must be very hot and trying in this climate. Then there is also a 'volunteer' force of all the eligible Europeans in the place, and everyone having such qualifications is obliged to join. Even the English men of business have to belong to this force, but I am told that, receiving no encouragement to rise in their profession, and having an easier time by so doing, most of them remain classed as 'recruits.'

The first place to visit from Batavia is always Buitenzorg, some two and a half hours' journey by rail. This is supposed to be a healthy resort up in the hills, but it is really only some 800 feet above the sea, and there is little about the place itself suggestive of hills. There are, nevertheless, some grand views of distant volcanic mountains rising out of the plains. On the whole, however, I was very disappointed in the scenery of Java. One expected something magnificent, but in my opinion there is nothing about here to approach the scenery of Ceylon. Rice is the great product; and paddy-fields, levelled and embanked, are to be seen stretching away for miles on all sides; and on some of the hills are large tea-plantations, with great sheds for drying operations.

Torrents of water from the mountains dash along their rocky beds, occasionally bridged by neat and scientifically-constructed bamboo bridges.

At Buitenzorg is the Governor-General's chief house, situated in some very fine, extensive grounds. These form a regular botanical garden, and abound in grand specimens of tropical trees. There is a splendid avenue at the entrance, all the fine trees (a species of fig), whose branches meet perhaps

100 feet overhead, having different creepers covering their stems. In these grounds one comes
across a curious relic of past times. There is a
small cemetery, in which many of the graves are
those of Englishmen who died here during our
occupation of the island. There is a large ornamental lake, and facing this is the Government
House, not unlike a small model of that at Melbourne.

The town of Buitenzorg consists chiefly of one
good street of Chinese houses. Wandering along
it in vague search for wondrous sights, we were
presently entranced with strange sounds of music,
and stopping before the door of the small house
whence emanated the mystic strains, we were cour-
teously invited within by a civil host, who placed
for our use a couple of good cane-bottomed wooden
arm-chairs. So here we sat and made ourselves
comfortable while we listened to the three musicians
who sat before us, one performing on a sort of two-
stringed fiddle, another on a similar though smaller
instrument, and the third on a 'san heen,' a sort of
banjo with a snake-skin drum, played with a small
piece of tortoiseshell.

The house itself consisted of a strong framework
of thick bamboo poles supporting the big roof of
large tiles, the walls being formed of a sort of
matting of split bamboo, and the floor merely well-
trodden-in earth. Pictures and Chinese placards
decorated the walls, and the usual religious arrange-

ment of a shelf with candles and flowers completed the ornamentation. Our conversation with our hosts was of the most animated description, though I imagine that when we left the hospitable portals they were no wiser than we were as to the purport of the colloquy.

The next place of importance up the railway-line is Soekaboemi. This is the great sanatorium, and here is a large military hospital, chiefly for the troops invalided from Acheen.

Soekaboemi is a most uninteresting place, and my experience of it as a sanatorium was not such as to convince me in its favour, as I promptly had another attack of fever there.

Tjandjoer is the next station on the line, and the nearest point to Sandangliya, to which place I wanted to go. It is but a wayside station, with a small village, so I at once got a ' sados ' to take me on.

The Javanese always had struck me as being intensely dense and stupid, but here I came across one worse than any. He was the driver of the sados. My very best Malay was wasted on him, Dutch had no effect, and at last I could only shout in English, ' Well, you *are* an idiot !' to which he at once replied, ' Ya, ya !' and seemed to thoroughly agree with me on that point. However, somehow we got off, though he would insist on turning back after a bit to get hold of a third horse, and eventually we proceeded on our way up a long hill on a fairly good road, mounting gradually higher and higher.

15

The scenery here is decidedly an improvement on what I had seen. The country is mostly open, covered with coarse grass. Natives, as well as houses, are numerous all along the road, for Java is very thickly populated.

After two hours and a half we got to Sandangliya, where there is a large Swiss-chalet-like hotel, surrounded by trees and gardens. Steep hills and valleys give variety to the view around, and the air strikes much cooler. Numerous paddy - fields extend in all directions, but there are some pretty walks about. The houses are all well built, mostly of a very neat kind of hurdle-work, the posts being sometimes formed of stems of tree - ferns, which one would hardly have thought a good wood for the purpose.

The natives seem to be hard-working people, dressed in their bright-coloured sarongs and peculiar round, umbrella-like hats. They were busy harvesting the rice at this time of year, which looked not at all unlike an ordinary cornfield at home, though of course it only grows at most a couple of feet high. They pick the ears of the rice, and bind them into little bunches, which are slung over a pole and carried off on a man's shoulder to the villages. There the ears are spread out to get an extra drying in the sun before being thrashed.

It is a very fine drive from here to Buitenzorg over the Poentjak. I went in a small two-wheeled vehicle, drawn by three ponies abreast, but after a

mile or so we began a steep ascent, and a fourth
pony had to be attached in front.   After a long pull
up we got to a small village near the top of the hill.
On descending the other side the road enters a very
pretty gully filled with fine trees and masses of tree-
ferns and undergrowth.   Several peculiar bridges
are passed over.   These are often roofed in ; I
don't know why, unless it is to keep off the rain,

JAVANESE BRIDGES.

which might assist to rot them.   Some of them
were made entirely of bamboo, and displayed great
ingenuity.

Still further up the line, between Tjandjoer and
Bandoeng, there are again some attempts at fine
scenery.   Rapid mountain streams dashing through
wooded gorges afford very pretty glimpses, and the
country becomes altogether wilder and less cultivated.

Bandoeng is a largish town, much spread out. There is a pretentious-looking hotel of three separate buildings in a garden, but after all it only contains about fourteen bedrooms.

Everything about seems damp, and although it is a good height above the sea, yet all the country round is very flat, and here, again, are plenty of well-watered ricefields.

All the principal houses in Bandoeng are built of stone, surrounded by the usual gardens and trees. The natives' houses in the country are built with a framework of bamboo, roof of grass thatch, and walls of split bamboo plaited, and sometimes made in black and white designs. Many of the houses have high poles with bird-cages hauled up by a string like a flag. I never could discover what these were for exactly, but imagined they must be some form of trap.

From here a number of distant volcanic mountains are visible, some of them being active volcanoes, emitting smoke.

In the hotel were several very good and life-like dogs and other animals, apparently made of china. One, a very large frog, I thought particularly good. It was presumably used as a weight to keep the door open ; but on my examining it closer it suddenly hopped away ! After that I steered clear of the glassy-eyed dogs.

I noticed in Bandoeng a simple expedient which I should have thought might have been advantageously followed elsewhere. The telegraph-wires

running along the high roads were supported on
insulators fixed to the stems of living trees. In
places where no convenient tree grew, budding poles
had been planted.

There was one place in Java which I was very
anxious to see, but I found that the journey would
take up altogether too much time. It is called 'The
Valley of Death.' It must be an extraordinary sight
to see a large valley without a sign of vegetation in
it, and which has apparently magical qualities, for
whoever attempts to cross it drops down dead! I
am told you can watch animals innocently wander
into it, and after a few minutes sink to the ground
never to rise again! But the explanation is easily
credible. There are exhalations from the ground in
this volcanic region of carbonic acid gas. This gas,
being heavier than air, lies in a mass in the hollow
like so much water, in which any animal would,
of course, soon be asphyxiated.

The same cause may be the origin of the fable
of the upas-tree, under which, it is said, anyone who
sleeps will never wake again. The upas-tree does
yield a poisonous secretion, though this could not
affect anyone at a distance, as the fables make out,
but it grows much in these volcanic districts.

The coasting steamers about Java (Dutch company) charge a higher price than any other I have
heard of. The fare from Batavia to Samarang and
back is £14, and the journey occupies twenty-two
hours each way.

At the east end of Java, and between that island and Bali, are the Straits of Bali, and very picturesque they are.

At a place with the peculiar and suggestive name Banjoewangie, on the Java side of the Straits, is a small town chiefly known as being the place where the Australian cables 'land.' There is here a grand view of the volcanic mountains, which rise up to a height of 11,000 feet, with a beautiful incline from the flat plains, clothed in rich green, and dotted over with trees.

All the coast at this end of Java is more or less picturesque, and several active volcanoes may be seen.

SUMATRA.

Of Sumatra I cannot say much from personal observation, having only gazed upon the vast stretches of flat, low-lying country, which continues for a thousand miles, between the Sunda Straits and the Straits of Malacca, though the western edge of the island is, I believe, more mountainous.

This extraordinary island, which contains probably a greater variety of big game, of useful plants, and of wonderful scenery than any other country of its size, is yet very little known. The long-continued and difficult war between the Dutch and the Acheenese in the north part of the island has been going on for nearly twenty years without the former having been able to gain much material advantage. It is a bad climate, and hundreds of Dutch troops are brought away every month from the seat of war suffering from fever or from an awful disease they have there called Beri-beri.

The capital of Sumatra is Padang, situated about half-way up the west coast.

Off the extreme southernmost point, and between this island and Java, lies the island of Krakatoa, where the extraordinary volcanic eruption took place in 1883, when half the island was blown up; and where formerly was the apex of a mountain is now a depth of water of over 160 fathoms. The wave caused by this disturbance dashed over the neighbouring lands, causing a loss of some 37,000 lives, and carrying a Dutch man-of-war two miles inland, while traces of the wave were even said to have exhibited themselves in the English Channel. Everyone remembers the extraordinary sunsets about that time, caused by the dust, which it is calculated was thrown 150,000 feet high.

STRAITS SETTLEMENTS.

The British Crown colony thus named consists of several settlements on the Malay Peninsula in or near the Straits of Malacca. Of these Singapore is by far the most important, Malacca, Province Wellesley, and Penang being, as it were, but dependencies of Singapore. There are also several large native States in the Peninsula under British protection, of which the best known is Johore, others being Perak, Selangore, Pahang, etc.

There is a great idea among those in Singapore that all these native States should, and will, form one British colony. They are all practically ruled from Singapore, and the garrison of the latter is rendered necessary, to a great extent, in case of disturbances in these places.

The first sight of Singapore on arriving from the south shows at once the importance of the place, for it is one of the greatest ports in the world.

After a tedious journey along the east coast of Sumatra, one presently descries a row of low hills ahead, and on getting closer the sea in front appears to swarm with vessels of all shapes and sizes. In Singapore roads lie men-of-war of all nations, large P. and O. and other steamers, fine sailing ships from China, dirty colliers, Chinese junks, and native 'prahus.' As we steamed in we passed a Russian man-of-war doing sail-drill ; away to our right was a piratical-looking junk ; while farther off lay a large new steam collier, flying the flag of Sarawak. But, passing all these by, our steamer wended away to the left, and, steaming in between several islands, seemed as if about to leave Singapore behind. We passed through some pretty channels, and watched the sailors at work on the new fortifications on the hills, and emerged into open sea beyond ; but then we turned again, and came back into the new harbour, and got alongside one of the many wooden jetties.

This is some way from the town, and a gharry

has to be hired — a conveyance not unlike the familiar 'four-wheeler,' only chiefly constructed of Venetian shutters, and without any glass to the windows. Just as the roadstead showed the trade by the number of vessels of all kinds, so the streets of Singapore have a very busy look. Bullock-carts, jinrickshas, and masses of Chinese coolies hurrying to and fro, present a very animated scene, and it is soon palpable that the town is almost entirely Chinese, although specimens of nearly every nation under the sun could be seen here ; for besides the Europeans and the Malays, there are many 'Klings' (from Madras), Armenians, Arabs, and Jews.

Along the Boat Quay, where runs a sort of canal packed full with native boats, are the principal Chinese shops. These are all just alike, each displaying knives, scissors, cotton, beads, brass wire. tools, and guns. The latter are mostly small-bore shot-guns, muzzle-loading rifles, and some flint-locks ; but there are also many Spenser repeating-rifles, new and good, which I hear were originally sent from America for sale to natives at the time of the French War in Tonquin. Here also may be seen many large wooden cases, which contain bird's-nests brought from Borneo for soup-making.

The Chinese quarter extends for miles, consisting mostly of good stone houses and fairly wide streets. Many details of Chinese life are to be seen here. Eating-houses are numerous. In front of these are the dining-tables, with low forms—not for sitting on, but for squatting on. Here the men squat round the table, chop-sticks in hand ; while on the table is put for each person a bowl of rice and two or three little dishes of fish, egg, etc., chopped up and made into a sort of curry. The rice is generally shovelled into the mouth with the hand, and then a dainty morsel from one of the other dishes is taken up and conveyed to the mouth with the chop-sticks. These are two sticks, about the size of a pencil, only

CHINESE AT DINNER.

longer and square-shaped, held between the fore-finger and thumb rather in the manner of a pen. They are so manipulated that the user picks up any object between them like one might with a pair of tweezers.

Then, of course, there are numerous barbers' shops, where customers get themselves shaved all over the face and head, except a patch round the root of the pigtail. They shave the neck, the cheeks, and even the nose. They then clean out

the ears with a small instrument, comb out the pigtail, and plait it up with a piece of silk (either black,
red, or white), so as to form a sort of tassel to end
the tail.

Here they all speak a kind of Malay, for the
Chinese language varies to such an extent that a
native of one part of China would not understand
one from another district.

This great Chinese population is a most awkward
community to deal with. There are numerous
secret societies, very difficult to detect, which are
almost as bad as some of the Irish leagues of which
we heard so much in times now happily gone by.
Some years ago they threatened to massacre all the
white people, and as a beginning to the revolution
shut up their shops. The then Governor, I believe
it was Sir W. Jervois, warned all the whites, and
told them to go up to the fort if necessary. He
then ordered the Chinese to open their shops and
resume business by twelve o'clock the next day.
But it was a ticklish business, as there happened
not to be any men-of-war in harbour at the time.
However, next day, by the merest chance, the
whole British squadron sailed in, and they soon
landed a strong force. The Chinese were, doubtless, very much surprised at their unexpected
arrival, and soon all their shops were opened, and
‘ business carried on as usual.’

But there is, of course, also a European quarter
in Singapore, with banks and offices and shops of all

kinds. Then there is the large rambling Hôtel de l'Europe, the cathedral, and the great green running along the sea-front, on which cricket matches are played, and bands perform, and the élite of the place assemble.

There is a good club and a well-built opera-house, also an interesting museum of local curios, and a good English library in the same building.

Government House is a very fine, comfortable building, situated in beautiful grounds, some little way outside the town. This is the home of Sir C. Clementi Smith, the Governor of all the Straits Settlements, and also High Commissioner of Borneo.

Fort Canning is situated on a steep hill at the back of the town ; and from here the guns could make fine havoc of the houses below in case of any serious rising of Chinese, which is a contingency always to be feared. Most of the artillery are quartered here. It is a roomy place, with space enough, as I saw, to have athletic sports within the fort.

The Tanglin Barracks are about three miles off, and here the infantry battalion is stationed. They are very unlike what we in England consider typical of barracks, being situated in well-kept grounds, more like those of a large country-house. A fine big mess-house with cool verandas stands by itself, surrounded by shady trees.

The Botanical Gardens are one of the shows of the place. They are extensive and well laid out,

and contain many beautiful plants.   One is struck
with the number of 'traveller's trees' here and all
about Singapore.   They are peculiar-looking plants,
like a big fan on a tall stem, and belong to the
banana family.   This name is derived from the
fact that on piercing the stalk of the leaves a good
quantity of cool drinking-water will flow out.   I
believe it is properly a native of Madagascar.   The

TRAVELLER'S TREE.

Victoria regia flourishes in the ponds of the grounds,
a huge kind of water-lily, with leaves sometimes five
or six feet in diameter, turned up at the edges like
a frying-pan.

Whampoa's Gardens are another sight.   They are
merely the private gardens of a wealthy Chinaman,
with some curious specimens of Chinese gardening,
and many miniature bushes cut in fantastic forms.

The waterworks of Singapore, some three miles off, consist of a prettily-laid-out artificial lake with well-kept gardens. Why should not water-tanks always be thus, so as to be ornamental as well as useful?

Singapore is, of course, hot, being only eighty miles from the equator, but it did not strike me as being very uncomfortably so. There is a good supply of shady trees to detract from the glare.

The only representation of the fauna of the place that one sees commonly are the Java sparrows, which flit about the streets just as their more familiar cousins do at home.

The town of Singapore is situated on an island of the same name, separated from the mainland of the Malay Peninsula by a channel nearly a mile wide. This island is about twenty-five miles long by about fourteen or fifteen across, and has several good roads running through it. The soil is not very fertile, although there is abundance of natural vegetation. Nutmegs, for instance, were at one time much grown, but after a time all the trees, from some unaccountable reason, died. Coffee is, however, grown in small quantities, and many cocoanuts. Occasionally a tiger is to be seen in the jungles, but they are comparatively rare now. Extraordinary though it may seem, it is known for certain that these tigers only visit the island from the mainland, swimming across the salt water channel to get a feed! There are several small native villages and occasional Chinese houses on the island. Some interesting Malay villages also exist on the sea-coast, built on piles over the water, very like those in New Guinea.

These Malays are not altogether a nice lot. They are as a rule stupid, and yet treacherous ; and they have an awkward way of running 'amok' every now and again with their 'krises.' These latter are peculiar instruments—a sort of big dagger, sometimes made wriggly like a snake, kept in a wooden scabbard with carved mouth.

Round the coast of the straits are found the curious king-crabs. They are generally about the size of one's hand, and covered with a crescent-shaped convex shield over the fore part of the creature, and a smaller shield over the hind part, with a long, hard, sword-like tail attached to it, the legs being invisible from above.

JOHORE.

Johore is the native State, occupying all the southern end of the Malay Peninsula, the town of that name lying on the straits which separate the island of Singapore. Across this channel one has to be ferried in a native boat with an awning of 'kadjang,' that is, one made of dried palm-leaves.

Johore is rather like a small edition of Singapore, the chief part of the town being inhabited by Chinese. An extensive building, looking like a market, is the Gambling Hall, and here is a large and motley crowd gathered round numerous tables, eagerly jostling one another to get their hard-earned pittance staked on the fickle board. Several kinds of games are indulged in. One is played with a cube put into a brass case and twirled round. The cube has red and yellow marks painted on top. Another game is 'fantan.' This is played with a number of brass 'cash' or coins with square holes in them. A heap of these is thrown on the table; a brass saucer is laid on this, and those coins not covered by the saucer removed. Stakes are laid in certain positions on a square sheet of lead, and then the coins are counted in fours, each one being pulled in by the dealer with a small stick, and thus no cheating in the counting is possible. The winnings depend on whether there are one, two, three, or no coins left. Beside this Gambling Hall runs the main street of the town, and on some rising ground at the back are the well-built Government offices, and lower down, nearer the water, is the Sultan's Astana, or palace. Unfortunately, when I was there the Sultan's uncle (or some such relative) had just died, so I was unable to see him, although he has the reputation of being very hospitable to all English-men, and is not unknown in London.

The Astana is a comfortable large house with cool halls. It is surrounded by shady gardens, and is guarded by sentries looking very smart in their big red turbans.

There is a small but comfortable English club

here, with bedrooms, reading and dining rooms, and billiard - table, etc., where I was comfortably housed. It is a curious little building, with a stream washing its walls in front. There is also a rowing-club down on the water's edge. I had an introduction to the English Postmaster-General, who kindly showed me round the place.

At the other end of the town are some large steam saw-mills, containing a lot of good machinery, and looked after by a Scotchman.

The prison is another object of interest, standing by itself, within large square walls with look-out towers at two opposite corners. Passing in through two wicket-gates, one gets into a good-sized courtyard with grass - plots and terraces. There is a big building used as storehouse, etc. ; near this is a large shed, or roof supported on columns, under which all the prisoners, mostly Chinese, were feeding. The food looked very good—in fact, just the same as they got outside, *i.e.*, large dishes of rice, and small ones of various sorts to eat with chopsticks. The Klings, in a separate lot, also had good food, and ate with their fingers. Many of the prisoners had big chains on their legs, but otherwise appeared to be well treated. The sleeping-house was just like some of the cages at the Zoo — each den (or cell), with bars in front, to hold six or eight men, being divided by a wall from the next, whilst a veranda surrounded the whole. There were plenty of warders in neat gray-and-black uniform, besides

16

soldier sentries. Altogether, it appeared a very well-regulated establishment.

For some miles along the edge of the straits runs a fine road and esplanade. Besides these places there is but little, I expect, to detain one in Johore.

CHAPTER VIII.

BORNEO.

Sᴀʀᴀᴡᴀᴋ (which, by the way, must be pronounced Sara*h*wk, not Sara*wack*) is situated on the north-western coast of Borneo, and though sometimes looked upon as an insignificant little place, is in reality nearly as big as England. It is remarkable as being an independent state (though lately placed under British protection), ruled over by an English-man. I may as well repeat, for the benefit of those who are wont to complain of bad memory, that the original Rajah, James Brooke, came to the country over fifty years ago, and found the natives engaged in intertribal wars and troubles. Siding with the Sultan of Borneo, nominally ruler of the whole island, Mr. Brooke was instrumental in quelling the rebellion, and was thereupon made Rajah of Sara-wak. He at once set to work, and most success-fully too, to keep in order the quarrelsome Dyaks, and to abolish the piratical and head-hunting expeditions which had made their name a terror. But next, the enterprising Chinee made himself objectionable in the country, and a very nasty massacre of Europeans was organized by him about the same time that the Mutiny was raging in India. The Rajah barely escaped with his life; his Astana was burnt down, and it was only because the Dyaks preferred Englishmen to Chinese that he was enabled with their assistance to quell the rebellion and restore the country to order. Those wily Chinese must have repented their act when they found themselves hunted down all over the country by the bloodthirsty head-hunters, who were only too pleased at being once again let out to do their horrid work!

In 1868 Sir James Brooke was succeeded by his nephew Charles, the present Rajah, who as a naval lieutenant had already visited the country.

Though well known to many Englishmen, the Rajah is a man about whom there is much speculation. He is the very opposite to what those imagine who picture him a semi-native adventurer living in Oriental lavishment. He is a quiet, unostentatious, typical English gentleman, ever anxious to do the best he can for his country and its inhabitants. He married an English lady (called the Ranee), and has a son at school in England, who is his appointed successor (Rajah Mooda).

The government of the country is now most perfectly organized; there are some thirty English officials, of whom a certain number, having the title of Resident, are allotted to the various districts, where they act as magistrates and general rulers of the country.

Then there is the army of some 300 well-drilled
natives, forming one regiment, the Sarawak Rangers,
neatly dressed in white with black braid, and armed
with Snider rifles. These are commanded by an
English officer, Major Day. There is also an
excellent police force; a navy, consisting of one
old gun-boat and some steam-launches; and all
other desirable institutions. On the postage-stamps
is a very good portrait of the Rajah, whose profile is
also delineated on the copper coins.

A small but well-found steamer plies regularly
between Singapore and Kuching, the capital of
Sarawak. She is seldom overcrowded with saloon
passengers, and there was, I believe, quite an average
number when one lady was the only other passenger
besides myself. The fore part of the ship quite
made up, however, for any lack of numbers aft, as
the entire deck was tightly packed with Chinese
emigrants. I was glad to find in my fellow-passenger someone able to give me information regarding the strange land I was about to visit. One of
my first questions was the very natural one, 'Which
is the best hotel in Kuching?' 'Hotels!' replied the
lady in extreme surprise, 'there are *no* hotels there!'
'But, then, where is one to go to get a bed—how
is one to live?' I asked. 'I'm sure I don't know,'
was the extremely disappointing answer. I did not
relish the idea of stopping in a Chinese house, still
less the thought of living with Malays or Dyaks;
but when one goes to Rome one must do as the

Romans do. However, before I got to the end of my journey my charming fellow-passenger, who was the wife of the Commandant of the Rajah's troops, very kindly asked me to stay with them.

The country for many miles around Kuching is comparatively low and flat, and thickly covered with forest ; further inland rise mountains, increasing in height as they get into the interior.

Kuching is some twenty miles up a narrow winding river, with small wooded hills on the left bank, and flats covered with mangrove and Nipa palm on the right.

This Nipa palm is one of the most useful of plants. In appearance it is like the branches of a cocoa-nut stuck in the ground, it being stemless. The fruit is edible, the leaves valuable for thatching and building huts ; salt is got from the leaves, sugar and 'palm-wine' from the sap.

Numerous voracious crocodiles frequent the river, and make themselves so unpleasant to the inhabitants that a reward is given by the Government for any miscreant brought in alive or dead. A young and innocent, but promising, captive was brought in one day alive, and was offered to me for a pet as an alternative to his being put to death. He would doubtless have proved a most agreeable companion, but I was cruel enough to leave him to his fate.

On the banks of the river, as with all the rivers of Sarawak, are numerous clear sign-boards, readily understood by any novice, and not presenting mys-

terious enigmas like the beacons in most rivers.
You read 'Hug this' and 'Rocks here'; or, when
puzzled at a branch in the river, you are directed
'To Kuching ▶→.' ·

Numerous Dyak houses and villages are passed,
built of palm-leaves and raised on piles.   As Kuching is approached you see to your right the white
castellated fort on a small knoll, and on your left the
town, composed chiefly of Chinese houses with
verandas and shop-fronts ; beyond are the public
buildings.   This side of the river (the right bank) is
low and flat, and here the steamer goes alongside
the wooden wharf, on which is gathered a crowd of
Chinamen and Malays.   Just beyond the wharves
and their sheds stands conspicuously the prison on
the river bank, its glaring whitewashed walls
formed so as not only to keep the malefactors in,
but also to keep rioters out, so that it would form a
useful outwork, in the event of another rising, to the
fort, which commands the town from the other side
of the river.   It has a small tower, with a command-
ing view, in which are the quarters of the Governor
of the gaol, who is also Chief of Police.   Behind the
prison runs the main road of the town, parallel to the
river.   Close by are the public offices, ugly high-
roofed structures, with grass plots in front, on which
are some beautifully-worked native guns, originally
made at Brunei, and captured during some expeditions against unruly Dyaks.   These buildings consist of the Law Courts (where the Rajah himself

presides over the Court of Appeal), the Post Office, Treasury, etc.

Further up the river bank is the fish market, in a large room over which is (or rather *was*, for I hear it is now removed to more commodious premises) temporarily placed the museum. This contains a most interesting collection of native products. Beautifully made grass-mats, baskets, and cloth woven in well-arranged coloured patterns; Dyak war-dresses with feathers, and cowhide cloaks; numerous native arms, chiefly 'krises' (daggers) and 'parangs' (swords); also skins and skulls of the human-like orang-utan and other interesting beasts; snakes in spirits, birds, eggs, insects, and numerous other curiosities, complete the collection.

On going up the road away from the river the hospital and public dispensary are passed on the right, the police station on the left, then the Rajah's stables, and a little further on is the church, a neat little building, well planned for coolness, and with what I have seen in no other church all the world over—large comfortable seats. It is a most peculiar sight to see at service here a number of Chinese choristers, their pig-tails hanging down over their surplices.

Then we get to the small building containing the public reading-room and library, a most useful institution in this small community. Opposite are the public gardens laid out with flower-beds, and having a band-stand in the centre, where the excellent little band of the Sarawak Rangers, consisting of about twenty Manila men, plays twice a week. On such occasions Kuching turns out in its little best. The European ladies muster in force (about half a dozen when all there) to hear the selection of music, which duly ends with the Sarawak national anthem.

Further on is the club, where, in the cool of the evening, all the male portion of 'the upper ten' assemble for lawn-tennis, and, when it gets too dark for that, retire inside to play billiards and American bowls.

So that Kuching is a gay little place, all things considered.

The Chinese part of the town does not call for much comment. It is much the same as other towns built and inhabited by Celestials, and is very like a bit of Singapore.

So much, then, for the right bank of the river. We must now cross to the fort and the Astana. At the landing-stage near the prison is a 'sampan' waiting. This is a sort of native gondola, with roofed-in seat, and a man at each end with a spade-like paddle, by means of which the boat is skilfully propelled across the rapid stream and arrives at the shed on the opposite landing-place, whence a short walk brings us up to the fort.

The Commandant's house is a cool, roomy building, the lower part containing hall and dining-room and offices, the sitting and sleeping rooms being above, with large and shady verandas. The fort itself is somewhat similar to the prison, also having a tower containing the armoury and loopholed walls with battlements. Here are a few small guns sufficient to announce the time of mid-day, if not to shell the town below on the other side of the river.

In the Commandant's garden I first became acquainted with some of the slightly less human inhabitants of the country. For here, chained to poles, are several monkeys of different kinds—one, a white one, supposed to be very rare, had taken a strong hatred to Mrs. Day, and would not let her approach him, though he did not seem to mind anyone else; in fact, he was very friendly disposed towards me.

By going down a pretty little path amongst some fine trees, and crossing a small bridge, you get into the large and well-laid out grounds of the Astana, or Rajah's palace. They extend all round the house, and at the back are very extensive and pretty, the ground being undulating, with ornamental ponds lying in the depressions. The house itself stands on rising ground, with terraces down to the river. It consists of a fine-looking old tower and a large bungalow-like building, with very high roof and wide verandas. The front-door is in the tower, and over it is carved the Rajah's coat-of-arms, while from the top turret floats the Sarawak flag (a St. George's Cross, half black and half red, on a yellow ground). A sentry of the Sarawak Rangers guards the entrance. Inside, the house is comfortable and well decorated. The large drawing-room

is surrounded with panels, painted by the Ranee, of
native orchids; and here also are several stuffed
Argus pheasants—those birds with huge wings of
brown feathers, with white peacock-like markings.
There is a very complete and representative little
library, and a billiard-room in the tower. I have
seldom been more luxuriously housed than when
staying at the Astana, having a complete suite of

RAJAH BROOKE'S HOUSE.

four rooms to myself, and every possible comfort.
At a dinner-party, with men in evening dress and
ladies in the latest Paris fashions, you might almost
imagine yourself in London, except for the gorgeous
blue and gold costumes of the servants—uniforms
rather than liveries—and for the soldiers who stand
smartly at the corners, waving great fans on poles
to and fro.

The neighbourhood of Kuching does not present any special features of interest. Roads are conspicuous by their absence in Sarawak, with the exception of the streets in the town, and one or two roads which have been recently made, chiefly for the Europeans to take their drives along. There are probably not half a dozen wheeled vehicles in the place.

There is a pretty little semi-natural reservoir on some rising ground near, for supplying the town with water. Not far off is a large mission-house, with schools attached, but in which, I hear, the scholars learn but little. Several prettily-situated bungalows for Europeans nestle among the fine trees and luxuriant shrubberies; and then, still further afield, we get to patches of cultivation, where may be seen coffee, pepper, tapioca, and other crops, as well as a great many betel-nut palms, whence comes the nut so much relished by all natives of the Far East. I once heard a great argument about this palm, one party stoutly asserting it was the betel-nut, while the other was ready to bet a large sum of money that it was the areca-nut. Reference to an impartial and knowing umpire taught them that both were right; for what we generally call the betel-nut is really the areca-nut! This confusion of names may be explained thus: the latter nut is chewed wrapped up in the leaf of the betel-plant (a variety of pepper); hence it gets to be called betel-nut and betel-nut palm.

The coffee which has been planted in these low-lands is of the Liberian variety, but it remains to be seen how far the experiment, for such it is, will succeed.

A field of pepper is not unlike, at a short distance, a Kentish hop-garden, the plant creeping up a thick pole, and having a leaf resembling that of a laurel. In cultivating the plant, the cutting is allowed to grow up to a certain height, when it is pulled down, coiled up in a bunch, and the whole buried except the top shoots. The plant, after being frequently pruned and richly manured with burnt earth, then grows strong and thick, forming a large root, and in time gets covered with bunches of berries like hard green currants. These berries are formed of the pepper-corn, or stone, surrounded by a little fleshy skin, and when ripe they turn red, and the skin is easily removed. The peppercorn thus cleaned forms 'white' pepper. But the berries ripen unequally, so that only those at the end of the branches ripen fully, and the bunch is picked mostly green, and these green berries with their husks are made into 'black' pepper.

The tapioca, or cassava, is a plant about five feet high, with big passion-flower-like leaves, the tapioca of commerce being got from its potato-like root, though the juice of the root is naturally very poisonous.

As our two breakfast beverages—tea and coffee—grow together, so also we find two articles of food closely associated in our minds—tapioca and sago—growing not far distant from one another; but the sago, of course, is from a very different sort of plant. The sago-palm is a large coarse-looking, thick-stemmed palm, not unlike a date-palm, ' only more so.' The tree is cut down and split up, the pithy interior hacked out, washed in water, kneaded, and the concoction cleared of fibre. The water is then evaporated and a white powder left, which is made up eventually into the glutinous globules which we know so well. One large tree may produce as much as 800 lb. of sago, and it is said that more than half the sago consumed in the world comes from Sarawak!

Many other plants are cultivated in the country (though not so close to Kuching), such as tobacco (which, however, is not a great success), cinchona (from the bark of which quinine is extracted), rice, and tea; a considerable trade is also carried on in rattans, indiarubber, gutta-percha, and in camphor, which latter is got from the sap of a very large tree.

Dyaks, like most other giddy young people, civilized or uncivilized, are very fond of dancing. One evening we witnessed a performance which, in the absence of the flickering glow of the camp-fire, was rendered visible by the more prosaic light of lanterns. The orchestra was composed of a number of performers, squatting on the ground, playing on ' gamelons ' (gongs) and drums. Two men came forward as the principal dancers; their costume con-

sisted of a round skull-cap with some long feathers
of the Argus pheasant, a cowhide sort of cloak, a
'seat' tied on behind looking not unlike a sabretash,
and various coloured scarfs. A shield and a sword
in its shaggy scabbard completed the outfit. A
lady also presented herself in gala attire. Over a

DYAK DANCERS.

dress of flower-pattern muslin, with black skirt
trimmed with red and gold. she wore a sort of
corset composed of some forty brass rings around
her waist. In her hair was a large ornamental silver
comb, besides which she had a profusion of gold
jewellery. The dancing chiefly consisted in the men

throwing their bodies into various not unpicturesque attitudes and contortions, and wildly leaping about between whiles.

I made journeys in three directions from Kuching. As there are no roads to speak of in this low-lying country, the only methods of travel are by 'sampan' up the rivers, or by 'batang' paths, which consist

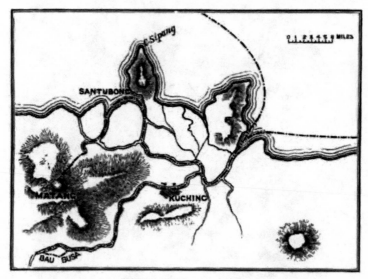

NORTH-WEST SARAWAK.

of felled trees, lying end to end, so that one walks along comfortably above the wet and rank growth of the swamps. I say 'comfortably,' as referring to the natives, for a novice unaccustomed to tight-rope dancing, and with slippery solid boots, is very apt now and again to find himself standing ankle-deep, if not deeper, in the mud below, rubbing his bruised hip and using unparliamentary language.

However, we will not bother ourselves with this just yet, but get on board the Borneo Company's steam-launch, which is just about to ascend the Kuching River.   We soon pass the flag-ship of the Sarawak navy, the *Aline*, and we now obtain a good view of the native village on each side of the water. Beyond the precincts of the town, we find ourselves in a pretty winding river, with thick jungle down to the water's edge and many fine trees towering above.   Now and then we pass a clearing, with cultivation and some Chinese or native dwellings.

After four hours' steam we arrive at Buso, quite a civilized-looking place, since here are some large antimony works, with furnace-buildings, sheds, chimneys, etc.   Cinnabar (quicksilver ore) is also got here, but the workings appear to be 'pinching out.'

I had a comfortable night in the house of an interesting host, Mr. Everett, who looks after the mining works, and next day we proceeded to the mines.   These consist of pits, say thirty feet deep and ten feet square, the sides lined with horizontal beams, behind which upright sticks are driven, making a good lining to prevent the earth falling in.   At the bottom, 'levels' or tunnels are driven in underground.   The earth, of a clayey nature, is put into baskets as it is dug out, and raised to the surface by means of a long horizontal pole pivoted near one end, which is heavily

17

weighted, the basket being hung by means of a light pole from the other end.

The country that we are now in is quite different to that about Kuching or along the coast. Here it consists of a series of small but steep hills, with much rock showing, and is intersected with good paths, which might almost be called roads, only, as there is no wheel traffic, they can hardly be raised to that dignity.

The gold workings are interesting to see, as for many years the Chinese have been accustomed to getting the precious metal and working it into jewellery. But the labour involved is so great as not to make it worth the while of Europeans to work it, though Chinamen, with their industrious, easily-contented ways, have taken greedily to it.

There are several methods by which the gold is obtained. In one place, in low-lying country, you see men standing knee-deep in swamps and ponds. In their hands they hold a round wooden dish, and with this they dig or scoop up some gravel from the bottom. Large stones are picked out and thrown aside, being at the same time examined for signs of gold or other metal, and promising stones are kept in one heap. The rest of the stuff in the dish is now carefully washed, by continually moving the dish in a circular motion, throwing out muddy water and all light earthy matter. After some time nothing remains in the dish but a small sector-shaped heap of sand running from the centre of the dish to the edge. On close examination a few specks of gold may be seen near the centre. These are carefully separated and kept, and the rest well washed again. The whole operation depends upon the centrifugal force caused by the whirling motion imparted to the dish.

The larger stones found in this way and supposed to be auriferous, as well as the pieces of gold-bearing quartz dug out of the rock, are passed through a primitive battery of stampers. This apparatus consists of a large beam of wood, supported on trunnion-like pivots; one end of the beam is heavily weighted, and under this end is an iron hammer-head, which pounds the ore lying in a hollowed stone below. At the other end of the beam a man stands, and by placing his foot upon it, and bringing his weight to bear, causes this end to descend, and the other, in a see-saw-like manner, to ascend and lift the hammer. On the man moving his foot the weight falls and the stone is crushed. In this tedious manner the ore is gradually reduced to powder, and is then washed with water in a dish, and the grains of gold separated as before.

But in other districts they wash the gold out of the earth directly. A stream is artificially diverted to pass the desired spot—a bank of clayey soil— and the water is thence thrown up by scoops and allowed to trickle back into the stream, carrying with it the gold and much mud; the latter is borne off by the water, but all the fine particles of gold sink to the bottom.   After the bank is all washed away, the bed of the stream is dug out and washed in pans.

Near Buso are some extraordinary rocky hills. The formation is suggestive of a huge sponge, for on all sides one sees large holes and caves, mostly round, and apparently water-worn.   They are formed of a hard limestone, and it is no easy matter to climb over them ; indeed, it would seem almost impossible, were it not for numerous batangs, plank bridges, and even ladders, by means of which the footpath is enabled to wind its way towards Paku.   About these rugged hills numerous orchids may be found ; but the soil is so scanty that the few bushes which grow here spread forth their roots in the most extraordinary way over the bare rock so as to catch any chance patch of earth, or to tap any damp fissure. Chinamen make use of some of the holes in the rocks as natural gold-mines.   They scrape up the deposit from the bottom, and in that find small quantities of gold.   They are also able by means of the natural shafts to follow up the quartz veins, which, by the way, often enclose a lode of antimony ore like a sandwich.

Clambering up these hills under the equatorial sun is distinctly warm work.   I actually had to wring the moisture out of my handkerchief after mopping my heated brow, and glad indeed I was to get my tub at the Resident's House at Paku.

There are many very pretty and interesting walks

to be taken about this district. Intermingled with grand forest scenery, we have the native cultivation and the Chinese gold-diggings. Near Bau is a picturesque reservoir, mostly, I believe, formed arti- ficially to supply the streams which wash the gold from the soil as before described.

At every village, as soon as the Resident approaches, two or three Malay policemen at once put in an appearance, smartly dressed in blue with silver buttons, red cummerbund, and number on collar, armed with 'parangs.' One or more of these men always came on to accompany the Resident on his tour around.

I was anxious to know how it was that the roads or paths about here were so very well kept, and was informed that all the Resident has to do, if he finds the road not good, is to let the Chinese people know that it must be repaired, and everyone at once sets to to get it done, any shirkers being immediately reported to the Resident, who can then impose a fine.

It is in the same limestone formation that exist the large caves wherein are found the bird-nests which form an important article of export from Sarawak, being sent to China for ultimate conversion into soup. Mr. Awdry, the Resident, and I, accompanied by several policemen and natives, walked off to explore, or we had better say visit, some of these caves. The natives made splendid torches by merely collecting a bundle of sticks split up and bound together at intervals, like· a sort of fascine. We entered the cave in the side of a cliff surrounded by beautiful green forest, and soon found ourselves wading ankle-deep in soft mud, with huge cracks and fissures extending on all hands, the cave varying from a narrow tunnel to huge caverns, of which we could hardly discern the bounds. There were lots of nasty holes and crevices to cross,

DYAK SUSPENSION BRIDGE.

bridged by rotten-looking poles and rattans; awkward ridges of rock, with deep black chasms on either side, with frail rattan railings to guide us. High up in the cracks overhead poles are jammed across in such a way as to enable an agile native to scale these dizzy heights and collect the nests, of which we could just make out several, as their swallow-like occupants flitted down past us and flew about in the flickering light of the torches. The nests form little brackets, attached to the rock, and are composed of a substance like glue or size, often intermixed with feathers.

There were only a very few stalactites, and but little beauty in the cave itself until we presently got. into a huge hall lit by two 'windows' high up, through which the green ferns and trees which surrounded them looked marvellously fairy-like and beautiful, reminding one of some pantomime transformation-scene. At last we got out by another 'entrance,' wet and muddy to our knees.

The natives of Borneo exhibit a wonderful skill in the construction of suspension-bridges, made of rattans and bamboo, utilizing large trees as piers. The bridges are often suspended at a great height above the stream, so as to allow for the rise in times of sudden flood. Some of them have been improved by substituting iron rods for the canes.

One comes across many queer beasts and insects during one's wanderings about here. 'Wou-wou' monkeys (a kind of gibbon) are often to be heard, though seldom seen, in the trees. There is a sort of chameleon, or rather lizard, which, although very unlike the Egyptian chameleon, changes its colour in much the same way, being usually of a most brilliant green. There are numerous tarantula spiders—great big hairy things with two large sharp fangs neatly tucked away under their bodies. They live in holes in banks, etc., sometimes eight or ten inches deep, and with a cocoon-like web round the entrance. It is wonderful how they make the holes, which are often bored into comparatively hard sand-stone. We noticed a peculiar domestic arrangement which is not easy to account for; in almost every instance out of some dozen where we found a spider at home, he was sitting with the more or less fresh remains of a dead one. Does he eat his wife? or does he go forth to battle and bring home his vanquished opponent for supper?

Orchids are, of course, one of the features of Borneo, and many grand and beautiful specimens are to be seen. Collectors often come out and gather them by hundreds; generally, however, but a small percentage reach England alive. I was very lucky in that, out of about a dozen I took away, the only one which was healthy and flowered within a few months was by far the rarest I had got.

Talking of orchids, it is not perhaps generally known that vanilla, which gives such a delightful flavour, is got from an orchid.

Another expedition I made took me eastwards. Mr. Maxwell, the 'Resident of Sarawak,' or second in command to the Rajah, kindly took me with him. We started early one morning in the fine steel Government launch, and went down the river. It was a beautiful calm, hot day, so that when we got out of the mouth of the river to go along the coast the sea was as smooth as glass. We noticed several large fish jumping out of the water. It is marvellous how they do it. Some of them must have sprung—if that is the right term—at least five or six feet straight up into the air.

On the shallows about the coast are some peculiar-looking fishing 'boxes,' or small huts, built on high piles, looking all very well in calm weather, but somewhat dangerous to be in, I should imagine, when a sea comes on. About here also are fisher-men sitting in their boats with their enormous umbrella-like straw hats—capital hats under the circumstances, but rather awkward for every-day town life, some of them being as much as three feet in diameter, and most beautifully worked in coloured patterns.

In due time we got to the mouth of the Sadong, and slowly steamed up it against its strong current. This is a good-sized river, with the usual low banks covered with mangroves and Nipa palms.

After a journey of some miles up the river we came to a branch, on the right bank of which stands the village of Sadong. On the point of land between the two streams is situated the Government bungalow, where we stayed. It is a comfortable little place built on piles, with well-kept garden, which, however, is low and very liable to flood. For this reason large ditches are dug alongside the paths, and in them are to be seen numbers of the very curious mud-fish who lives out of water, hopping about on the mud and making—or, at all events, using—holes in which to hide himself.

Near here is one of the coal districts, which are becoming of such importance to Sarawak. A rough wooden wharf fronts the river, and sheds with 'attap' (plaited palm-leaf) roofs protect the stores of coal. From this runs a tramway, the rails of which are formed of 'billion,' a very hard dark-coloured wood, useful not only for standing the wear and tear of the wheels, but also for resisting all attempts at destruction by the white ants. However, there is no comparing it with iron for rails, as it requires continual repairs, and it would probably have been cheaper in the end to have laid iron rails from the first. The line is about three miles long, and the trucks are drawn by water-buffaloes. It passes through the densest jungle, which, at all events formerly, was the home of orang-utan. We passed a 'cemetery,' or space fenced in, where some sixty Chinese, who had died of cholera the year before, had been buried. The fence had to be erected to keep out the wild pigs, who used to make the place hideous by exhuming the ghastly-looking victims.

On arrival at the mines one returns to civilization once again after the journey through the wild jungle. Here is quite a considerable Chinese village, for the miners are all Chinese. We went up to the house of the mining superintendent, a young Scotchman just out from home, having come straight to this outlandish spot, where he lives without another European within reach, and unable to speak either Chinese or Malay! Yet he seemed quite contented with his lot, and was rapidly learning the 'lingo' from his Chinese clerk, who could manage a few words of English. Whilst here I heard for the first time a loud and peculiar noise. I thought it must be some large bird with a powerful voice, and was much surprised when I was informed that it was simply the note of a small beetle! It seemed almost impossible that so small an insect could emit so loud and startling a note.

We are now at the foot of a high and steep hill, into which four tunnels are bored, which form the mine. This is, of course, a most satisfactory mode of mining, as all the 'levels' are made on a slight slope upwards, so that the water drains itself out and the loaded coal-trucks run down the tram-lines right from within the mine down to the level country below. It must be a great advantage to do without pumping-engines and elaborate hauling gear.

The coal obtained is said to be very good, especially for use with engines, and a great quantity is now being shipped across to Singapore in a fine new steamer which only arrived from England whilst I was there. It sells there for about six dollars (Chinese) a ton.

I was very anxious to see a real live orang-utan and to get some shooting, so started off one day with this object, passing the mines and through the village till we got on to a 'batang' path, leading over swampy ground, covered with long rank grass.

The inhabitants of this district must live a peculiar life. The marsh around may be compared to an unnavigable sea, and their houses to ships or islands. One follows the batang track as surely as a train sticks to the railway till one comes to one of the Dyak houses ; but these domiciles, erected on high piles above the swamp, are really entire villages, for the house contains a number of rooms, one for each family, with a large public veranda in front. Thus, in making a journey, when you come near to a house, you find—as on a highroad in England on coming to a village—that the path leads straight up to it, so that you mount the ladder and appear upon the public veranda, and, passing among the inhabitants, you descend at the other end and continue your walk along the batang. The Dyaks are a wild-looking lot, with long, straight black hair, a 'handkerchief' round their heads, and a dirty cloth round their loins. Such is their entire costume. But they are always civil and ready to assist one in every way. and, what is more, don't expect any pay for it.

· We walked on for miles on the timber, through marshes, up and down hills—often as wet on top as in the depressions below—and across streams (which often required some nerve to accomplish), and at last got to the base of some large forest-clad hills, and ascended on a good path. Here we met some old, shrivelled-up, stooping brown natives, whom I almost mistook for monkeys, and brought my rifle to the ready. We were now surrounded by splendid forest scenery—grand trees, with numerous creepers, orchids, and ferns. After a time we left the track and ascended a hill. A Dyak guide went in front, plying his 'parang' (a very sharp, scimitar-like sword) to cut away the numerous vines and undergrowth, and clear a path for me. I noticed him cut clean through a sapling in one blow, which I measured, and found to be as thick round as my wrist! We passed numerous places where wild-boar had been digging and lying, and also where natives had been digging pit-falls for them. We had a great climb, the hill increasing in steepness, till at last we got to the top, whence doubtless a splendid view could have been obtained over the plains were it not for the dense growth, composed chiefly of a species of stemless palm which grows thickly here. It was near this that I saw a curious instance of the practical utility of some plants. The climbing was warm work, and one of the natives wished for a drink. He suddenly ran on one side among the bushes, stopped, and picked something from among the leaves on the ground. It was a large leaf of the pitcher-plant! He held it as one would a teacup, and raised it to his lips, and drank the water it contained. The liquid always present in these leaves is a natural juice of the plant, and is not only rain or dew water collected there, as is sometimes supposed.

We could now hear the roar of water, and I was anxious to see what sort of waterfall it was, so we pushed on through the bush, and were finally rewarded by finding ourselves beside a beautiful, clear-running stream, which but a little farther down leapt over the cliff and fell a height of some fifty feet on to large fern and moss-covered rocks below. Here we stayed for lunch in a really beautiful spot, with the grand forest scenery, the sparkling stream, and numerous ferns, pitcher-plants, and orchids all around. Later on we started on our return journey, going by another route, and at last we espied a 'mias' house. 'Mias' is the native name for orang-utan, 'orang' being the Malay word for 'man,' and 'utan' for wood or forest. But the word is often spelt in England 'orang-outang,' 'outang' being the Malay for 'debt'; so, instead of saying a man of the woods, we, in our ignorance, often speak of a man in debt! However, we have seen the domicile of the beast (though I think it rather a shame to style the dear old mias 'beast'). This consists of a large nest of sticks and leaves high up in a lofty tree, but it is doubtful whether it is made as a regular habitation, or only as a nest, such as birds have, for rearing the young in. Anyway, we knocked, by hitting the stem with a parang, but Mr. Mias was apparently not at home, so we continued our way.

Just when getting tired and disappointed at not having seen any mias, the rain commenced. First we took shelter under a rock, but seeing that the rain didn't mean stopping for that, we continued, and plodded on, with rain overhead and dripping trees, wet bushes brushing against us at the sides, and sopping wet ground below; and then, just as we were getting our tempers well up, the guide owned he had lost his way! However, we were not long in finding it; we could see glimpses of the plains through the trees, and soon got into an open part; there we saw some felled trees, and from these led a track which took us to a batang path, though old and much overgrown, and in many parts rotten. However, we followed it up, and finally got to a Dyak house, and, after a short rest and long discussion between the guides and inhabitants, started straight off for the mines. We passed a large tree, with one of the peculiar native ladders on it. This consists of a number of pegs driven into the trunk, so as to form the rungs of the ladder, the outer ends being joined together by rattans, etc., so that each peg assists in the support of the others. On my return to the manager's house, and whilst eating a well-earned tea, my two Dyak guides requested to speak to me. I thought they wanted their payment for their hard day's work; but not a bit of it: they only wished to shake hands and say 'good-bye,' as they were about to return home!

The next day I started off on an expedition up

the river, where I was assured I should not only see orang-utan, but should also come to some open country, where deer and wild cattle were to be got in herds. Among the trees by the wayside I might also perhaps see some of the great 'boa constrictors' hanging like creepers among the boughs. But I understand that this term, though frequently used, really applies only to a comparatively small snake of South America, 'python' being the more correct designation for the large serpent of Borneo. I am told it is a marvellous sight to see the lightning-like rapidity with which these creatures can coil themselves round their victims, which they then crush to a pulp, and swallow leisurely.

There is an amusing tale told of the absolute terror of a sportsman who one day met what he naturally believed to be some awful unheard - of monster. It proved to be a python at his dinner, who was just enjoying a piece of venison ; but the head and antlers had not yet been partaken of, and were left protruding from the creature's mouth. Seeing this extraordinary apparition wending its way through the forest, he imagined he had really this time seen the old gentleman. I am not prepared, however, to vouch for the accuracy of this yarn, so it must be taken 'with a grain of salt and a pinch of cayenne pepper,' as Mr. Jorrocks would say.

These serpents are peculiar as having two small claws, or rudimentary hind-legs, which are of assistance to them in climbing.

I brought back a piece of the skin of a python. It measures twenty-three inches across, so that the animal must have been bigger round than most ladies' waists!

To ascend the river I had a large and comfortable sampan, with a crew of six. In the stern sat the pilot, then came the attap-covered part, in which I lay at full length (there being scarcely room to sit upright under the roof, and only a flat flooring to recline upon), forward of this sat the Chinese interpreter and the Malay servant, a policeman and a 'shikarri,' and two other natives, all the latter sitting in pairs to paddle the boat. This sounds certainly a most luxurious and easy way of going big-game shooting, yet it was more tiring and irksome than one would imagine.

The river soon narrows and gets wilder, with dense bush on both sides, and a sort of pandanus tree growing in the water all along for some distance out from the banks. Numerous orchids, with pretty flowers, hang from the boughs of the trees. Lots of small birds and butterflies flit about (which, by the way, were conspicuous by their absence the day before).

At last we got to a native house near the river-bank, on the usual high piles, all below and around being long grass and bushes, through which, I imagine, one could hardly crawl. No wonder if they now and again get a huge boa-constrictor squirming itself about the roof. After having dinner

18

here we again continued to ascend the river. The scenery now changed, the dense undergrowth ceased, and on either side was a great forest of large trees, the ground being entirely covered with water. It all had the appearance of a flood; but I understand that so it always is. This is the country wherein the mias delights to disport himself, and here we see at once the reason for his peculiar figure. Legs would be but of little use in such a place, so the mias 'goes in for' a second pair of hands on some very short, stumpy hind-limbs. It was only occasionally that we could find a dry spot of land whereon we could get out for a stretch and to light a fire to cook our frugal meal, and mile after mile was passed without any change of scenery. Towards evening many monkeys came down to the river-side, carrying on an animated conversation, and a few pigeons flew over to be shot at. As darkness came on the fire-flies lit up and illuminated the bushes along the banks in the most marvellous and brilliant manner. There are certain kinds of trees which they frequent, and these were a perfect blaze of stars.

At last we got to the native house where we were to remain the night. The owners were very civil and hospitable in their way, laying down numbers of native mats for me to lie upon. These mats are beautifully made, and beat anything of the kind I have seen elsewhere. They are finely woven of grass, and are worked in most artistic patterns of various natural tints of yellow and brownish grasses. With four or five new mats on top of one another laid on the floor of the public veranda, and a mosquito-net (very necessary) rigged above me, I was perfectly comfortable and slept well, notwithstanding a squalling baby (for they *do* squall even in these parts) and the men treading rice all night. This latter is a peculiar operation : the ears of rice are laid in a heap on the floor, a man seizes hold of a rafter above and 'marks time' with his feet, occasionally kicking aside some of the old straw and drawing in fresh.

Next morning we started off again in the sampan and passed on through the forest, plodding along against a strong current. In due course of time we arrived at a dryish piece of land where a batang path led into some scrub ; here we were to land, and, as I understood, were to commence our march to the plains, where the deer and wild cattle were to be found in abundance. We landed accordingly, and I apportioned each man his load of the provisions and ammunition for the day, my gun and rifle, etc. Gaily we started off. After a few hundred yards we came to a small knoll with a house on it, and an attempt at cultivation around. At the house the path ended ! I made inquiries of my interpreter and guide, but they both seemed perfectly satisfied, nodding, and implying, 'Here we are. These are the deer-and-cattle-covered plains.' It was certain we could go no farther in this direction, the knoll being quite surrounded with swamp and forest, so back we went to the boat, and then I gathered that that was merely a little diversion and we had much farther to go. So off we went once again up the river.

PROBOSCIS MONKEY.

In the evening we saw numerous monkeys as usual, amongst many others some of the very extraordinary-looking proboscis monkeys (*Larvatus nasalis*), one of which I shot and brought back home. This monkey, which is peculiar to this district of Borneo, and found in few, if any, other parts of the world, has, unlike the orang-utan, long legs, long tail, and a long, bulbous nose, which seems to hang in front of his mouth. He has a thick coat of a yellowish colour, being prettily marked with a reddish 'jacket,' hence the native story of their being the ghosts of some British troops who were killed in Borneo many years ago. This animal utters a most alarming noise, sounding rather like a tiger laughing— that is to say, a deep and sonorous 'haw-haw.'

We had a great job to land (or, rather, embark) our specimen, as, although the bullet had entered his side just below the shoulder, he was not quite dead, and the men seemed very loath to tackle him, but as a matter of fact, I should imagine his ponderous nose would get very much in the way of his biting anyone, and he certainly has no other means of defence. However, he soon died without requiring any *coup de grace*, and we got him on board.

We had much more difficulty soon after with another peculiar - looking monkey, which I had descried clambering up a large tree. I had shot him with a shot-gun, and he was only wounded in the lower portion. He sat on the ground at the root of a tree in some inches of water, evidently meaning fight, and in this instance his *mouth* was more like a tiger's than his voice. He had, unlike any other monkey I had heard of, huge tusks protruding below his jaw when the mouth was shut, and, as may be imagined, had consequently a most ferocious aspect when he opened his mouth. Several hard blows on the head from an iron ramrod seemed only to make him the more angry, although, as the skull now before me shows, it was actually cracked and smashed in from the blows. He turned out to be a peculiar species of long-tailed macacus.

MONKEY'S SKULL.

The happy hunting-ground we never reached! The guide evidently did not know his way, and after several landings without result we returned down the river again.

I managed to get, through the shikarri, a live young orang-utan, whom I christened Mias. His age I could not ascertain, for the estimates given by those up in such matters varied between six months

'MIAS' AT HOME.

To face page 279.

and two years ; but he was certainly a precocious child. He was very strong, and stood (or rather sat, for he seldom stood erect on his legs) about two feet nothing. He could be very bad-tempered when he liked ; but I must say for him he never once attempted to bite me. Twice over, however, when a stranger, following my example, gently stroked his little nearly-bald head, he quietly but firmly seized the stranger by the wrist, raised the hand to his mouth, and deliberately gave it a good bite. It was extraordinary how quickly he grasped the principle of the soda-water bottle ; when he had had his pull at the bottle he would not attempt to lay it down as he knew that the water would be spilt, so he always held it upright until he had had enough 'pulls,' winking his eyes and sucking his lips meantime. Mias, I may here mention, accompanied me in my future travels. He had to have a special cab all to himself in Singapore, as he then travelled in a large cage. In Batavia he lived in the courtyard of the hotel. On board the ill-fated *Quetta* he was a great source of amusement to the passengers, and finally at Brisbane he lived (and died !) in an old aviary in the grounds of Government House. The cold westerly winds were doubtless the chief cause of his untimely death. But he had sickened gradually of an obscure disease, and I was much perplexed whether to send for a doctor or a veterinary surgeon ; the former appeared insulted, so I had to confide in the latter.

But I am anticipating. Mias, like all his kind, had a fine human-shaped head, with high noble forehead and beautiful (yet, I must confess, rather *bestial*) eyes. They say that the skull of a young orang-utan more nearly resembles that of a man than does that of any other animal; later on their teeth become comparatively coarse and large, and the forehead recedes. His nose was small, very; but his lips made up for it. They were most peculiarly mobile and expansive. The grimaces he would make after he had done his dinner—I suppose to clear his teeth—were extraordinary. He had not much of a neck to speak of, and was rather given to stooping; his body was covered with long reddish-brown hair; hands and arms human-like, if thin. He delighted in a shawl, even in his native country, and it was comical in the extreme to see him throw it over his head and round his shoulders, just as any old woman would do.

One day we put a small monkey, much to the little thing's fright, in the orang's cage. Mias looked at him in a scornful, dignified way; then, curiosity overcoming him, he stretched forth his hand, gently touched the newcomer, and then smelt his fingers. Satisfied with that, he took no further notice whatever of the intruder.

Mias ate just like a child. Almost anything would suit. Bread, meat, pudding, etc., were all relished. But his great delight was, of course, fruit, and he was always very careful about peeling his bananas, and spitting out the stones of such fruits as had them.

I dare not think what would have happened had Mias lived. In course of time, I am told, he would have grown as big as me (except for his legs), and about as strong as any three men. What if his liver got a little out of order *then*, and he had had a difference of opinion with me?

At Sadong I again joined the Resident, and before returning to Kuching we went up another branch of the river Sadong in two sampans, though, with the exception of a few pigeons and some common monkeys, saw nothing. But what a night we had in the steam-launch after it! The veriest tyro would say that it would probably not be comfortable to sleep on a small steam-launch in the mouth of a river in Borneo without mosquito-nets. But if the Resident could do it, why not I? As it was, we neither of us did it—at least, not for long. After dinner we enjoyed ourselves fairly well shooting mosquitoes, not exactly with guns, but with bits of leather. However, later on they had *their* turn, and did their little best to kill us. We tried everything. First lying completely covered with a blanket; then, suddenly finding this unbearably hot, we covered our faces with handkerchiefs. But then our hands and arms suffered. Feet we stowed away in canvas bags, and we tried lying on our hands, but 'pins and needles' were worse than mosquitoes. Occasionally, just as one of us was dosing off nicely, he was rudely awakened by a frightful oath from the other, who would get up to 'rearrange.' Then I tried getting up on top of the attap roof, which was cooler and more airy, and less liable to disturbance from my companions' shiftings. But I soon found it very damp from dew, and not extra comfortable to lie on. In turning over I *very* nearly rolled clean over into the river ; and finally the mosquitoes found me out, and were as bad as ever. So I retired below again. At last I was just getting off to sleep, when the men woke, and proceeded to coal up the fire and make other noises. But soon afterwards we were again under way. A cool draught was caused by our progression, and the mosquitoes vanished. So, leaving them behind in their happy hunting-ground, we continued our journey down the river, and enjoyed at last a real good sleep.

Again we were lucky in finding a calm sea, so soon got to the Kuching River, and were back in the capital next day in time for church.

My next trip was with the Rajah, to visit his mountain retreat on Matang, a steep thickly-wooded hill, some 4,000 feet high, which rises from the plains to the westward of Kuching. We started off in a steam-launch and went downstream. Turning off down one of the many mouths of the river, which form the delta, we came out eventually beside a fine-looking peninsula called Santubong. It is just like a small Gibraltar, being

SANTUBONG.

To face page 282.

a rugged mountain, only connected with the mainland by a flat spit of sand. We stopped opposite a
large village, with numerous fishing-boats and native
craft drawn up along the beach. Behind the village
rises the precipitous hill, thickly covered with trees
most of the way up, but with the bare rock standing
out boldly at the top. Here we landed, to visit
another very pretty little bungalow belonging to the
Rajah, with a garden full of bright crotons and
tropical plants. Near this many old remains have
been found of some ancient Hindoo colony.

We then continued our journey inland again up
some very complicated windings of a small river.
Mangroves hemmed us in on both sides, standing
perched up on their curious roots, as though it would
not make much difference if the tree were inverted
and put roots upwards. But presently the river
shallowed and we had to change out of the steam-
launch into a large boat manned by Rangers.
This craft had been presented to the Rajah by the
King of Siam. In due time we landed a short distance from the base of Matang near a small house
whence a broad, well-kept path led in a zigzag
direction up the mountain. We had a hot trudge
of some three miles to the bungalow; but the
scenery was very fine in the forest jungle, with occasional glimpses of an extensive view of the plains,
and frequent trickling streams and waterfalls.

We then got to clearings where are the tea and
coffee plantations, both of which seem to be thriving

well. And finally we arrived at the Rajah's bungalow, most prettily situated with a background of
forest trees, tree-ferns, traveller's palms, and plenty
of rose-bushes all around. From the veranda a
glorious view is obtained of almost all the low-lying
country, which appears quite flat and thickly wooded.
On the left Santubong stands up boldly in the sea.
Glistening streaks of river sparkle here and there
amongst the forest plains, while the town of Kuching (ten miles off as the crow flies) stands out white
amongst the trees. The hills about Sadong are
seen in the distance, and other hills at still greater
distance dimly form a horizon. In the evening
we sat and watched for the eight o'clock gun to be
fired in Kuching, the flash of which is distinctly
visible. The wooden house is small but comfortable, having, as by the way is the case in all houses
here, no glass in the windows. Next morning we
took our baths in a peculiar manner. Close behind
the bungalow is a fine little waterfall dashing its way
over the mossy rocks from higher up the mountain.
Just on a level with the house it is made to shoot
off a ledge of rock, and under this shoot a bath-
house has been made, so that you walk under the
fall, and gain a very agreeable sensation from the
powerful fall of water on your head and shoulders.
All around you hear in the early morning the
peculiar warbling noise of wou-wou monkeys,
sounding like water being poured from a bottle.
These monkeys are very difficult to see, as they

keep hiding themselves as you approach ; they are long-limbed and agile, and are about the highest order of the smaller monkeys. In the cool of the evening we made the ascent to the top of the mountain, clambering up a rough path. Near the summit is a clearing where is a cinchona (quinine) plantation.

On the very top of Matang a light wooden platform is erected, from which a truly grand view is obtained, not only of the plains towards Kuching, but also of hills and mountains in other directions, extending into Dutch territory.

In the clearings on the hillside, or, rather, in the scrubs surrounding them, are numerous wild boar, said to be of very large dimensions. We got up a shoot, but, with my usual bad luck, found nothing except recent tracks of some evidently very large animals.

The woods on Matang also contain Argus pheasants, fine large birds with magnificent plumage; but they are very wary and shy, and, although often caught in traps, are seldom indeed approached sufficiently close to get a shot at them. There are also numerous rhinoceros-hornbills about. Curious-looking birds they are, with their huge beaks, which, unlike the New Guinea species, have an upturning horn rising from the upper mandible. Although giving an absurdly unwieldy, top-heavy appearance, their beaks in reality weigh but little, being thin and hollow except for a fine sponge-like substance partially filling them.

Tame cattle also thrive well in these clearings and supply fresh meat. The manager of the coffee estate, with whom we spent a day, must have a very lonely time of it. In a rough little house, with glorious out-look, he lives here from week to week, and month to month, once and away being able to get a few days' dissipation in gay Kuching. Yet here he is surrounded by all the latest (a few months old) English illustrated, sporting, and society papers, so that he is not as much out of the world as some might think.

In due course we returned to the capital by the same means by which we came, and shortly after I found myself once again on board the ss. *Normanby* heading for Singapore, with feelings of the utmost thanks to those who had made my trip one of the pleasantest experiences of my life. I then returned to Brisbane, and later on to New South Wales.

CHAPTER IX.

NEW ZEALAND.

THE journey from Sydney to Auckland takes about four days, and the passage is generally a rough one. The steamer I crossed in had, moreover, a reputation for rolling, and I soon had occasion to endorse the opinion of previous passengers. The captain, however, assured me that the motion was solely due to the fact that we had a beam sea, otherwise the vessel would have ploughed her way onward as steadily as a duck in a pond. But the steward confided to me that it was only because she carried so light a cargo, while one of the officers declared that *any* ship would roll in such a tremendous sea as we were encountering. I, however, convinced that neither sea nor cargo were to blame, remained ' of the same opinion still.' Among the passengers on board was Peter Jackson, the Australian negro pugilist, and a quiet, unassuming man he seemed to be.

The coast about the north of New Zealand is very lovely. Many picturesque islands and headlands are passed, such as Cape Brett, which, by the way, appropriately reminds one of Brett's pictures, and Piercy Island, with its natural arch. Then we turn, and, passing inside the great volcanic island Rangitoto, enter the harbour of Auckland, which is, I think, just as pretty as Port Jackson, especially when viewed from one of the numerous heights in the neighbourhood.

Auckland itself is not a particularly interesting town, for, although the largest and most important in New Zealand, it is not the capital, so that it lacks such interest as might be derived from the Houses of Parliament and Government buildings, which are in Wellington. But, still, it has a few fine buildings, some well-planned public gardens, and some pretty suburbs. There is a residence for the Governor here in well-timbered grounds, but it is not the chief Government House.

The principal hotel is a good one, as Australian hostelries go; but, then, all the New Zealand hotels seem better than those of the main continent. I noticed, by the way, in most of the inns I went to in New Zealand, an efficacious yet simple arrangement for escape from fire. Under the inside of every window an iron ring is fixed, and to this a good-sized knotted rope is attached, and hung in a coil. In some places there was even a wire-rope ladder, and in the passages notices pointing out the nearest means of escape.

Playgoers may find a good theatre in Auckland,

and here I again came across Toole and his company, who had now been all round the colonies.

There is in Auckland, near the club, a very well-stocked curiosity shop. Though small to outside appearance, it is really a most complete museum of relics of New Zealand and the South Sea Islands. Every variety of native spear, club, carving, dress, etc., can be got here. It only makes one sigh over the uselessness of taking any trouble to collect curios on the spot when everything can be bought here without trouble. The old greenstone or bone clubs, the 'meres' of the Maoris, are peculiar weapons. They are the shape of the back of a hair-brush, and not so very much larger, but doubtless a very nasty wound could be inflicted by a good blow from the edge of such an instrument.

The greatest celebrity in Auckland, or, indeed, in New Zealand, is Sir George Grey, and I was glad to get an opportunity of seeing him. He has a wonderful history. Early in life he was in the army, and went out to explore Western Australia in 1839. He became Governor of South Australia a couple of years after, then went to New Zealand as Governor, and afterwards to the Cape in a like capacity. He then became Governor of New Zealand again, and when his time was up settled down in the colony, and, taking a great interest in local politics, held in time the comparatively subordinate post of Premier of the colony. Till recently he lived on an island not very far from Auckland, surrounded with a manifold collection of plants and animals; but now he has retired to a smaller house in Auckland. Although getting old, he still has all his wits about him, and is ever keen to hear about new and strange places.

The surroundings of Auckland are mostly hilly and fertile. Mount Eden is one of those curious conical volcanic hills common to the district. It was years ago converted into a Maori fort, and a lot of labour they must have spent in cutting it to shape. The principle of the Maori system of fortification appears to be to cut a hill into a series of terraces, each of which has to be contested before the summit can be captured. The view from the top is extensive, and gives a good idea of the lie of the land. In every direction bays and inlets of the sea are visible, dotted with islands, and in the foreground stretch flat green fields and dark trees, mostly a kind of fir, with numerous extinct volcanic hills round about.

On the other side of the harbour, reached by a service of steamboats, is a small suburb, and from here one can take many walks and drives around. There is a lake within a few miles which one is supposed to admire, but I much preferred the harbour as a thing of beauty.

The extreme northern part of New Zealand is peculiar as being the only place in the world where the far-famed Kauri pine lives, though in certain districts of Queensland there is a tree very like it.

In order to see these trees one has to make an expedition to the bush. I went off by rail to a small place some distance to the north of Auckland, where I had been told there was a good hotel. On alighting at the station late in the evening and asking my way to the hotel, I received the encouraging answer, just as the train left, that there was none! However, bed and food must be procured somewhere, and I was directed to a small temperance place, which was also apparently vegetarian, for they had no meat of any sort! But eggs they could get, and got, and I fared very well. In the morning, however, when I wished to make an early start, no one was to be found, so I had to break into the larder and help myself, and, leaving what I considered a fair charge for the lodging on the table, I took my departure on a walking tour to the hills.

Most of the country about here which is not bush is open heath-covered plains, and it is here that the kauri gum is got. It is the gum or resin from ancient trees, the idea being that these plains used to be covered with kauri forests. The gum-digging is a peculiar operation, chiefly indulged in by those temporarily out of other work. The tool used, called a spear, consists of a piece of iron rather like a straight sword, but with a spade-like handle and square 'point.' With this implement the ground is probed, and whenever any hard lumps of gum are felt (for there are no stones in this ground) they dig them up. The gum is usually about two or three feet below the surface, but in the more marshy places it lies deeper and is not of such good quality. In some localities, on the other hand, it is found nearer the top, and is then got by turning the surface after the manner of ploughing. This gum is chiefly used as an ingredient in the best varnishes, and it is surprising what vast quantities of it are obtained. In 1889 eight thousand tons, approximating a value of £400,000, were exported.

, When well in the bush the scenery is really most beautiful. Splendid great trees with creepers and pines (wild pineapples) growing on them, tree ferns, lance-trees, and numerous bushes grow in profusion; whilst several streams with pretty waterfalls dash among the rocks below.

Amidst such surroundings the great kauri rears itself. This tree is in appearance not very unlike a thick-stemmed Scotch fir, only that the bark is gray, not red. One of its peculiarities is that the stem rises in an almost perfect cylinder without any branches for a great height, which is, of course, a great advantage in a timber-producing tree, and is especially desirable for the making of ships' masts. It grows to an enormous size, and some that I saw measured quite eight feet in diameter; but they have been known almost double this size, and then the trunk is the same size round, perhaps, forty or fifty feet from the ground. It is said that this tree cannot be propagated, and it therefore seems as if it must inevitably soon become extinct.

In travelling south from Auckland the railway passes for many miles over flat open plains, mostly covered with 'ti-tree,' which in this country means a plant very like heather, but often growing up to a height of eight or ten feet. In some places fine grassy meadows are passed, thickly dotted with sheep, which appear to be more closely distributed here than is usual in Australia, and it is quite homely to see some good old red and white Herefordshire

NEW ZEALAND FLAX.

cattle grazing on the sward. Then, by the banks of the rivers and streams grows the New Zealand flax-plant, with its sword-shaped leaves and tall (almost aloe-like) flower. The leaves of this plant—which, by the way, is quite different to the common English flax—are cut and gathered into bunches ; they are then split into shreds and dried in the sun. This fibre, the strongest vegetable substance known, then forms a good material for rope-making, but requires further preparation to transform it into the soft flax from which linen is made. It is a most convenient plant, for at any moment a leaf may be picked, or rather cut (for it is not easy to break with the fingers), which, when shredded and twisted, makes, without further preparation, a good strong piece of string.

Oxford is about the nearest station to the hot lake district, which is, of course, *the* sight of New Zealand. But there is not much similarity between this place and the old university town, for it consists altogether of about five houses, including the hotel!

Early in the morning I left by the coach for Rotorua. Four good-looking horses, sleek and fat as compared to the Australian horses, drew the buggy at a good pace along a not very good road, through bleak open country of a sandstone formation covered with heather and bracken. Then as the road entered the bush it became worse and worse. The wheels sank in the mud up to the axles, and sometimes it seemed as if it would be impossible to proceed. I wonder what would have happened if I had tried, as I so often do, to walk, especially as but very few houses are passed, and these only of the roughest description of timber huts.

There was only one other passenger, a commercial traveller, who evidently knew the road well. The chief topic of conversation between him and the driver was on the amount of whisky various local people could consume.

On getting clear of the bush with its many fine

trees, the road improved again, and presently a new passenger was picked up in the person of a very dirty-looking tramp who hailed the coach. The driver welcomed him as ' Captain,' and offered him a lift. But one could at once see that 'thereby hangs a tale,' for our new fellow-passenger at once brought out some interesting yarns in a voice that had certainly been heard in more aristocratic quarters, and afterwards I was told that he had run through several fortunes. Now, however, he was working on some new railway near there, and had been on the tramp to get to Ohinemutu, having walked on right through the night, taking an occasional nap by the roadside. He told us how in their navvies' camp the pigs, semi-wild, robbed the tents of all eatables while they were away at work. To put a stop to this, they had tried putting big bits of broken glass in the potatoes. But this seemed to make no difference to the pigs. They had then invested in a quantity of strychnine, but that had all been consumed without any apparent ill effects, and now they were busy trying to invent some method whereby a little dynamite secreted within some luscious morsel might be made to explode during the process of digestion.

After a six hours' drive we arrived at Ohinemutu, the small town situated on Lake Rotorua. Here are several good hotels, a few shops, and a good-sized native Maori village. All around the lake is a large plain, and in various directions over this plain are to be seen little clouds of steam rising up like smoke from camp fires. But these are all geysers and fumaroles. Just before getting into the village one sees the first sign of a hot lake, consisting of a small ordinary-looking pond, close to the road, emitting volumes of steam, and containing water which is quite hot to feel. But it is on going about the village that one sees these hot springs put to good use. There on open bits of green, like any English village green, you may see a hole in the turf, perhaps only a foot across, with a boiling spring in it. The water bubbles up as in any other springs and trickles away in a small stream to the lake. The hottest of these holes are used for cooking ; there a Maori may be seen sitting boiling his potatoes, or, more curious still, dipping a reed basket full of eggs into the boiling water. In other large pools, less hot, the women will be washing their clothes, and other places, again, are built in with flat stones so that baking operations can be carried on.

The Maoris did not impress me very favourably. They are very like English gipsies—dirty and fond of begging. In fact, they demand money on your entering their villages as a sort of right. There are said to be about 40,000 of them left, though they are fast decreasing in number. Natives living amongst civilization in this way never are so interesting as the free savages. All their primitive arrangements are supplemented by 'civilized' materials. The modern 'whares' or houses are generally built of wood with glass windows, the only peculiarity being the arrangement of gable boards in front, which is built in imitation of the original native buildings. And though some of the houses are now built of reed thatch, these are often covered by a galvanized iron roof. There is generally one big house in each village used as a place of assembly, which has a front of true Maori pattern, with grotesque figures carved upon it, and shells, etc., inlaid or nailed on.

In the garden of the hotel there is a natural hot bath. At first one feels a bit nervous at all this hot water springing from the ground. One imagines that at any minute the whole place may go up as a big geyser, but, somehow, one soon gets accustomed to it. At Rotorua are a number of hot baths of different kinds. They are said to be a wonderful cure for all rheumatic complaints. The patient is supposed to have two or three baths a day, remaining in about a quarter of an hour each time. I want to know whether an equally good effect might not be produced at home if one had two or three hot baths of fifteen minutes every day.

The 'Priest's bath,' enclosed in a large wooden building, is like an ordinary swimming-bath, with sandy floor and wooden seats round the edge, so that one can sit down in the hot water with the head out and soak for the specified time.

The Government baths are situated in well-laid-out gardens, in which are several 'tame' geysers. These are surrounded by concrete ponds, and a drain-pipe is stuck in the ground over the geyser, so that the water shoots up like any artificial fountain.

The natives also have their hot baths, small pools among the bushes, much frequented as the shades of evening fall.

Lake Rotorua is a fine-looking piece of water, with high hills in the distance and a large island near the middle, which it is the proper thing to do to visit. This island, Mokoia, like so many other conspicuous features in New Zealand landscapes, is the scene of some romantic Maori legends. Here Hinemoa is supposed to have lived, and her bath is still on view, which is curious to see, as being actually part of the lake, merely enclosed by a few loose stones, and yet it is quite hot. Then they took us to see an old skull and bones in the fork of a tree, which are said to be the remains of a Maori who hid in the tree to escape capture at the time of the war. The next object of interest to which the guide conducted us was the native god, interesting, no doubt, but not visible to such as us. The building which contained it is all that may be shown, but it was very disappointing. I did expect to see some real native work this time, but found a little wooden structure rather like a large sentry-box, with locked door, glass windows, and ordinary-looking blinds drawn down inside. Then we went to visit the typical native 'whare,' and to see the native ways when really at home and unconscious of the presence of strange white men. However, it would not do to spring upon them too suddenly, so the guide had to shout his directions, and several children who were at play some distance off came running in, got hold of a pack of cards, and sat down in a ring on the floor to play cards as we entered. They continually looked round to see if we were watching them play, but certainly took no interest whatever in the game, and directly we came out the children followed too, to resume their ordinary vocations. The whole thing was a farce, and the house evidently solely prepared for the inspection of the tourist.

Away on the other side of the lake is Tikitere, a place full of hot springs. The first object of interest is the boiling pond, and marvellous it is to behold. A pond, say, forty yards across, all boiling and steaming, but especially in one place, near the side, where the water rose in a sort of mound, boiling hard, just as one sees the water in a saucepan boiling. They *say* that a Maori woman committed suicide by jumping in here. I should think this yarn was true, for I felt a sort of inexpressible desire to do the same myself.

Round about this were numerous hot springs and mud geysers. The latter are generally deep holes or pits, from three to ten feet deep, the bottom being covered with soft mud, which in the centre is thrown up in jerks, sometimes several feet high ; the mud thus thrown up often takes the form of an octopus as it ascends, and then breaks up and falls in splashes around.

There are also numerous sulphur holes of all sizes, from that of a rat-hole to that of a cave one can walk into, these being lined with beautiful yellow sulphur crystals, and from the depths of them a hot sulphurous air comes out.

The whole place was most uncanny. Barren sand and mud heaps all around, without any vegetation, and then steaming pits, with roaring and bubbling noises, altogether very suggestive of Dante's Inferno.

Driving back along the side of the lake we passed some curious country. It is all soft sand covered with thin heather and a quantity of sweetbriar. This country is cut up into deep 'nullahs' by water, these being often as much as ten feet deep and thirty wide, with perpendicular sandy cliffs.

We passed the cemetery, where is an elaborate tomb to Mr. Bainbridge, a young Englishman who was killed during the great eruption of Tarawera in 1886. There is an elaborate description on the tomb, with an extract from the poor man's diary, which he wrote up to the last minute, and in which, after describing the scene, he says, ' It is the most awful moment of my life.' Within a minute afterwards he was killed by the veranda falling on him.

We then crossed over a plain of sulphurous sand

with remains of old geysers. Sulphur is got here for commercial purposes and carted away. They say this place, a bare stretch of dry sand, once got on fire, and could not be extinguished for days!

Within a few miles of Rotorua, across the plain, is Whakarewarewa, where are several large geysers and a native village; but the whole neighbourhood is full of hot springs and mud-holes. There are many ordinary - looking ponds about with muddy edges, as if the tide was low; but in this mud one sees numerous little mounds, and from the centre of these there is a continual bubbling, and drops of mud are continually thrown up, generally only a few inches high, but occasionally the bubbling increases and the mud may be thrown up a foot or two.

It is not a district I should care to cross at night. Among the ordinary-looking heather one may suddenly come upon a pit, perhaps six feet deep and ten across, with soft, bubbling hot mud in the bottom.

The geysers seldom form a steady shoot of water like a fountain, but rise in fits and starts. There is a fine-looking one rising out of a sort of pyramid of white formation, which may be seen from a long way off. But it pulsates up and down; sometimes the water jumps up fifteen or twenty feet, with, of course, volumes of steam rising from it; the next moment it falls, and sometimes actually ceases for a few moments, and only a steaming mound remains; then the water belches forth again, jumping to a few feet only, and so on.

There is a much larger one close by, but although I hung about for an hour or two to see it 'go off,' I saw nothing but steam.

Some miles from here were the pink and white terraces, so famed before they were destroyed by the eruption five or six years ago. Now they (or rather anything that remains of them) are buried under a thick stratum of mud. But the district in which they were, for the exact locality is difficult to determine, is in itself a marvellous sight. The whole of the hill of Tarawera, almost split in two by a large rift, and all the country for some miles round, is covered with light-gray mud, looking almost like snow; not a blade of vegetation is to be seen within a couple of miles, and nothing but hard dry mud worn into numerous channels by the rain-water. It is a marvellous spectacle, especially when one considers the extraordinary change that must have taken place in a very few hours. Thickly wooded hills, a beautiful lake, native villages, and the fairy-like crystal terraces, all lay serenely one evening, and by next day there was nothing but a still, quiet desert, bare and desolate!

The Waitapo Valley is another hot spring district. It seems as if one would get tired of going around all these different places, each with its geysers and mud-holes and boiling lakes; but somehow every district varies, and new wonders are to be seen in each. Here we pass two small lakes close together, but while the one is a deep coppery green colour,

the other is a purplish brown.   A little further on
is a 'sulphur terrace,' which is a pretty heap, about
ten feet high, of glistening sulphur, formed by water
issuing from a hole in the hillside.   We then passed
more mud-holes and boiling springs, and in one
place, seeing some bubbles bursting through the
mud by the side of the path, I dug my stick in a
few feet; on withdrawing it quite a little fountain
of hot muddy water sprang up a foot or so high.
On returning about an hour later it was still 'playing,' though I now found on probing it that there
seemed a hard strong bottom just under the mud!
I tried another similar-looking place, pushing my
stick right down to the handle, but without any
result.   There are some nasty big pits about here,
perhaps thirty feet deep, the bottom being composed
of big loose stones, in the crevices between which
boiling water can be seen and heard, for in some
the sound is almost like that of a steam-engine
at work.   More sulphur caves are to be seen,
where the sulphur crystals cover the sides, looking
just like yellow snow, and being of much the same
powdery and compressible nature.

The 'champagne lake' is another interesting
object, though I would rather not try a glass of the
sparkling liquid.   It is a round pond, about 100
yards across, on the top of some rising ground, and
looks like a piece of ornamental water in some
public garden, especially so as it is raised a little
above the level of the surrounding sand by a beauti-

ful border of silica formation. The water is boiling hot, with volumes of steam rising from it, and on throwing in a handful of earth, the water fizzes like champagne. It is very clear, and all round the edge one can see beautiful, almost coral-like, formations sloping down towards the centre, and I expect the pond would be a pretty sight if it were emptied, as it might be with a large siphon. On one side the water gently overflows, and runs smoothly down over a creamy-coloured terrace, which some day may become like the great destroyed terraces. At present it looks very much as if frozen, and one can walk all over the glistening slope, since, although it is all wet, it is so formed that the water is nowhere more than about a quarter of an inch deep. Near the bottom of the terrace the material changes, and here one can see the process of formation. All the loose pebbles are covered with silica, though remaining loose. These later on become attached and 'frozen' together, and so finally form a continuous bed of silica. Many little sticks and other objects were found partially coated with silica.

The stream starting from the 'champagne lake' goes through some curious episodes during its life. After flowing over the silica terrace it becomes an ordinary-looking stream, but soon after flows over what appear to be rocks of pure yellow sulphur, making quite a pretty and very peculiar waterfall. It then passes on along a narrow gorge, the sides of which are white cliffs of pure alum. These look almost as if composed of chalk, but on putting a little of the material in the mouth, there is no doubt as to its being of a different nature, being salt and bitter, and the wonder is that it does not dissolve and waste away quicker. The stream then forms a small lake, shut in with cliffs except in one narrow opening, and later it flows into a low flat-shored lake, the edges of which are formed of a 'shingle' of pieces of silica, each of which on being broken open is found to be formed round some nucleus, such as a bit of stick, small leaf, seeds of ti-tree, etc.

Then yet another lake is visited, on the banks of which sulphur is found in another form—that is, in grains of a bell shape. In one part of this lake boiling water can be seen, yet the remainder is quite cold, and wild-fowl may be seen swimming about on it. On the way back a large 'porridge-pot' is passed. It is a conical mound of hard mud, perhaps ten feet high, the 'crater' of which is full of boiling mud continually 'blobbing' and shooting up splashes.

Here we found some of those extraordinary curiosities—the vegetable caterpillar. It is supposed that the caterpillar, about the size of one's little finger, eats the seed of a certain plant. The seed grows, kills the caterpillar, and the plant fills out the skin, and takes the form of the insect—the result a thing exactly like a caterpillar, legs and all, and yet it is really a growing plant!

The journey between Ohinemutu and Taupo

(nearly fifty miles) has to be done by coach—that is, if a coach happens to be going; but if not, as when I wanted to go, a buggy has to be hired. The country passed over is generally most uninteresting, consisting of undulating plains of bracken on a sandstone formation. Some hills of volcanic appearance in the distance are, I was assured, to be the site of the next volcanic eruption; but I am not at all sure whether there are any really scientific grounds for this supposition. After a bit some fine-looking cliffs appear away to the right, and from them juts out a pinnacle of rock called Hinemoa, with, as usual, a Maori fable attaching to it.

It is a bad road, and very badly laid out, for it seems to make every twist and turn it can, and yet to take advantage of every little bit of up and down hill! But, then, our coachman says 'naturally,' and relates some queer accounts of how things are managed by the New Zealand Government. I might have believed some of his statements had he not ended up by the assertion that 'There's not a single man in the Legislature that's worth a pin's head.' For as I suppose that body *must* represent to some extent the greatest ability in the colony, all I can presume is that no one in New Zealand is worth the small piece of metal to which he referred.

Atiamuri is the half-way house. It is a picturesque spot, the small inn lying in a valley near a rapid river with rocky foreground, and a magnificent

hill rising behind, with bold cliffs almost all round
it, and a rounded top which was formerly a Maori
stronghold.

After a big lunch off sucking-pig we continued the
journey, and the scenery improved. For some way
we drove alongside a curious kind of valley with
precipitous sides, which *might* have been a volcanic
rift rather than a watercourse. Then the country
becomes more hilly and steep, with fine views, till
presently we get a glimpse of the great Lake Taupo
and the mountains behind it. We then descend to
the level of the lake and, crossing over the river
Waikato, which is deep and marvellously clear,
arrive at the little township of Taupo, from which
one gets a glorious view; but I, ill-advised, continued my way to ' Joshua's,' a small hotel, or rather
collection of huts, down in a hole, whence no view
was obtainable of this grand scene, which I consider
one of the finest sights I know. Across the lake,
with its clear blue water and distant islands, rise the
mountains, thirty miles off—Tongariro, an active
volcano, with volumes of thick smoke ever curling
away from its summit, in the foreground; Ngauruhoe
(don't ask *me* how it's pronounced) standing proudly
by its side; while the snow-covered Ruapehu rises
to 8,800 feet behind.

An old inhabitant of the place told me a startling
anecdote, in which there may be *some* truth.
Ruapehu was never supposed to be volcanic; but
one fine day Lord Onslow, the Governor of New

Zealand, arrived to have a look at the place, where-upon Ruapehu promptly erupted! But it did this in a peculiar way. This old gentleman tells me he watched it carefully through a telescope. A column of what appeared to him to be water shot up several times during the day to a height quite equal to that of the mountain above the lake! But since then no further signs of activity have occurred. There is said to be a lake near the top, which is probably hot, as, being above the snow-line, it would other-wise be frozen.

Most of the interesting sights, in the way of numerous geysers and boiling springs, etc., are situated along the banks of the Waikato. Fore-most among them is the great ' Crow's Nest ' Geyser. You see on the flat shore, close to the river-side, a mound, chiefly composed of large sticks covered with layers of silica, and thus looking rather like a large gray nest. It is only four or five feet high, and you can safely go up to it and look in, and the crater is full of clear water with nothing suspicious-looking about it except that it is slightly steaming. But then you go away to a safe distance and sit and watch. Presently—it may be after half an hour's wait—with an awful suddenness, a rumbling is heard, a mass of boiling water rises out of the nest, and then it shoots up amid a cloud of steam, just as the water would from a hose, varying in height with every pulsation, but going at least thirty or forty feet (and they *say* it goes a hundred) in a slanting direction into the air. It has quite an alarming effect in its suddenness, and, before one could count ten, it slowly falls, and all is quite quiescent again!

All the country for many miles round is completely covered with pumice-stone, the pieces varying

GEYSER.

in size from a foot across to mere sand. Through and over this a scanty vegetation thrives.

Some miles further down the Waikato are the Huka Falls, a grand shoot of water coming through a narrow rocky channel, and falling some fifty feet into a large pool below. A small and difficult path leads down among the ferns and moss to a cave right under the falls, where the roar of the water is appalling.

Wairakei is yet another district of geysers which has to be visited. A small and uncomfortable hotel is situated near the narrow gully, in which all the principal sights are to be seen. There are a dozen or more separate geysers, mostly small, but nearly all having the same inexplicable character of only going off at certain intervals. It is an awful place to visit. As I sat on an innocent-looking bank to watch for a geyser to start its performance, I suddenly felt that the place was becoming most uncomfortably warm, and I believe if I had sat there a very little longer I should have had to have got my nether garments patched!

Here one can see the 'Eagle's Nest,' a pretty and quite innocent-looking heap of silicated sticks ; the 'Prince of Wales's Feathers,' consisting of some holes in a beautiful salmon-coloured coral-looking formation, whence watery feathers occasionally shoot up. Then there is a big mud-hole, with a mud geyser playing in the bottom, and into which they told me a pack-horse had recently fallen and disappeared ; and a most artificial stage-like place known as the 'Witch's Caldron,' where is a steaming, bubbling pool surrounded by dark rugged cliffs covered with a peculiar iridescent colouring.

It was most jumpy work sitting by one's self in this little valley trying to sketch the geysers, with alarming and often unaccountable noises and sudden outbursts of the erratic geysers going on all around.

Not far from this is a hill on which is a 'blow-hole,' *i.e.*, a pit from which volumes of steam rise; so powerful is the rush of steam that, if you throw your hat into the hole, it will be blown out again.

After having thus seen quite enough of these unearthly places, I returned by coach to Lichfield, about forty miles off, passing over large open plains whereon wild horses are occasionally seen. I am told that these horses, unlike those found in Australia, are generally very good ones; but the best are difficult to catch, being naturally able to gallop away from any horse handicapped with a rider.

At Lichfield is a very rough but fairly good hotel. The *table d'hôte* I found most entertaining, the host presiding at one end, and the hostess, a Maori woman, at the other. The 'guests' were all sorts and conditions of men, the railway - guard, in his uniform, being quite the ' boss.'

Near here may be seen a very pretty waterfall, which, though not much talked about, is quite as fine as any I saw in the Blue Mountains.

From Lichfield one can return by train to Auckland.

There are several very curious birds in New

Zealand. The kiwi or apteryx is a queer-looking little fellow, without outward sign of wings, covered with hair-like feathers, and having a long pointed beak. The kea is the extraordinary parrot who has lately taken a fancy to sheep's livers, so settles on a live sheep, and, digging its sharp beak into the animal's back, kills the sheep, and devours that portion it likes. It does not seem to be understood why it should have taken to this peculiar carnose diet, or what it may have fed on before sheep were introduced into the country.

One hundred and thirty miles north of Auckland is the Bay of Islands. This is a curious place. It is really a large inlet full of picturesque islands covered with ti-trees ; it becomes very difficult at times to see where you are, for you cannot tell which is mainland and which island, nor can you see in which direction the sea lies.

At Opua is a small wharf for coaling the steamers, there being a mine not far off, and some pretty walks may be taken in the bush during the operation. Whenever I went into the bush in New Zealand, I was always thankful for one thing, that there were no snakes. In Australia one always feels nervous, and continually when one is enjoying the scenery one is rudely startled by a horrid wriggling thing jumping from almost under one's very feet.

Russell is a more pretentious town on the Bay of Islands, but still is not more than a village.

This neighbourhood was the scene of some hard

fighting in the Maori War, chiefly about Flagstaff 'Hill, a mile or so beyond the town, and from which a lovely view may be got over the bay.

Russell used to be a great whaling centre. Along the beach may be seen several of the long whale-boats, pointed at each end, and with a large row-lock for the steering-oar, so well known in pictures of whaling. I heard many interesting yarns of whaling adventures in the south seas.

The country about here is mostly covered with a variety of New Zealand ti-tree, and there are also many aloes, which appear to be indigenous.

CHAPTER X.

THE TONGA OR FRIENDLY ISLES.

SOME 1,500 miles to the north-north-east of New Zealand lies the first important group of South Sea Islands. The steamer which plies thitherward is small indeed for so long an ocean journey, but we must only be thankful that there is any such convenient mode of progression. And what a dusting we had at starting! The Pacific Ocean certainly belied its name. However, on getting beyond the bad influences of the rock-bound coasts of the 'England of the South,' we entered more genial tropical climes before we arrived at our destination, Tonga. There is often not a little confusion in the minds of the uninitiated with regard to some of the groups of the Pacific, and as to exactly which island or islands form the country known by a particular name, as, for instance, that of Tonga. On looking at a map one may see a group of islands named (by Captain Cook) the Friendly Islands. The largest of them rejoices in the name of Tongatabu, or Sacred Tonga, and this one, being at present the most important

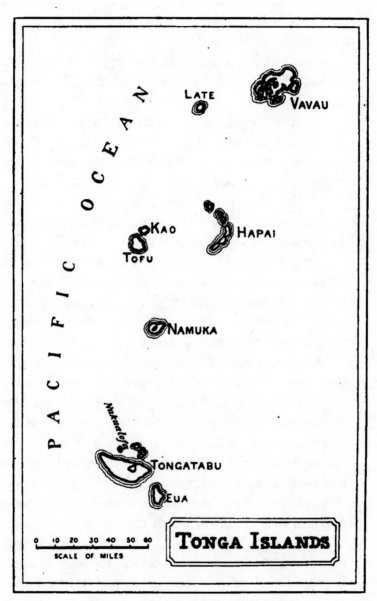

LATE

VAVAU

KAO

TOFU

HAPAI

NAMUKA

Nukualofa

TONGATABU

EUA

P A C I F I C   O C E A N

0 10 20 30 40 50 60
SCALE OF MILES

TONGA ISLANDS

Tongatabu is about the size of the Isle of Wight.

politically, gives a name to the whole group and to the nation inhabiting it.

More confusion may arise unless I explain that Nukualofa is a small town, the capital of Tongatabu and of the group.

The next largest of the Friendly Isles is Vavau— at one time the seat of the Government—which lies some 160 miles to the north of Tongatabu. The other important islands are Haapai, Eua, Namuka, etc. There is a great difference in the natural formation of these islands, some of them, including Tongatabu, being coralline, and lying perfectly flat, and only a few feet above the sea ; while others, of which Vavau is a specimen, rise to some thousands of feet in steep volcanic hills—one island (Tofua) being an active volcano. Nearly all are covered with dense luxuriant vegetation.

In approaching Tongatabu, the island, from its very low elevation, is not seen till one is close upon it, when it has the appearance of a mass of trees growing out of the water. Some of the detached islands, with thick undergrowth and a few tall cocoa-nut palms, have a great resemblance to a large ship, and appear to be ploughing their way through the ocean, on account of the narrow border of white surf which surrounds them.

On getting close to the island one is struck with its immense size. Accustomed to seeing these South Sea Islands marked on a map of the Pacific as so many small dots, one expects to see a mere rock standing by itself in mid-ocean ; but when one looks upon the mass of green verdure, stretching almost as far as the horizon in each direction (for Tongatabu is over twenty miles long), then one may realize that these islands have some size, and may be of some importance.

Situated around the coast are numerous sunken reefs, the position of which is only rendered visible by the deep blue sea becoming emerald green as it

A TONGAN ISLAND.

shallows, and in places dashing in the whitest of foam over the tops of the coral formation.

The harbour of Nukualofa consists of a large open bay, somewhat sheltered by the islands and reefs, though affording no very secure safeguard against a hurricane from the north. But here, unlike many of the primitive harbours in these islands, the steamers draw up alongside a good wooden wharf, connected by a causeway with the shore, a nasty-looking reef bordering the coast closer in.

On the wharf are crowds of natives, fine-looking,

muscular men, all decently dressed in shirts, jerseys, or jackets, and 'lava-lavas' (loin-cloths). Those who wish to be up to fashion wear mats round their waists, or pieces of cloth woven from reeds, clumsy-looking garments, kept in place by a girdle of

TONGAN NATIVES.

knotted cord. They wear nothing on their heads, which, by the way, strike one as being of peculiar shape, the cranium appearing high and flat behind (it may be only from the way of cutting or dressing their hair). The hair, which grows back from the forehead, and in almost an *upward* direction behind, is nearly always dyed with lime to a reddy-brown colour, giving it a pleasant appearance, not unlike sealskin, it being lighter at the tips than at the roots. Some of them, with the lime still plastered on their heads (which has to be done about once a week) at once recall to mind the London flunky. The men have fine, open, if somewhat coarse-featured, faces, and are of a dark, coppery colour, although, of course, much lighter than negroes or Papuans. It is absurd to describe them, as some have, as no darker than Southern Europeans.

The women, whose hair is generally made up in a tuft behind, bound with ornamental tortoiseshell rings, or cut short when in mourning, are mostly attired in coarse dark-blue cloth shirts, with lava-lavas and mats. Many of both sexes wear garlands of flowers, with strips of fibrous bark, around the neck or waist. The unmarried damsels may always be distinguished by a loose lock of hair or plait over each ear. This is cut off with great cere-mony after marriage. The young children are not obliged to dress in so elaborate a style as their elders, and mostly only don the lava-lava.

We have often heard of the female beauty of these islanders. Do not dispel any pleasant concep-tions simply because my experience of the natives was not sufficient to endorse such description !

It may be as well at this point to take a glimpse at the history of these people of the Friendly Isles. And first as to the origin of the islands themselves, for the generally acknowledged account of their first appearance is somewhat remarkable.

One of the Tongan gods was out fishing one day, presumably sitting on a cloud, since no dry land existed at that remote period. Suddenly he got what he thought was an undoubted bite. He struck, but was disappointed to find that, like many another fisherman after him, he had only hooked the bottom! However, in *his* case he put so much divine strength into his tackle that he pulled the bottom right up above the surface, and there it remains to this day as the island of Tonga. I have seen it myself, so can vouch for the truth of this story.

Later on the place became inhabited, and after many more years was visited by Tasman, and later still by Captain Cook.

At the beginning of the present century an English vessel, the *Port au Prince*, was attacked and looted, and most of the crew massacred, off Haapai Island. One of the escapees, William Mariner by name, lived with the natives for four years, and was finally rescued and brought to England. A most remarkable and interesting book was the result of this man meeting a Dr. Martin, who wrote a full description of the manners, customs, and language of the Tongans, from Mariner's verbal description, which is pronounced on all hands to be perfectly accurate in every detail, and is to this day a standard work on Tonga.

At the time of Mariner's visit, the Friendly
Islands, or at least Vavau and Haapai, were
governed by a king named Finow, Tongatabu being
in a state of continual war amongst different would-
be potentates.   There was also at that time a
curious personage designated 'Tuitonga,' or 'Chief
of Tonga,' a kind of sacred noble higher than the
King, evidently something of the same sort of being
as the Mikado of Japan.   This great demi-god,
however, died while Mariner was there, and, for
various sensible reasons, it was determined that no
successor should be appointed.   But the Tongans
are very particular about their rank, precedence,
and privileges, and a descendant of the 'Tuitonga'
is still considered as of higher family than one of
royal—that is, kingly—blood.   Mariner relates some
most interesting details of his visit to the islands.
One can easily imagine the extreme surprise felt
by the natives when they discovered that the
stranger could read and write.   At first, what the
white man did was quite beyond their comprehen-
sion, when he made marks on a piece of paper; but
when he explained that it was a means of com-
municating with other people, they, being sceptical,
determined to put him to the test.   Finow the King
said : ' Put me down on the paper.'   Mariner wrote
'Finow.'   'That is not like me,' said the King.
'Where are my arms and legs?'   And, sending for
another one of the crew, he asked him : 'What is
on that paper?'   All were quite dumfounded when

the man at once read ' Finow !' What a change
now, when not only can most of the natives read
and write, but many of them can even report a
speech in shorthand!

The present ruler of all the Tongan Islands is
George, an ancient monarch, said to be somewhere
between eighty and one hundred years old. He is
assisted in his rule by native Ministers and a Parliament. The Tongans always have possessed plenty
of *amour propre*, and consider themselves, as they
probably are, superior to all the other Pacific
islanders. This may be imagined when I say that at
the time of the Franco-Prussian War King George
thought it necessary to issue a proclamation of
neutrality!

Although the period during which Mariner was
on the islands was one of much discord, yet troubles
more peaceful, but quite as harmful, have since come
over the natives. And by what cause? Solely by
jealousies among the so-called Christian missionaries!
I would not, if I could, describe exactly how the
disagreements originated or were carried on. It
will be quite sufficient to say that there were difficulties between the missionaries; that there are
now two Wesleyan churches (besides the Roman
Catholic) in Nukualofa at bitter enmity with one
another!

The Rev. Shirley W. Baker, who was probably
chiefly responsible for this state of things, is one
of the best-known men in connection with Tonga,

and as I shall have more to say about him personally later on, I must refer briefly to his career. He started as a Wesleyan missionary many years ago. He rose in the favour of the King, till finally he was made Premier of Tonga, resigned his 'missionary-ship,' and started a Free Church in opposition. But he was not content with this; he was soon able to assume other offices as well. At the time of his enforced retirement, shortly before I was there, he 'united in himself the offices of Auditor-General, Agent-General, Minister of Foreign Affairs, Minister for Lands, Minister of Education, President of the Court of Appeal, and Judge of the Land Court, and in one or other of these capacities he alone had the exclusive control and knowledge of the finances of the country.'* The Treasury funds were wisely paid into the Bank of New Zealand, and, as Agent-General, he therefore had the sole control of these foreign-invested funds.

He, with his family, had quarters in the King's palace, or, rather, the King was allowed one room, the Premier occupying the rest of the house. He lived well, and kept his public accounts carefully. To show with what accuracy and attention to detail the accounts were kept, I will quote some actual extracts. One item reads:

'Police Uniforms, Hardware, Parliamentary Expenses, Tanks, Medicines, Building Materials, etc. ...   ...   £769 6 2'

* Report of auditor.

But other entries are simpler; thus:

'Freight ...   .   £700 19 5'

without any further details.

Then we find the name of a gentleman, who, by the way, is supposed to have written a series of articles in a certain colonial newspaper on the Government of Tonga, credited with £50 without explanation. These articles, oddly enough, were written in a strain very favourable to Mr. Baker and his rule.

Certain other expenses were entered in the books, which, although personal, might reasonably be charged to public funds. Naturally travelling expenses were allowed him, and on a visit to Auckland for one month, £46 for 'cab hire, etc.,' shows that he lived in a style not derogatory to his position. His annual subscription to the club in Auckland had, of course, to be paid from the revenue of the country, in order to maintain the dignity of the Premier of such a nation in the eyes of the civilized world. Photographs had to be taken of this important official at Government expense in order that the nation at large should be able to see what kind of a man they had as chief civil servant. Details such as bootmaker's bills, groceries, and suchlike, I need not criticise.

But all pleasures must have their end, and the greatest of men will sometimes fall. One fine day an English man-o'-war arrived at Nukualofa, having on board the High Commissioner of the Pacific. A message was sent ashore to the King asking for an interview. The answer came promptly, that the King would send his Premier at once to discuss any matter. A second message to similar effect elicited the reply that his Majesty was indisposed, and again that the Premier was ever ready to convey any matter to the King. But a private personal visit by the English Consul disclosed the fact that the King had not even heard of the High Commissioner's messages. Within a day or two Mr. Baker left Tonga, with pretty clear instructions as to what course would be taken should he again visit his old home. Poor man! It is hard indeed to be turned out of house and home (even though it be another's house), and to be deprived of such a privilege as utilizing the moneys lying idle in the Tongan Treasury!

Mr. Basil Thomson, my old New Guinea friend, was appointed by the British Government to officially audit the accounts (which must have proved a somewhat arduous task), and to remain to lend his assistance to the Government of the country, much needed after the loss of such a valuable official as Mr. Baker, and here he was when I arrived.

Thomson was styled at this time 'Assistant Premier' pro tem., but I rather expect a more descriptive title would be 'Assistant King'—unless, indeed, that title were applied to George Rex.

Thomson thoroughly entered into the position,

and, were it not such a very out-of-the-way part of the world, would doubtless have liked to remain on as practical ruler of Tonga. But he was very loyal, and begged me not to laugh when he told interesting anecdotes of the kingly behaviour of his Majesty, or when he introduced me to a royal Prince, the aide-de-camp in chief to the King, whom we met in a semi-nude condition strolling on the wharf. But this brings us back to the wharf again, whereon we landed.

The town of Nukualofa consists of a number of detached houses, mostly of native build, with reed walls and thatched roofs ; but there are also one or two more pretentious edifices. Of these the King's palace, with its church, stands foremost. A handsome wooden two-storied house with small tower and large verandas, standing in an enclosure, with pretentious rails and gates, forms the residence of his Majesty. Inside it is a simple, comfortable house. Without in any way being palatial, it is quite sufficient (too much so, Mr. Baker would probably say) for the requirements of Tongan majesty. Here is the reception-room, with its three thrones ; here at the back is the King's own private room— scantily furnished, a native mat on the floor alone forming the bed, the decorations consisting of a few portraits of the King, by various local artists I suspect, and a Tongan school-like map of Europe.

In the hall are busts of the last two German Emperors and of Bismarck and Moltke—wonderful

relics of a bygone power! Hanging on the staircase is a huge life-sized portrait of the old Emperor
when young, seated on a mottled-gray horse, the
latter having evidently been faithfully copied from
a lay figure in the form of a rocking-toy. We need
not ask how all these German works of art came
there; it is not likely that they were bought. But
a few years ago it is supposed that the iron Chan-
cellor had fixed his eye in the direction of far-off
Tonga, as a vast vessel for receiving the overflowing
stream of the superfluous population of the Fatherland. The large portrait, doubtless the work of
some *German* local artist, was probably a good
riddance from the art galleries of Potsdam, yet a
magnificently suitable gift to a potentate whose
critical eye was inexperienced in modern art.

Close outside the palace is the King's church.
This is a handsome edifice of wood; its steeples
and buttresses and architectural embellishments
giving it quite the appearance of a good stone
building. The inside is fitted with pews imported
from New Zealand, a small squeaky organ, a
splendid red throne, a number of tawdry lamps in
green-bronze style, and a fine peal of tubular bells,
with their ropes collected in a wooden frame so that
one man can pull the lot. Outside the church is a
monument to the late Prince Wellington, a very
clever son of the King's. It was decided, so I am
told, to erect a marble monument to his memory.
So Mr. Baker was despatched to Auckland in order

to negotiate with some celebrated Italian sculptor worthy of the task. Happening to pass a tombstone-carver's establishment, his eye fell on the very article required. The figure happened to be that of a lady—Hope or Faith, or someone, leaning on a little rustic cross—but that did not matter: the monument was bought, conveyed to Nukualofa, and erected, as the Tongan people now believe, as a representation of Mr. Baker's youngest daughter.

Nearer by the wharf are the Government offices, plain wooden buildings without architectural pretensions. Outside the court-house is always quite a crowd of women, numbers of these daughters of Eve being brought up daily, charged with certain offences unrecognised as such in most countries. All prisoners used to be kept in a novel and convenient manner. They lived at home, but had to do so many hours' hard work; the system, however, did not prove a success, as the prisoners found it pleasanter to migrate to other islands.

Beyond the palace, again, is the private residence of the Treasurer—it must be seen for one to appreciate the tale it tells of how far the Treasurer may be accused of appropriating to his own use any of the deficient funds from the Treasury. It stands by itself, surrounded simply by the green grass sward. One end of the native-built house is past repair, the roof actually falling in. The other end is only kept watertight (if it is that) by patches of rusty tin laid on the rotting thatch. The walls are repaired and patched with boards, stones, and bits of tin, the whole looking like a very disreputable barn on a small farm. But we Britishers cannot afford to laugh at this! Only a little further on is the English Consulate—another large native-built house, which, if it is in better repair, is certainly not all we could wish for our representative to live in. It is, however, a cool style of building, consisting really of one big and lofty room, but divided up by a number of partitions. The Consul must have a pretty easy time of it in Tonga, for I don't suppose he has a 'job' more than once or twice in a year. Still, I believe that what Mr. Leefe does, he does well and with all possible ceremony.

The ordinary Tongan house is of an oval plan, the walls being some four or five feet high, and made of reeds laid diagonally together. The roof, rising up to a considerable height, is formed of a thick thatch of cocoanut leaves, the whole being, of course, supported on a strong framework. The door is in the centre of one side, and is generally the only means of light and ventilation.

One peculiarity of the houses here is that the roofs are generally chained to the ground, so as to keep them down when a 'blow' comes.

Shops are conspicuous by their absence in Nukualofa. One or two good-sized iron-roofed storehouses are all there is to remind one of trade. But talking of trade, there is a very peculiar inter-

national system of coinage in this country. It is in
dollars (4s.), shillings, and pence ($ s. d.).

Besides the King's church, ecclesiastical edifices
play an important part in the scenery of Nukualofa.
'Mount' Zion, the only place worthy of the name of
a hill, and that not much over fifty feet high, is
surmounted by a plain-looking church; farther away
lies a large stone Roman Catholic place of worship,
and the Wesleyan and the Free Churches stand side
by side in rivalry not far behind the palace. At
times open hostilities are carried on between these
two by means of loud and prolonged bell-ringing
during one another's services. The Free Church is
a magnificent building—as native buildings go—
and when inside it is difficult to realize that so
large a structure could be erected without the use of
stone or iron—for no nails or bolts are used to join
the beams or rafters, but all are fastened together by
being bound round with cocoanut string in an ornamental way, one of the principal bindings having
been done by the King himself. The roof is constructed in a wonderful manner, there being a
number of *curved* beams of great size, formed of
several lengths of wood scarfed and bound together.
Although all the roof is thus done in native fashion,
the walls are made of ordinary wooden weather-
boards, with windows of coloured glass. The pews
here also have been imported, as well as the rest of
the 'furniture.'

Mr. Thomson lives in a comfortable ' European '-

made wooden house. (Again I wish there was another word for 'non-native.') It is tastily decorated by Mrs. Thomson with curtains of 'gnatoo,' carpets of grass mats, and many other native curios. Here were some teeth of the sperm-whale, which are always considered by the Tongans as objects of the greatest value. For food, fish, chicken, and pork form the chief ingredients, other fresh meats and eggs being rare.

On first landing one is struck with the greenness of the place—none of that intense glare so often experienced on getting ashore at any tropical place. The reason of this is that everywhere throughout the town grow trees—cocoanut, hibiscus, casuarina, and others, while underfoot all is grass. It may sound peculiar to hear that all the main streets of the city are grass-covered, but such is the case: the only reason for its not wearing out is the great rainfall and the fertility of the soil. Over the whole island the cocoanut palms grow in profusion, enabling the natives to make a good revenue from the 'copra,' which is collected by the European firms. Indeed, the trade of Tonga consists almost entirely of copra, bananas, and oranges. The large yellow hibiscus gives the bark which makes lace-like appendages to the dresses, as well as a most useful tough fibre for rope-making, and many similar purposes. Pine-apples grow almost wild, and the 'Chinese paper mulberry' is cultivated, from which to make 'tappa' and 'gnatoo,' the native cloth.

The manufacture of this is a great industry. Quite young saplings of the plant, two or three inches in diameter, are taken, and the bark, being split down one side, is removed from the stem. This bark is then manipulated by the women by laying it across a beam of wood, about 20 feet long by 6 inches square, and beating it with a small piece of wood, about a foot long, of square section, grooved or fluted, as a mallet. This beam, being supported only by logs near the ends, has a certain spring about it, and at the same time gives forth a sonorous sound every time it is struck. To hear a number of people in the act of making tappa has a most curious and pleasant effect, onlookers often 'assisting' the work (so they say) by beating a sort of tattoo with another stick on the beam as an accompaniment to the steady beat of the mallet. The sound of this tappa-beating quite fills the air round Nukualofa.

The bark, meanwhile, being continually wetted and moved while the process of beating continues, gradually expands, and becomes thinner—very slowly but surely—until at length it becomes a firm, strong, papery cloth of considerable size, 6 feet by 30 feet not being unusually large. It is then known as 'tappa,' and requires to go through various improving pro-cesses, and a coloured pattern printed upon it ere it can be designated 'gnatoo.' In Samoa, by the way, it seems to be always known as 'tappa'—plain or coloured.

The island of Tongatabu being so flat, and the

roads all being grass-covered, excellent rides may be taken to all parts of the island. One of the chief objects of interest to be visited being the 'Stonehenge,' two massive upright stones supporting a third laid across their tops, the horizontal one being cleverly let into the others. There is great discussion as to the origin of these, some declaring that, like Stonehenge, they are relics of a very ancient time, and even asserting that the stone has been brought from a great distance, while others attempt to prove that they are but a portion of the tomb of a comparatively modern Tuitonga, and that the stone was got on the spot. One hears of remarkable remains of very antique buildings on some of the Pacific islands, notably Easter Island and Ponape Island; but there is, I understand, but little similarity between them and the remains at Tonga. Some miles to the east of Nukualofa is a deep bay, that is, deep in plan, but unfortunately *not* in depth of water, else it would make a splendid harbour.

There is not much to be seen here in the way of animal life. Some weedy horses, a great number of pigs, a few mongrel dogs, is about the lot. We must not, however, despise the horse when we take into due consideration his value. We do hear of a horse having fetched as much as £5 in Tonga, but this was quite a fancy price. Half a crown is sufficient for those to give who do not expect a 'flyer.'

Cava-drinking is, and has been from time immemorial, one of the great institutions of Tongan life. It forms an important part of all ceremonies, and is also as much in vogue with afternoon callers as a cup of tea would be at home. In Samoa I was lucky enough to witness the ceremony in its highest form, and will therefore here only describe its introduction at a humble homely visit.

First, the root is produced. It is the dried root of a pepper - tree — gray, hard, and woody in appearance. This is broken in pieces. Formerly these were chewed up by the ladies of the party and then put in the bowl to make the beverage; but now, I am thankful to say, this practice has given way to a less repulsive one. A large round green stone is laid on the ground, with a mat under it, and the root is pounded on this with another stone. When well crushed the cava is put into a large wooden bowl, and some water poured in. The lady presiding now commences to apparently wash her hands in the beverage, but is only thoroughly stirring up the mixture with her hands. The liquid then becomes of a milky consistency, of a light-brown colour, like weak *café au lait*. And now the curious straining process begins. A bunch of tow (of hibiscus bark) is taken in both hands, and laid on the liquid at the far side of the bowl. It is then slowly immersed, and drawn towards the cava-maker. As it is drawn up the near side of the bowl, most of the coarse husk and grits are drawn out, and the tow is well shaken out on the grass. This process has to be repeated again and again, the fibre being well shaken between each immersion. At length all coarse matter is removed, and only the pure milk-like beverage remains. As soon as it is announced that the cava is ready, every-one round solemnly claps his or her hands, and the doling out commences.

The drinking-cup is formed of half a cocoanut shell. The tow used for straining is now employed as a sponge for filling the cup. The first cupful must never be given to the guest or greatest person present. It is taken to some one connected with the household. The second or third is the cup of honour. It is said that this originated from a servant of some old Tuitonga who discovered the beverage. He tried to persuade his master to partake of the nasty liquid, but the latter ordered that, when made, the servant should be the first to drink of it, and if no bad result followed, then the Tuitonga himself would indulge in the glorious potation.

But you will be anxiously wondering what this much-prized drink is like to the taste. Were you ever in your youth forced to take a dose of Gregory powder? I was; and the cava exactly recalled it to my mind. Others have compared the taste to that of soap-suds with a dash of pepper; but I have never tasted this latter mixture.

To the south-east of Tongatabu lies the island

with the euphonious name of Eua, rising to a peak over a thousand feet high. But it has no sort of harbour, though it was once utilized as a sheep station.

Haapai is another low, flat island like Tongatabu. A white coral beach skirts the shore, whereon is a straggling village of native houses, a few large and well-constructed European stores, and some comfortable-looking bungalows.

Here are more Government buildings, containing offices kept up just as though managed by Europeans, with ledgers, inkstands, iron safes, and cash-boxes ; and yet when some important functionary calls in on business, bare-headed and bare-footed, he generally prefers to squat cross-legged on the floor than to utilize the modern innovations for comfort, such as stools or chairs. Near by, the King is having a new house built for himself, and under his auspices a large church is being erected, or at least constructed, for in this part of the world the roof is built first, and the walls finished later on ; so that the church at this time had the appearance of a big umbrella. But, talking of building the roofs of churches before the walls, I must digress to relate an incident in church-building which occurred to Mr. Baker in Nukualofa. The greater part of the church being completed, and having given full directions to the native carpenters as to how to put together the steeple, Mr. Baker left the island for some weeks. On his return the foreman joyously told him that everything was done—even the steeple completed. ' But where is it ?' asked Mr. Baker, gazing at the church from afar. Imagine his delight when they pointed out the steeple quite complete erected on the ground ! ' But that is to go up on top,' says Mr. Baker ; ' how are you going to get it up ?' ' Yes, that's what we want you to tell us,' was the simple reply. However, the missionary Premier was not to be beat. A bank of earth was raised against the wall, and the steeple drawn up to its place on rollers.

An ordinary native house is commenced with four posts planted upright in the ground. On these two frames are laid in a slanting way, like the roof of an ordinary house. These being fixed in position, semicircular ends are added on, and the whole carefully thatched, the walls being then filled in with rushes.

Several old whale-boats, used by the whalers who used to frequent these islands, are lying on the beach, and by the stores are some platforms covered with copra, put out to dry. This copra is the white internal lining of the old cocoanut—well known to schoolboys at home. The shell is broken and laid in the sun ; the lining cockles and becomes detached. This is then spread out by itself in small pieces and left to thoroughly dry in the sun, after which it is carted off in shiploads to be converted into cocoanut-oil.

We next come to Vavau, the second most im-

portant island of the Friendly Group. Here we
have a great change in the formation, the extensive
island standing boldly before us, with considerable
hills rising inland. Numerous thickly-wooded islets
are passed before we enter the fine picturesque
harbour. Even these little islands rise abruptly
out of the water, with perpendicular cliffs around
their base, cut into by the sea, so as to overhang in
such a manner as to prohibit almost any chance
of landing on them. In these cliffs many caves are
to be seen, and there is one here which can only
be entered by diving into the sea and swimming
under water until one is well within the large dark
cave. Mariner relates a most romantic anecdote
connected with this cave, which is so good I must
repeat it. Once upon a time a certain chief medi-
tated insurrection against the oppressive Governor
of Vavau ; but the plot being discovered, he was
ordered to be put to death, and not only he, but all
his family as well. Now, this chief had a beautiful
daughter, and she was betrothed to a gallant young
prince, who happened shortly before to have discovered this cave while diving after turtle. He,
grasping the situation, carried off the girl to save
her life, and hid her in this submarine abode. There
he frequently visited her, and brought supplies of
food. Months elapsed, and when the attempted insurrection had been almost forgotten, the unsuspected
hero announced his intention of making a journey
to Fiji, accompanied by many of his retainers.

Then people suggested that he ought to take a Tongan wife with him, but he replied that he would get one from the sea during the voyage. The party duly started, and as they passed along the coast, he presently announced his intention of jumping into the sea to get his wife. They thought him insane, and when he plunged overboard, and did not reappear for some time, they imagined he must be drowned or caught by a shark. But suddenly, to their intense dismay, he rose to the surface, accompanied by a lovely damsel ; and even when they recognised her, they could but suppose she must be the ghost of one of that family who were known to have been annihilated months before by the irate Governor of Vavau.

Vavau harbour is certainly a splendid one. I will not undertake to say that, like so many others we read of, it is capable of holding all the navies of the world ; but it is very commodious, with plenty of deep water, and is well protected from all sides. Besides the harbour proper, the numerous islands outside form a good shelter or outer sound.

We never know what diplomatists may be up to, but I do hope that something has been, or may be, done to place this great harbour under our protection, or, at all events, to prevent any foreign nation annexing the place. It is all very well to say that we don't want any more of these islands, or to spend any more money in maintaining them. Only we are apt to forget that had we not allowed any foreigners to grab islands and lands in these parts, it would hardly be necessary for us to spend money on the defences of places near, as we have to do at present. If a foreign nation was established in Vavau, on an outbreak of war they would menace our position in Fiji, and cause us to devote great energies to its defence. With Fiji in their possession, a descent on Australia might be attempted, which otherwise (except for French New Caledonia and

A WOODEN GONG.

German New Guinea) would be quite beyond the range of practical warfare. It was once supposed that we needn't go to New Guinea because no other European nation would go there. Now there is a powerful German settlement there, with good coaling-stations and sources of supply.

When I was in Vavau there was a German man-o'-war, the *Sophie*, there. But it was the season for peace and holiday, and they were busily preparing for Christmas festivities on board.

Niafu, the capital of the island, is a pretty little place. A straggling village extends amongst the numerous trees and orange-groves about the shores of the harbour. Opposite the coral-built wharf is a good building containing the Custom House and Post Office. There is a Roman Catholic church on some rising ground, and under a small shed in front of it is one of the peculiar wooden gongs which represent bells in these parts. It is a large block of wood hollowed out, and when struck with a club can be heard at a great distance.

I much regret to have to say that the filthiest house in the village is kept by an Englishman and his wife, and is called the hotel. I pity anyone who has to resort to it as such.

The King has yet another 'palace' here, and he was living in it at the time of my visit. He is a dear old man, and I was very glad to be able to get an interview with him. His Majesty was sitting in a back room at a table, on which was nothing except a Tongan Bible. Around the scantily-furnished room were two or three cane-bottomed chairs, a sideboard, and some German oleographs.

The King hardly looks as old as I expected, since he *says* he remembers the wreck of the *Port au Prince*, which occurred in 1806. He was dressed in a check shirt, a claret-coloured (royal purple) cloth round his body, with a grass mat outside it, legs and feet bare, and with wisps of green reeds tied round his ankles. But I must announce that, like other royalties, he has an extensive wardrobe of apparel for wearing on special occasions. He has been known to don a complete suit of naval uniform. His Majesty appeared to be pleased and interested with my visit, and asked many sensible questions of

THE KING OF TONGA.

me through Thomson (as he is not very proud of his English). He was particularly anxious to know about the strikes which were then going on in Queensland. He said truly, 'But what can these people gain? Surely it is no good the poor holding

out against the rich; the latter are in power and
have the money—it would only be the poor man
who would lose, for he would starve, while the rich
can always buy food.'

Outside the palace is the village green, whereon
numbers of children play merrily. They are wonderful adepts at throwing up and catching three or four
oranges in rotation, à la juggler. Some could even
manage six at a time.

Farther inland is the cemetery of the chiefs, raised
above the level of the ground, and embanked with
large and ancient stones; the more ordinary people
are buried on some bare promontories in the bay.
The graves are covered with dark pebbles got from
the volcanic islands, and many are sheltered with
wooden roofs.

In the outskirts of the village we passed a house
where someone had just died. All the grieving
relatives were sitting around weeping and wailing.
One man, who I hear is hired in on such occasions,
cries out aloud in a most mournful way, jabbering
off strings of words—I dare say chanting the praises
of the departed one—and now and again bursting
into a (dry) flood of tears, and roaring in his
anguish.

Delightful walks and rides can be taken about the
island—along the bush tracks among the dense and
luxuriant trees. Around the village oranges and
pineapples grow in profusion, looking quite wild, and
the ground is everywhere so covered with grass

and green stuff that one hardly gets a sight of the red, loamy soil. As we get up among the hills, occasional glimpses of the pretty harbour may be got through the trees. There is not much sign of animal life, large dark-coloured lizards being the only common living thing.

But it is Christmas Eve. My boat is about to depart for Samoa, and, taking leave of Thomson, who is to adjourn to the *Sophie* to join in their festivities, I step from Tongan soil to sail forth and battle with the threatening-looking elements.

CHAPTER XI.

THE NAVIGATORS.

SAMOA is the native name of that group which Captain Cook re-christened Navigator's Islands. There are three large islands—Upolu, Savaii, and Tutuila—and several smaller ones, all more or less hilly, if not mountainous, and thickly clothed in verdure.

Apia (pronounced Arp*ee*a) is the capital, and is quite a fair-sized town, situated on the northern coast of Upolu.

Everyone knows that the Bay of Apia is comparatively unsheltered from the north, for all will remember the account of the awful hurricane in 1888, when so many lives were lost, and how the only British vessel there, H.M.S. *Calliope*, saved herself by steaming out to sea. Three or four wrecks of men-o'-war were still there when I visited the place, testifying to the destructiveness of the storm, though they were in course of demolition, and must have quite disappeared by now. On entering the harbour one of the German vessels was seen to the right, lying on her side, almost high and dry, upon the reef. On the left the American *Trenton* was sunk, close in shore, with some remains of another ship showing above water close to her, while other pieces of wreckage were to be seen in all directions along the beach. The reefs, which extend to some distance on each side of the harbour, have a most nasty appearance. Even in quite calm weather a

APIA.

big swell rolls in from the Pacific. At one moment all appears smooth water on the top of the great billow ; then the whole sea sinks, and a kind of table of water seems to rise, smooth and shiny, from which the water pours off on all sides, and then a treacherous big flat rock appears, just showing itself before it is again completely covered by the swell.

This bay, nevertheless, often has quite a number

of vessels moored about it.   One or two men-o'-war
are generally there, several good-sized sailing ships,
small German trading cutters, and numbers of
native boats.   These latter are of two kinds : there
are the small outrigged ' dug-outs,' similar to those
of other parts of the world, except that they go in for
' schooner bows' and spade-shaped paddles ; and
then there are the larger boats, somewhat similar to
a whale-boat in design, but *sewn* together.   It is a
peculiar but very good idea to make a boat by
sewing it together, and I was anxious to know how

CONSTRUCTION OF SAMOAN BOAT.

it was accomplished, for it is different to the method
employed in Madras.   I soon found out by examining an old smashed-up boat.   The pieces of wood,
seldom long boards, but planks two or three feet
long, and about an inch or more thick, are made to
fit very neatly together, edge to edge.   Holes are
bored, say an inch from the bottom of the upper
board, and an inch from the top of the lower board,
in an inclined direction, so as to come out in the
centre of the edge.   Pieces of sinnet, or string made
of cocoanut fibre, are passed through these holes
and tied inside.   The result is that the boards are

neatly and strongly joined together, with a smooth surface outside, the joins being filled up with the gum of the bread-fruit tree. These boats are always built near the place where the wood grows, the builders camping out there for the time, and thus much transport is saved.

A few miles behind the town the country rises in steep ascents to some very fair-sized hills. These are all thickly wooded, and they say there is not a bit of land on the island that is naturally clear. But one or two artificial clearings are visible, and some fine waterfalls may be made out among the trees.

SAMOAN CLUB.

Away to the west is seen the island of Savaii, rising to a considerable elevation.

The natives here are very like Tongans, but they go about with much less clothing on than those in Tonga, and the men at once strike one as being fine, tall, muscular specimens, though I hear it is seldom that you can get a Samoan to put his strength to any use. The usual costume is only a linen lava-lava about the loins, and they have a peculiar way of tattooing their legs. They make themselves nearly black from the waist to the knees, so that they look, when without their lava-lavas, as if they had thin knee-breeches on. Nothing is worn on the head, the hair being kept rather short. The men generally have small black moustaches and a little beard.

As for the ladies, it may be only a matter of taste, but, whatever anyone may say, *I* certainly never saw a single woman in Samoa that, in my opinion, had the slightest pretensions to good looks.

I noticed among the natives a good many cases of elephantiasis, and, curiously enough, a great many hunchbacks.

The language, which is akin to both Tongan and Maori, is certainly very pretty and musical.

Wherever you go you are constantly greeted with the salutation, ' Tah-lo-fah,' signifying ' My love to you.' Many of these barbarous races know no means of expressing thanks, but the Samoan euphoniously says ' Fah-fah-tai ' whenever the occasion demands.

There is a peculiar custom in Samoa for each village to have as a social representative a young girl—I suppose the beauty of the village, though, as I have already implied, I am no authority on this latter point. But this young lady, called the ' Taupo,' has to receive and entertain any illustrious strangers, and to act hostess at all functions.

Native houses are either circular or oval. They consist of a number of posts placed round the edge, and sometimes one or two in the centre, supporting a large thatched roof. Walls are conspicuous by their absence ; but narrow mats of plaited palm-leaves are hung around so as to let up or down, somewhat after the manner of venetian blinds. The floor is covered with small loose dark pebbles, and on them thick reed mats are laid. Bamboo pillows or ' head stools' lie about, something similar to those used in South Africa, and, indeed, in almost all savage countries. Various clothes, etc., hang from the rafters above. But these are the country houses. In the town the domiciles are of more ordinary build.

Apia is a straggling town, mostly of wooden houses, extending along near the sea-beach. In one part the narrow road has houses on both sides, with several shops and so-called hotels and restaurants ; but they are dirty and uninviting. Farther on the houses on the seaside of the road cease.

Towards the west end of the town is the principal hotel, a big stone church, and a large one-storied wooden building between the road and the sea, which is the German Consulate.

Near the centre of the town is the building which we may designate Government offices, or Houses of Parliament, or Council Chamber. It consists of a not extra large and rather dirty native house, but with a big flagstaff in front, on which floats the Samoan flag. This is a red flag, with white St. George's cross and a five-pointed star in the inner top corner. Here the chiefs meet and all important transactions take place.

Right away to the east end the road gets into

more aristocratic-looking regions, and runs beneath shady trees past detached houses. Going on right beyond the promontory forming the bay, we get to the English, and then to the American Consulate.

The British Consulate is a wooden, iron-roofed, verandaed structure, very much after the typical Australian style. It has a small garden in front, with a big flagstaff, on which the Union Jack proudly floats, and cocoanut-trees grow all around.

Mr. Cusack Smith, the Consul, very kindly put me up during my stay. The three Consuls (English, German, and American) were at that time ' everybody.' Dr. Stuebel, the German Consul-General, was ' boss ' of the triumvirate, and he had a Vice-consul under him. The American Consul, Mr. Sewall, has vital interests to look after and arduous duties to perform. They say there are not half a dozen Americans in the islands, but then, it is a very usual thing for an Englishman in trouble to claim protection as a citizen of the United States. Many American vessels also call here.

As anything in the way of a state carriage is out of the question in Apia, the Consuls have to content themselves with a boat to keep up their state ; for, after all, functions are rare, except calling on men-o'-war. The English consular equipage is a very fine turn-out, consisting of a good large boat, with four stalwart natives dressed in blue bird's-eye lava-lavas, white jerseys, and red cloth turbans, who row very well together.

At the time of my arrival the ·consular board practically ruled the country. King Malietoa nominally reigned, and his Ministers nominally assisted him ; but he always received the advice of the Consuls. Mataafa was, and indeed *is*, always giving trouble. He is pretender to the throne, and has a powerful following. Tamesese is yet another pretender, and is looked upon as the German nominee to the throne.

King Malietoa is a dark, quiet-looking man, with black moustache, about fifty years of age. He dresses in ordinary white linen suit, pot hat, and yachting shoes, and carries a smart-looking gold-topped cane. He did not impress me favourably, and when I had the honour of an interview with him, he did not seem to have much to say, or to take much interest in anything we told him.

During my visit to Samoa, a very great and important change took place in the political organi-zation of the country. It was the appointment by the three Powers of a Chief Justice, who, besides being chief adviser to the King, would also act as a sort of referee between the three Consuls, and thus become the most important man in Samoa.

The King of Sweden was asked to nominate this great personage, and Baron Cedercrantz was duly appointed, and left Europe to take up his post. Great preparations were in progress to receive the Chief Justice in befitting style. But awkward questions will always crop up. First, all the principal chiefs of the group were summoned to come to Apia. But then it was remembered that arrangements here were such that it might be impossible to feed all these and their retinues. So the chiefs were requested not to bring a larger staff than necessary. Then there was the question of disturbances, for many of these chiefs and their people had strong political opinions, which might very easily end in a free fight. So the order was sent out that no arms were to be brought. But soon the town began to fill, and numbers of men were to be seen carrying rifles! And then things seemed getting serious, when the news got about that Tamesese had come into the town, and had applied to sleep in what was practically the old royal palace. The German Consul had given him leave. But to let him stay there would be almost tantamount to recognising his claim to be King, so he had to go, doubtless very offended.

One day the news flashed through Apia that the ship with the Chief Justice on board was in sight! All was hurry and scurry to prepare for his reception. The Consuls got into their boats; Suamana, the Chief of Apia, went off in a splendid big boat, as representative of King Malietoa. Then followed boats conveying committees of reception, the mails, and many other people and things—all going out to meet the ship.

The *Alameda*, from San Francisco, could only stop outside the harbour, so in a short time the

23

fleet of small boats was seen returning. Then did the Consuls begin to discuss where the landing should take place, and it was decided that the pier near the hotel would be the most suitable place. But when everyone was assembled there it was seen that the boats were making for a landing at the other end of the town! So off went all the officials and the crowd and everybody hurrying down the street to head the boats.

Here we met the King's guards, a really fine body of men, who looked very business-like. They were not numerous, there being some twenty to thirty all told, but they had an imposing effect marching along to the beat of a side-drum. They were fine-looking fellows, their dress consisting of a turban and a tappa lava-lava. The turbans were mostly also of tappa, but those who wished to be extra *chic* wore bath-towels. Round their necks hung large necklaces of the red fruit of the pandanus, and the lower part of their faces was blacked. They were all armed with guns of sorts, but it will be immaterial to specify the details of the mechanism. There was one great big fat man, I suppose a sort of sergeant-major, who looked splendid. Instead of the turban he wore a huge head-dress, not unlike a large bearskin, but made of hair, said to be human, with red feathers in front. Then he had a sort of sporran of red feathers in front of his lava-lava, and wisps of green reeds round his ankles. The officer in command, however,

was a sad come-down, though doubtless he did not
think so, for he was dressed in a shabby blue
European uniform, with proper sword and a white
helmet. But, unfortunately, the latter was very
small—I think it must have come from the Lowther

THE KING'S GUARDS.

Arcade—and he had not been to his hairdresser
lately, so that the result was most ridiculous.
Another officer wore a blue uniform coat and a sword,
but the remainder of his person was unadorned.

In this manner the new Chief Justice, Baron

Cedercrantz, was received, and conducted to his hotel.

Next morning was to be the great public reception of the Chief Justice by the King.

The Consuls and the King's guards and officials, all in full uniform, were drawn up at the pier, to which the Chief Justice was brought by boat from his hotel. We all then went up to the Government House I have already described, before which floated the royal standard (consisting of the Samoan flag, but with a crown under the star). The house is oval in plan, perhaps thirty feet by twenty, the floor covered all over with mats, tappa curtains all round (now drawn up). The structure of the roof was very much like the church I have described in Tonga, with curved beams at the ends, supported by a large wooden pillar in the centre, and the usual pillars all round.

At one end sat the King on a chair ; on each side of him three or four chairs were placed for the Chief Justice, his aide-de-camp, the Consuls, and myself. Then the twelve principal chiefs came in, dressed in tappa lava-lavas, necklaces of pandanus fruit, and carrying what is considered as a staff of office—a fly flap. Each went up in turn to shake hands with the King, *squatting on the floor* as they did so, a Samoan sign of humility, after which they seated themselves on the floor, in order of precedence, round the edge of the ' room.' Behind the King stood his interpreter. Outside were many other chiefs sitting on the ground, the guards, police, and a large crowd of natives behind them.

Then, amid a solemn silence, the King began his speech, in a loud, clear voice, in Samoan. It was really well delivered, though the dreadful attempts of the interpreter when he endeavoured to translate each sentence into English would have been very amusing, had one dared to smile ; but the awful solemnity of the whole affair was such that it only became painful to endeavour to keep one's countenance, till the German Consul interposed and took upon himself the interpretation.

The speech was merely a flowery-worded welcome to the Chief Justice, with flattering references to the three Powers, etc. After the Baron had made suitable reply, the old Chief sitting at the opposite end of the room addressed the house, saying that the arrival of the Chief Justice was like the rising of the sun, and that Samoa, hitherto in darkness, was now flooded with light. More speeches then followed from the other chiefs, all to somewhat the same effect, clearly and loudly expressed, and on what seemed a very good system, viz., making a good pause between each sentence.

Then began the cava ceremony. This was a great event. None of the Consuls even had ever before partaken of ' King's cava.' But there was a certain amount of sham about it. First, the root was produced—genuine enough, I dare say. Six men then sat in a row outside the house, the nine-legged cava-bowl before them. Each man was then given some water to wash his mouth out, and a packet of cava wrapped in a bit of leaf was given to each. I shuddered at the awful thought of what was about to happen!

In true native fashion these nasty old men were undoubtedly going to chew the root, and I, with the eyes of the King and the assembled multitude upon me, would *have* to swallow the nauseous stuff! I watched very carefully, and was much relieved when I saw the packets collected again and put in the bowl. It was ready prepared, and this little ceremony was only to represent formally the mode in which it ought to be done, the cava being 'taken as chewed.' Then the bowl was solemnly brought into the house and put on the floor at the end opposite the King.

A big fat man sat down behind to preside at the preparation of the cava. The water was brought and the tow, and all was ready. Meanwhile the old semi-naked gentleman set to work to scratch himself all over, preparatory to the task before him, after which he plunged his hands in the bowl and started the mixing up. He performed the operation in great style, putting in the tow, drawing it towards him through the liquid, then carefully lifting it out, squeezing it, and wringing it out with a great deal of 'action,' and then throwing the tow to a man behind, who, after shaking out the refuse of the cava, flicked it several times in the air, and thus completely dried

THE CEREMONY OF KING'S CAVA.

To face page 358.

it. And at last the cava was ready, and all the people around clapped their hands.

Then the fat man retired, and another took his place in order to serve out the beverage. Yet another man comes to do duty as waiter and hand around the cup. He stands up before the bowl, and receives the filled cup from the server, which he then with both hands holds high in the air. The man presiding over the cava then shouts out in a loud voice the name of the person to whom the drink is to be taken. The 'waiter' turns slowly about, and goes to the person named and delivers the cup. The King was the first named, and to him it is handed in a cringing position. Next, after it had been taken back to refill, it was handed to the first chief on the right, then to the first on the left, and after that to the Chief Justice, who drank his potion like a man. Then it was brought to each of us in turn. I forced the stuff down somehow—for, of course, one had to drain a whole bowl at once—no sipping allowed at such a ceremony. Afterwards it was handed to all the other chiefs in the house in turn. And then the cava-bowl was removed.

The next event was a spokesman from the people outside, who shouted out a long speech, at the conclusion of which a lot of baskets of food (chiefly roast pigs, fish, cooked chickens, and yams) were brought as a present to the Chief Justice. Poor man! I expect the cava must have proved a struggle to him, but now, when he saw the food and was told it was all for him, he must have felt some misgivings, doubtless thinking he would be compelled to eat the whole of it then and there. But he was evidently much relieved when Dr. Stübel explained that all he would have to do was to thank the people, and ask them to distribute the food among themselves ; and by the aid of an interpreter it was soon said. This brought the proceedings to a close, and everyone took leave of the King and went his way.

It was after the reception of the Chief Justice that I first met that extraordinary man, of infinitely more interest to me than even the Chief Justice himself, Mr. R. L. Stevenson. And, to anyone who knows anything of him, it can easily be supposed that his dress and general get-up were not of the ordinary. At first—I hope he will excuse me if ever he sees these lines—I mistook him for a postman, and a very peculiar - looking one, too ; but directly he opened his mouth and began talking (and it was some time before it closed again), one could not fail to realize that he was no ordinary mortal : the Doctor Jekyll then appeared.

He lives in a small house right away up on the hill at the back. He intended building a large house, and started to make a road up by which to transport his materials ; but road-making is expensive, and by the time the road was finished, so was all the money he had. At least, that was *his* story. He asked me if I came up to lunch to bring my own provisions, and, indeed, hinted that I might bring two portions! Such is living in the exalted sylvan retreats of glorious Samoa!

The German flagship *Leipsig* came in just too late to receive the Chief Justice; and later all the officers (or a good proportion of them) came ashore and went for a ride, looking like a cavalry regiment. The Admiral came up for a game of tennis at the English Consulate.

The native police of Apia are a smart - looking body. They have a dark-blue uniform coat with silver buttons, and white trousers. They are armed with Remington rifles, and wear bandolier web belts. But they have lately been instructed in a new species of salute. The first time the English Consul was made the object of it he fled, believing a mutiny had broken out; and it is said that several of the police were at first had up for attempted assault. But custom breeds contempt, and now the salute goes unheeded.

Another interesting event, which I had the luck to witness, was the marriage between Mr. Girr, an Englishman, and one of the leading business men in the place, and Miss Fanua, the Taupo of Apia, and daughter of Suamana, the chief of Apia. The ceremony took place in the British Consulate. The bride's trousseau was magnificent. Ladies may like to have it described: On her raven locks was a large wreath of white flowers; her bridal dress was composed of that fine grass matting so much prized in Samoa, with little red feathers all round the edge. The fit was not quite of the same style that Madame Elise would make; but, then, the dress was seamless, and, I imagine from the bulkiness of her figure, there must have been a good deal underneath, probably several more mat dresses. The bridal train was absent, as, indeed, was much of the lower part of the dress; in fact, it rather looked as though something had been forgotten, for stockings and shoes were not considered necessary. The jewellery consisted of a marvellous necklace of big white things—something like long boars' tusks. I'm told they were made from whale's teeth.

The bridesmaids' dresses were very similar, the only peculiarity being that each had a long pointed red feather, got from the tail of the 'bos'n bird,' stuck in her hair.

The service, which was *not* fully choral, was simple. The Consul read it out of a Foreign Office list, and the only thing suggestive of 'the voice that breathed o'er Eden' was the yelling of the undressed children in the garden outside.

After the ceremony, the whole wedding-party went off in the chief's big boat, among showers of rice, but without any slippers, since no such articles were forthcoming.

Later on we attended the wedding-breakfast, or breakfasts, for there were two. The first was of European fashion at Mr. Girr's house. I had the

great honour conferred upon me of taking in one
of the charming bridesmaids. We all sat round
and feasted ourselves. I was not able to carry on a
very great flirtation with my partner, but by various
signs and grimaces endeavoured to make a few
remarks, which seemed to be duly understood and
appreciated.

After the customary speeches, we rose and proceeded off for the native breakfast to a house profusely decorated with tappa, mats, and green stuff.
All the guests, mostly native ladies, sat round on
seats. The first trying ordeal was that I had to go
round and shake hands with every lady there, and
then I had to seat myself down with my partner, and
again endeavour to keep up the conversation. Mr.
Stevenson, who was there as a guest, seemed quite
at home, and talked away as if he had been wound
up. But soon we ' processed ' off again for *more* food.
This was the native wedding-feast. Just outside the
house, on the green, a long strip of tappa was rigged
up on poles as an awning. The food was laid out
on the ground beneath, and very tempting it looked
to me, just after having dined to repletion. There
were yams, sugar-cane, and plantains, cooked fish of
various kinds, lobsters, chicken, and, finally, whole
cooked pigs. And to see that wedding-party eat!
We all sat round on mats, and the viands were distributed. Plates and knives and forks were, of course,
dispensed with ; and to see the ladies in their wed-
ding garments tearing the pork with their teeth and

biting into huge yams was a really refreshing sight. For drink we had some nice fresh cocoanuts.

It was only after the feast was over, and I had come away, that I was told that *my* bridesmaid had been specially told off to me because she spoke English so well. And we had not exchanged a word!

One of the characters of the place, who, I regret to hear, is since dead, was Mr. Hamilton, retired pilot, harbour-master, and American Consul. We went one day to call. Mrs. Hamilton was a charming bright native, beautifully dressed in a pink night-gown, and engaged in reading Stanley's 'Darkest Africa.' As in England the hostess might ring for tea, so Mrs. Hamilton called for cava. Here, however, it is prepared out of sight, though the clapping of hands announces the completion of its preparation, and soon the cocoanut-cup is brought in, and taken away each time to refill; meanwhile, we are regaled on pineapples and bananas.

One day there was a great Christy Minstrel performance given by some of the 'white' amateurs of the place. The audience was most select—at least, as regards the stalls. This part of the hall was mostly filled by native ladies, and their toilets are worthy of mention. To begin at the top, many of them had gorgeous hats—generally big straw things, with a profusion of red and blue flowers and a few green ostrich-feathers. Others, however, considered hats rather out of place in evening dress, and so merely had their own (at least, we'll hope so) raven locks tastefully arranged and decorated *à la mode*. The dresses were in some cases magnificent. Tasty arrangements of many-coloured bows and ribbons, and some beautiful edgings of lace, added greatly to garments not possessing much character in other respects. Per-

AN APPRECIATIVE AUDIENCE.

haps we ought not to go farther. I do not know exactly what the ladies' feelings are as regards their foot-coverings. It may be they were proud of the symmetry of their toes, or it may be that they thought their feet would not be noticed under the chairs ; but certain it is that the tight-fitting, patent-leather, high-heeled shoes worn by some were by no means universal. The back part of the hall was given up to the 'gods,' and here was a mass of naked humanity of the male sex crowded together squatting on the forms. Such performances are seldom really good, so I will not criticise the Apian amateurs; but they certainly succeeded in the main object of the entertainment, for I have seldom heard such shrieks of laughter from any audience. It mattered not in the least what the performers did. If one of them stood up it was enough; and when a long-haired, spectacled German came forward to recite a thrilling poem, the audience were more convulsed than ever, and every time the poor man held out his hand to add expression to his harrowing descriptions, roars of laughter filled the hall.

There is a small Protestant church well filled on Sundays with Europeans, half-castes, and a few natives. The latter (ladies) were dressed in their best, and on the whole, I thought, in much better taste than those I saw at the concert. It may be they considered a more sober style better fitted to the occasion, or it may be that they were other ladies less frivolously inclined.

I noticed that prayers were offered for Malietoa, but not for the Queen of little England.

The mission-house is a good-sized, cool-looking building of one story, with substantial walls. Here they have a lawn-tennis court, at one time the only one in Apia. But it is not good. The grass is very coarse; there are mounds and valleys, and in places the rock crops out. Then, by way of improving it, the gardener starts to cut the grass with an old dinner - knife! Nevertheless, some of the native ladies are very good at the game.

There is a race-course in (or rather *out of*) Apia but I would defy any stranger to find it. So thickly overgrown are the few level places in the neighbourhood that the riding has to take place on the beach, which, however, is only some three or four yards wide, and this is on a slope seawards! Otherwise, all the level ground is covered with cocoanut palms. However, I had several good gallops over the course.

Along this part of the beach some beautiful bits of coral may be seen, collected by the natives, and laid out in the sun to dry and bleach. The marvellous patterns and great variety are astounding.

Going along the sea-shore to the east of Apia, toward Vailele, one passes Mataafa's house, a very good one of its kind. This is more of the Tongan style, having regular 'walls.' Beyond this is the 'battle-field,' where the German sailors were landed some years ago, and were fired on by Samoans under Mataafa from the bush, which, by the way, is by no means dense, and some twenty of them shot. The Germans, having thus demonstrated, at all events, their ability to land, then thought it best to make a masterly retreat, and returned to their ships. It is difficult to get at any more reliable details, as the accounts given by each side vary considerably.

Inland of this is a large cocoanut plantation, owned by a German. The land is tolerably level, and the trees are planted in rows, allowing plenty of room between each tree. The nuts are cut down, gathered, and put into panniers on donkeys, and thus taken to the road. Four-wheeled bullock waggons, with two bullocks each, come along the road to collect the heaps. The roads are very bad, and though there are numerous boulders available, I suppose it is not found worth while to mend them.

There are a few date palms about, but they say they never bear fruit. I saw also a very fine banyan, with its many stems. Large mobs of cattle are kept, tended by cowherds, chiefly to eat away the undergrowth in the plantation, and also to manure the ground.

Much of this country is covered with the sensitive plant. It grows very readily, and is looked upon as a useless and undesirable weed. It is curious to watch one's track through it in crossing a piece of open ground. Before one is a green mass of vegetation (about a foot high) ; on looking back one sees what appears a well-worn track up to where one stands, but after a few minutes all is the same again.

The only animal life one sees here is in numerous black lizards, which run along at a great rate and clamber up the tree-stems.

I went out for a ride one day in the other direction from Apia. This time we went inland, going along a narrow footpath for the greater part of the way, very muddy or even under water in places. Most of this country is under cultivation, and many native houses were passed. Then we went through a regular cocoanut plantation and up to the house of the German manager, an ordinary wooden house, prettily situated in a garden of oleanders, crotons, acalifa, date palms, and umbrella trees. The latter are peculiar-looking trees with horizontal spreading branches covered with thick leaves, having a very artificial look, the tree from a distance looking like the mast of a ship with yards.

After a rest here we continued our ride, and went through miles of cocoanuts, finally getting to the cotton plantation which we wished to see. The land here is high and undulating, with a good view seawards. The cotton bushes are now all cut low, for they have to be cut down every year. The cotton is gathered by Kanaka labourers, and taken to a shed, where it is packed in sacks and sent to Apia, where it is cleaned, etc., and shipped off. Here, near the homestead, are groves of bread-fruit-trees, grown to supply the Kanakas with their native food.

It was in Apia I first made the acquaintance of the Rev. Shirley Baker. He was staying at the International Hotel, and I was, after all I had heard of him in Tonga, very anxious to see the man who had done such a lot for the country and for himself. I went with Cusack Smith, and Mr. Baker, who had been there several weeks, was profuse in his apologies for not having called on the Consul, but

24

he really had not had any time. I only wonder how one could get through two or three weeks in Apia without having any time to one's self!

Oddly enough, Mr. Baker—who is a stoutish man of about fifty-five or so—did not seem very keen to tell us all about Tonga, but preferred changing the subject.

The mail-boat for San Francisco touches off Tutuila to call for letters, so passengers wishing to go thitherward from Apia must go first to Tutuila. But to get to this island the usual plan is to go with the mails on a small cutter, which leaves Apia so as to get to Tutuila in plenty of time to meet the steamer. Occasionally, too, a man-o'-war is going, and on this occasion the U.S.S. *Iroquois* had been expected in Apia, and she was then to go to meet the mail-steamer. The U.S. Consul had promised me that if she came he would apply for a passage for me. As she did not turn up, however, I found it necessary to go with the smaller craft.

On getting on board the mail cutter *Vailéle*, I found her to be a very dirty-looking boat of about twenty tons, somewhat similar to, but even smaller than, that lovely boat in which I crossed to New Guinea. However, I was not to be alone this time, for I found my interesting friend Mr. Shirley Baker on board, as well as a crowd of natives. The captain, a German, seemed a jovial sort of a chap (but used the filthiest language), and at once opened three bottles of beer, which we consumed. In due time we sailed, and gently glided out of the harbour. There were now on board this small vessel, besides ourselves, the captain, five Kanaka 'sailors,' and twelve natives, and the very small captain's cabin was full of 'gear' and the hold full of merchandise. How we were all to pack away for the night remained a mystery to me. But this was *the* mail-boat, and I had paid £2 for the passage. Imagine, then, my horror when I heard a rumour that these natives, packed like so many sheep on board, and with whom we were to live in close proximity for perhaps two or three days, were *lepers*, poor loathsome outcasts being sent away from their homes to go to Molokai! I could scarcely believe it till I demanded an explanation from the captain. He could not deny it, but casually remarked, 'They won't hurt you. You don't catch leprosy like that.' Mr. Baker quietly remarked that he did not at all like the idea, but finding I could get no further 'change' out of anyone, I settled myself down to ponder over the not very reassuring fact that, as these people didn't seem to mind at all, it could not be so bad as I imagined. And now the more cheerful thoughts of dinner came up, and the meal was served on the hatch. But what a dinner! Some filthy stuff out of a tin bucket was called soup, and other courses followed of a very repulsive nature. However, we had plenty of beer, which the captain supplied. Then darkness came on, and we had to think of bed. But where were we to sleep? The captain, however, had got a splendid idea. The dinghy, which had been towing astern, was hauled on board, and this was to serve as the private cabin for Mr. Baker and myself. An old sail was laid on the bottom to make it soft, while another was rigged over the boat as an awning. Then a small and indescribably filthy pillow was thrown in, to do for the two of us.

As soon as all was announced as ready, two or three (leprous?) natives at once jumped in. But they were soon pulled out again, and Mr. Baker and I entered our cabin. The little pillow was rather a source of trouble between us, and there was a certain oleaginous perfume to which I objected. My companion was soon asleep, but I *could* not get settled down. The sails on the bottom, with their rope edgings, did not make the most comfortable of mattresses, and the ribs of the boat projected in a very awkward manner.

At last I got up and found a board about a foot wide, which I put on the bottom and laid upon, and found it an infinitely more agreeable mattress. Then, just as I felt fairly comfortable, I suddenly found myself nearly crushed beneath the weight of ponderous masses of human flesh. Mr. Baker had turned over! I plunged my skinny elbow deep in his side, and he rolled back again. Soon after, however, I was again overwhelmed, and again I plied my elbow. But this only gave the recipient bad dreams, and he shuddered, till at last I woke him and he got farther afield. Now things were going

a little better, till I discovered that the weight I felt
on one of my feet was the head of a leper, who had
slipped into the boat unheeded. Now, I had not,
under the circumstances, taken my boots off, and I
am afraid that native soon had cause to remember
the fact—at all events, he found a fresh, and doubtless softer pillow, elsewhere.

Now, surely, all is well for a bit, thought I ; but
just at that moment my companion began the most
awful snoring right into my ear ! Oh, it was terrible!
I could have fixed a dagger on the end of my elbow.
And next I began to find it very hot. I could stand
it no longer, so I got up and lay on some spars and
boards which were lying across the bows of the boat.
There was a big heavy pole laid along over the
boat to keep the awning up ; and suddenly, as I was
arranging myself, this slipped and fell in. I think,
from what I heard, that it must have caught Baker
in the face, but I lay low. At last, after many more
very weary hours, day dawned. Baker was up like
a lark, and now at last for peace and quiet, and the
pillow all to myself! But no! I was *too tired* to
sleep. Soon the captain came and offered me some
beer. Fancy beer under such circumstances !
Then other noises began, and I found sleep impossible, so got up and had a wash in a bucket of
water (the same which had been used as a soup-
tureen), and a wipe on a dirty towel, and then we got
to breakfast. This consisted of very nasty coarse
ham, stale bread well fingered with black hands, and

some undrinkable coffee, with dirty, wet sugar. Then the hot sun shone forth, and we rigged up a sort of awning, which seemed, however, to let all the heat through. I lay and gasped on the booby-hutch, my head on the dirty pillow, and my legs tucked under me (there not being room to stretch them out). So I lay and dreamt, rather than slept, all day, till the captain reminded me that I was on the dinner-table! More meals, equally dirty and uneatable. The swell was now increasing, and the awful darkness of another night of misery approaching. Tutuila was now fast ' growing near,' with a bold outline, with some rocky islets jutting out from the north end like the Needles.

Meanwhile the captain had some more beer, and his language and remarks became about as bad as any I have ever heard, which is saying a good deal. I looked to see what my reverend companion thought of it, but he only smiled placidly. The captain now informed us it would be quite impossible to land that night; even if we 'fetched up,' we would anchor there for the night. Then a ' sail ' was sighted. Gradually we approached. All eyes strained on the mysterious vessel. And soon there was no doubt. It was the *Iroquois*. How my hopes rose! How well and even happy I felt! We made for her to sail close past. We hailed one another. She hove to, and we shouted the news to the ship. They asked us if we had any letters for them. ' No !' shouted our captain, and we were

about to proceed and leave the *Iroquois* to sail
away in the darkness to Apia. One has heard of
the shipwrecked mariner watching the ship sail past,
unable to attract its attention—I felt like that. I
was frantic ; and my awful position, the prospect of
another night on board, flashed through my mind in
an instant. I had an idea. ' Yes, we have a letter
for the captain !' I shouted at the top of my voice.
My companions stared at me as if mad. ' Have
you a letter ?' asked our captain. ' Yes, I'm just
going to write it,' I replied. Soon the man-o'-war's
boat was alongside. I was very determined, and
utterly regardless of consequences. I bundled my
baggage into the boat and jumped in. With a
flourish of farewell to my recent *compagnons de
voyage*, I left that ship as one would fly from a
nightmare. ' Saved !' I said inwardly, feeling like
the shipwrecked mariner. There was a big swell
on, and when we did get near the ship, it appeared
impossible to board her. One moment we seemed
to be above her decks, and the next were down
almost under her bottom ; and she looked so huge
and black, with numbers of lights shining from all
parts. The captain hailed me and asked what the
letter was. I then explained that the Consul had
promised to get me a lift in the man-o'-war if he
could. ' That's all right,' he said ; ' but we may not
be back in time to catch the mail.' However, mail
or no mail, I was *not* going to have another night on
board that cutter ; and soon a line was thrown to us,

the whole boat bodily hauled up on the davits, and I stepped out on her quarter-deck, feeling as proud as Nelson boarding a Frenchman. Captain Bishop was very kind and hospitable, and soon, after a good wash, I was being regaled on the first food I had enjoyed for over twenty-four hours.

Seldom have I felt so relieved as I did sitting on that deck in the dark, talking to the American officers, and feeling that every minute I was getting further and further from that awful phantom ship.

Next morning I awoke in Apia once again. I am a little mixed as to what date it was, for I found that the American ship had American time, whereas so far we had been keeping Australian time, twenty-four hours' difference. The *Iroquois* is a fine vessel, quite of the good old sort. From the quarter-deck one had a bird's-eye view of the main-deck, with broadsides of muzzle-loading guns. She has played her part, and well, too, in the American War. The officers, all of whom struck me as being very old as compared with officers of similar rank in the British service, were, nevertheless, thorough good fellows, and I had a most pleasant trip. After waiting a few hours in Apia we steamed back to Tutuila. We came to anchor in Hübner Bay, and there was our old friend (?) the mail cutter. I would not have gone back on board for anything; but Mr. Baker came on the *Iroquois* and told me that the last two nights were *worse* that the first—food had run out, and the captain was by that time fairly intoxicated.

This island of Tutuila is a beautiful place, rising in bold, thickly-wooded hills, but is sparsely inhabited, and but little cultivated. The town of Leone, on the shore of Hübner Bay, is the most important place, but that is not saying much. There is, however, a stone Roman Catholic church, some missionary houses, and a store kept by a white man. Towards the other side of the island is a splendid harbour, Pago Pago (pronounced Pango-Pango). Not so large as that at Vavau, but still, deep and land-locked. This ought, one would have thought, to be an important place, being in a line for the mail steamers passing from San Francisco to Australia, and as being about the only good harbour in the Samoan group; and I believe the Americans have wisely determined on making a coaling-station here.

During the day the smoke of the mail steamer was descried above the horizon, but it was several hours before she appeared.

Lots of hearty natives came off from the island to sell curios, etc., to the ship, in their large boats, singing lustily. In due time the *Zealandia* arrived, and I got on board, and soon after we sailed for Honolulu, many of the natives who had come on board waiting till the ship had started and then diving overboard and swimming back to their boats.

CHAPTER XII.

SANDWICH ISLANDS.

ONCE again, as with Tonga and Samoa, I have to make an explanation to those who do not know the ins and outs of the Pacific. The Sandwich Islands consist of a group situated in the Northern Pacific, about 21° latitude. The largest of the islands is Hawaii (formerly spelt Owyhee), and this gives a designation to the nation inhabiting the group. Then Honolulu is the capital town, and this is situated on the island of Oahu.

These islands are of increasing importance, since they lie on the direct route between Victoria, the Western port of the Canadian Pacific Railway, and Australia. They are also just on the line between Panama and China. Honolulu is, therefore, bound to be of great value as a coaling-station, especially if the central American doorway between the Atlantic and Pacific is ever to be unlocked and opened. The islands are over 2,000 miles from San Francisco, and rather more from Samoa, these being the nearest civilized places to the group.

Unfortunately, time did not permit of my visiting

the island of Hawaii; the chief attraction of which is the huge active volcano, said to be a marvellous sight, where one may gaze on a lake of molten lava, watch fountains of liquid fire, and walk about on the ' frozen' surface in parts of the fiery lake.

The harbour of Honolulu is to all appearances nothing much more than an open roadstead; but is, nevertheless, well enclosed by shallow coral reefs, which makes it a fairly safe anchorage. On these reefs a lighthouse and several queer-looking houses have been erected on piles, and some good wharfs have been made on the flat shore, so as to enable large steamers to lie alongside.

Some English, American, and other men-o'-war are usually lying in the harbour; and I enjoyed many merry visits to the hospitable officers of H.M.S. *Nymphe.*

A mysterious flag at once attracts attention flying from many of the vessels in the bay. It has the Union Jack in the corner like any ensign, but the rest of the flag consists of stripes of red, white, and blue. This turns out to be the Hawaiian flag; but why it should have the Union Jack in the corner I am unable to satisfactorily explain.

A short distance along the coast is an extensive land-locked harbour, at present inaccessible for large vessels, but which, I am told, could at a moderate expenditure be formed into an excellent haven.

The country close round Honolulu is flat, but a few miles inland bare rugged hills rise, which, except for a covering of brown grass on the less steep parts, reminds one of the Red Sea coast.

The town itself is like a mixture of Cairo, Singapore, and St. John's Wood, but with none of the special attractions of either. The streets are mostly narrow and dirty, yet there are some good shops and offices. Then there are a few pretentious buildings, such as the royal palace, which is a fine large villa, standing in its own well laid-out grounds of ten acres, with stables and carriage sweep complete. Opposite this are the Government offices, with a statue before them, in bronze and gilt, of King Kamehameha (pronounced Kamay-ah-may-ah) in native costume, *i.e.*, feather cloak and sporran.

The back streets of the town are mostly full of wooden houses, and there are suburbs with wide avenues and detached villas. But the place is well lit with electric arc lights, and is supplied with a telephone system, which even extends to ships in the harbour by being permanently attached to the mooring buoys.

Another noticeable institution, but one which I did not often patronize, is the Chinese Young Men's Christian Association.

The Hawaiian Hotel is a good-sized, comfortable hostelry, with cool verandas, and surrounded by a lot of shrubs and shady trees. The waiters here are mostly Japanese, and are very attentive.

Not far off is the small English club, rather like that at Johore, with a couple of American billiard tables. There are also several of these tables in the hotel. They are so arranged that when a ball falls into a pocket it goes under the table, and rolls back to a trough under the bottom end of the table. The marking is done with a number of wooden beads on a string suspended above the table.

The English cathedral is a fine stone building, but I hear that the service, when conducted by the Bishop (Dr. Willis), is only attended by his few special friends, and one or two entire strangers; it is, however, well patronized when the Bishop does not officiate, as I can vouch for. I went there one Sunday morning with a naval officer, who was in uniform. We were a little late, and, feeling somewhat ashamed of ourselves, intended slipping into some back seat. But he that humbleth himself shall be exalted. Once inside the place no vacant seats were to be seen, but the officious verger was delighted to get us in his clutches. With great solemnity and state, the verger preceding us, we marched up the aisle, the eyes of the whole congregation upon us. To the very front we walked, yet I could see no vacant place. At last we arrived at the king's pew, bedecked in red velvet and gilded crowns, and there the verger stopped, turned, and, with a grand and graceful sweep of the arm, ushered us into the vacant throne. I almost expected a round of applause, but it came not. Doubtless tongues were wagging later in the day—if not indeed even then, within the sacred precincts—asking who was this new royalty attended by his naval aide-de-camp.

The poor King Kalakau was at this time in America, the people only talking of, and planning for, his return. Little did I, or anyone else, expect that before I got to San Francisco he would be dead, and that I should there witness his funeral; so now his sister, Princess Liliuokalani, reigns in his stead. Her name may seem peculiar, but the heiress-presumptive, daughter of another sister, rejoices in the name of Princess Victoria-Kawekiu-Kaiulani-Lunalilo-Kalaninuiahilapalapa Cleghorn!

Major Wodehouse is the British Commissioner and representative, and is, of course, quite one of the leading men of the place. He has been a very long time in the country, and therefore knows the place well, and used to be much consulted by the King.

There is plenty of society in Honolulu, for, besides several English, there are many Americans, both resident and visiting the place from California.

There are some small public gardens, where the band plays on occasion, and then many of the fashionable world attend on horseback. But the manner in which the ladies here ride, though I believe it is almost unknown elsewhere, is a matter discussed with much interest at home. Most of them stride their horses. It has a peculiar effect, but certainly does not look bad. The garment worn is like a riding-habit, divided and gathered

in round the ankles, not unlike Turkish trousers,
but I am inclined to think they would look much
better if longer.

There are dinners, dances, and 'at homes' here,
just as in England, and it was surprising to find,

LADIES ON HORSEBACK.

in talking to some of the young ladies, who con-
versed just as any English girl would, that they
had been born and brought up in Honolulu, and
had never left the island! Yet, of course, novels,
illustrated and other papers, and occasional visitors,

keep them well informed of the ways of the world, and all that is going on ; and I do not know that I should be far wrong in saying that even *more* interest is taken there in the doings of our Royal family than in England.

On the whole, however, the place seems, not unnaturally, more American than English.

The natives of the place bear a strong affinity to the Samoans and Tongans, and also to the Maoris of New Zealand. The language of all these is similar, and they are supposed to have the same origin. But the Hawaiian is more civilized, and many of the upper-class natives are as well educated and well-mannered as an average European.

Those born of a Hawaiian and a European parent, of which there are a considerable number, are always here called 'half whites.'

The natives are generally dressed in ordinary European clothes ; the only peculiarity noticeable, perhaps a relic of their former feather cloaks, is a band of peacock feathers often worn around their hats.

There are two 'Houses' of Parliament, though the members of both sit together. They are the 'House of Nobles' and the 'Representatives.' They usually only sit once in two years.

There was a great deal of talk about the Queen of Hawaii in London in Jubilee year, and as to her official position and proper escort. I wonder what would have happened if the Queen of Samoa had been there, too. She might have demanded an escort of life-guards, but would probably have attended the functions barefooted.

And this brings us to the subject of the Hawaiian army. As may be imagined, it is not very colossal, amounting to some five regiments, or rather companies, of volunteer rifles, and one of cavalry. The uniform is white with brass buttons, and an English-like white helmet with spike.

One of the finest views to be seen in Oahu is at Pali, about six miles from Honolulu. The road all the way runs in a gradual ascent up a valley, rocky, volcanic hills rising on either side, with ragged-looking tops, and a few bushy trees in the hollows.

Finally, the road appears to come to an abrupt end, going straight up to the edge of a great cliff, but it dips over the ridge and descends the ' Pali' (or precipice) in a steep zig-zag. A splendid prospect is obtained of the plain below and the sea on the other side of the island, with many rugged and precipitous cliffs in the foreground.

Coming back one obtains a good view over the harbour, and just before getting into the town one passes the cemetery, where is the grave of Captain Hope, R.N., who was killed here by a fall from his horse.

One day a roving Englishman and I rode out on a couple of good horses, with Mexican saddles, to a sugar plantation called Waimanalo (which means ' fresh water'). After passing Pali, and going down the very steep rocky track, an awful place for the horses, we got to the plains below, and rode along for some miles through fertile country, with the grand line of precipitous cliffs and high peaks, now rising into the misty clouds, some way off on one side, and the sea a mile or two away on the other. Our road became more hilly after a time, and we passed near a most extraordinary-looking hill, rising to an absolute point at the top, just as one has occasionally seen in some very exaggerated

HILL IN OAHU.

picture of the Matterhorn; but on passing it, it proved to be ridge-shaped, and not a mere cone.

There was not much cultivation here, except an occasional field of taro, flooded like a paddy field, and some guava bushes.

We forded several small streams and passed some native houses, which looked like a thatched roof on the ground, with a doorway dug through the thatch.

At last we arrived at the sugar plantation, and rode up to the homestead, where were three or four neat-looking wooden houses in a nice garden, with the large mill, labourers' quarters, etc., close by.

This plantation is peculiar as being owned by a native, Hon. J. A. Cummins, the Minister of Foreign Affairs, and entirely worked by Chinese labour. There is not a single European employed about the place.

We were very well received by the manager, who gave up for our use one of the clean and well-furnished four-roomed cottages, and, after a bath, we partook of an excellent breakfast. We tried some of the national dish, 'Poi,' which simply consists of taro (root) crushed and mixed with water, and then left for two or three days to ferment. It looks like thick gooseberry fool, but tastes more like rhubarb, though without any sugar, and altogether I thought it very nasty; but the rest of the food was excellent, and the table was most prettily decorated with flowers, which grow in profusion in the garden outside.

We then started to go over the plantation. The estate is almost level ground, bordered on one side by the sea, on another by some steep hills (over which we had come), and at the back by the rocky precipice, which, rising to the ridge, continued all along to Pali. The place was formerly a cattle ranch, and must have been well suited for this, as no fence or boundary riding would be necessary.

We went off on the engine of the narrow-gauge railway, which runs right through the plantation. This not only serves to bring in the cane to the mill, but also takes the sugar down to a pier, whence it is shipped away. It was a beautiful day when we were there, and the sea looked intensely blue, with a very white sandy beach, while away in the distance lay the island of Molokai, where the lepers are sent, and where Father Damien made such a name for himself. Whilst on this subject I may say that almost everyone in these parts to whom I spoke about it agreed in saying that they did not consider Father Damien deserving of any very special praise. Of course he did a lot of good among the lepers, but so have hundreds of others. There seems no doubt that he was a very dirty man, and, moreover, that if he had been of the more cleanly habits of others who visit and live with the lepers it is very improbable that he would ever have contracted the dread disease. There was another celebrity in the same line in Honolulu. Sister Rose Gertrude started from England with a great flourish of trumpets, but I believe I am right in saying she never even got as far as the leper island. If she did, she did not remain there long, and is now (or was then) a nursery governess in the family of a native in Honolulu. There are over a thousand lepers on the island, who are well looked after, having a doctor resident on the island, and are supplied with plenty of amusements.

However, to return to the sugar plantation. As I began by saying, all the employés are China-men, even to the engine-driver and the foreman of the plantation, the latter a most courteous old gen-tleman in large, round, stage-like spectacles. The yield of sugar averages five tons per acre without artificial irrigation (one ton being a fair yield in most other places). The mill was very like any other sugar-mill, and the machinery all looked very good and well kept, and was of quite a modern type. The only peculiarity that I noticed, as being different from the usual processes in Queensland, was that the sugar was taken straight out of centrifugals and put in bags without drying.

We returned to the homestead and had a sumptuous lunch, in a large room with polished floor, a billiard-table, and a bed!

Afterwards we laid ourselves down on the grass lawn in front, while the lady of the house made us up some beautiful 'lai-lais,' or wreaths of flowers, to hang round our necks. Now I am not of an æsthetic nature, and although all the surroundings, with the brilliant sunlight, the blue sea, the grand cliffs, the green cane-fields, and the shady foreground with roses, hibiscus, and many-coloured flowers, were truely poetic, yet I felt that this Arcadian form of decoration might become our friend R. L. Stevenson, but not me. However, *nolens volens*, we were decorated, and felt it would indeed be bad form, after all the hospitality we had received, not to seem to appreciate the attention. We accordingly rode off flower-bedecked on our return journey. On approaching Pali it looked truly grand, and I think the precipice, 1,500 to 2,000 feet high, is a much finer sight from below than the view one gets from the top. And what a journey we had to surmount that terrible stony track ! As for me and my horse, I found it necessary to dismount and lead him. Even then the stupid brute slipped at the side of the track and rolled over on to his back among the bushes. My companion, however, insisted on riding up. But bit by bit his saddle worked back, and presently I saw him, with a terrified look upon his countenance, lying along the horse's back, clinging on to its mane, and vainly shouting ' Woa !' though still gripping with his knees the saddle, now insecurely balanced on the root of his horse's tail !

Oahu does not abound with any startling birds or beasts. Minah birds are common, though I think they are a peculiar variety.

Here I found they had yet another ' ti-tree.' I have explained how in Australia this name is given to a species of eucalyptus, how in New Zealand it refers to a plant like heather, but in the Pacific islands it applies to a kind of dracæna with a big green leaf ; and it seems to be as useful a plant as some of the palm-trees in other countries, for its leaves make good thatch and a fibre, its root is edible, whilst sugar and an intoxicating beverage are obtained from the juice.

The departure of the steamer for San Francisco is apparently a great event in Honolulu ; large crowds gather on the wharf, and all the *élite* of the place is there. Many of those going away, even including old gray-bearded men, are profusely decorated with floral wreaths. Then the band attended to play us off, and, by direction of the British Commissioner, who kindly came to see me off, as we steamed out they struck up ' God save the Queen.'

CHAPTER XIII.

HOME THROUGH THE STATES.

To enter the United States by the Golden Gate (as the entrance to San Francisco harbour is called) is calculated to start one with a favourable impression of the beauty and grandeur of the country. Big, rugged, bare hills rise on the left, and smaller and more 'civilized'-looking ones on the right. These are really the heads of two promontories, the one running down from the north, the other running up from the south ; and here at the Golden Gate they approach within a mile of one another, thus enclosing a splendid harbour of some 600 square miles. On the extremity of this southern promontory, thirty miles long, stands the city of San Francisco. The harbour, with numerous islands, is decidedly picturesque—more so in my humble opinion than Sydney Harbour.

San Francisco may be disappointing at first acquaintance, if too much has been expected ; but after you get to know your way about, have visited the Cliff House, Golden Gate Park, and some of the very numerous places of amusement, your opinion will probably change for the better.

The city itself, with a population of 300,000, is decidedly ugly and dirty. The streets are badly cobble-paved, with lots of straw and paper lying about as if to hide the mud. Yet they are straight and regular, with fine shops, and huge masses of brick and mortar rising up skyward on every side ; everything is new—everything suggestive of money laid out with a purpose. Several very large and well-kept hotels exist. The 'Palace,' a huge ugly pile of bow windows, claims to be the largest hotel in the world (capable of accommodating 1,200 people); and the 'California,' according to my limited experience, is certainly one of the best. The 'feeding' at the latter is all one could expect in Paris itself ; and there are numbers of other hotels.

In addition to several good theatres, there is probably no town of its size which can boast of more places of evening entertainment than San Francisco. I believe I should not be far wrong in adding that there are very few that could not beat it as regards public morality. There is every kind of amusement, from the regular theatre, variety entertainment and music-hall, down to the lowest of the 'dives,' which are underground drink-shops, in which there is generally some kind of free entertainment going on, which, however, is hardly of the sort a man would take his daughter to. It is in some of the 'dives' that the chairs and tables, placed about for the convenience of guests, are often raised and moved about overhead in an uncomfortable manner, till the 'pop-gun' has done some execution, and the hall is cleared by the 'marshals' or police. And this brings me to another place of interest, especially to those concerned in such disturbances, and that is the police court and its cells—not, gentle reader, that this was the place to which *I* had to adjourn after visiting the dives. But I was fortunate enough to have a letter of introduction to the chief of the Detective Department, and in consequence saw much which I might not otherwise have seen. The police court itself was not unlike an ordinary English court, except that there was even more noise and less chance of hearing what went on, the court being crowded with people, most of whom were busily discussing their affairs. But the cells, situated in the basement, with their wretched oc-cupants, formed one of the most remarkable sights I have ever seen. We went along some passages, and entered a large cellar lit by gas. All along one side was a series of iron-barred dens, just like the lion-house in the Zoo, only much lower and darker. In each 'cage' were perhaps eight or ten men, seated on small benches, clinging to the bars and eagerly looking out, or restlessly pacing up and down. One 'cage' was full of women, one of whom was shrieking in a most distressing manner; but on my asking what was wrong with her, I was told in the most matter-of-fact way : 'Oh, she's just come in ; she'll be quiet presently!' There were other similar cellars, also accommodation for more respectable prisoners, and separate cells for murderers and dangerous characters. My first remark to a friend who accompanied me was: 'How like a menagerie! I wonder what time the animals are fed?' But as it so happened, we had arrived just in the nick of time, and the similarity to the menagerie was even more intensified. First a man came around with an iron bucket full of 'soup,' very suggestive of pig-wash. To see the eagerness with which all the poor creatures crowded to one corner of their cell, and pushed through the bars the small oblong tin dishes with which they were provided, to be filled with this hot mess, was pitiable indeed. And later on, when the man came to distribute dishes of bread and potato, it was extraordinary to see how they eyed the food, and vied with one another to get the best dish, although, to all appearances exactly the same. I need hardly say that the ventilation of this place was not all that could be desired, and it made me sincerely hope that I should never fall out with the powers that be in San Francisco, and I felt glad of my intro-duction, which in such case might possibly have enabled me to fare a slight degree better.

Although the police here do not go into such care-ful anthropometric details as do the Parisian police, yet it is interesting to see their books of photographs and descriptions. Some of the gentlemen who are forced to become acquainted with this place have strong objections to having their portraits taken. One of them gave the photographer a great deal of trouble, and spoiled many of his plates; but one fine day—at least, fine it may have been above, but he was down in the cellars—he was requested to step out of his cell, and while standing there in a dimly gas-lit passage, never for a moment suspecting that a photographer could frequent such a dismal place, there was a sudden lightning-like flash of magnesium. The instantaneous plate had received its indelible impression, and the very much startled prisoner had to own: 'Well, you got me *that* time!'

From these low scenes one naturally turns to China Town, populated by a pure Chinese colony, forming the lowest slums of San Francisco, and known throughout the world with an unenviable reputation. The chief marvel of this place seems to be the enormous number of human beings who can provide themselves with quarters in a given space. You go through streets, you turn up narrow lanes, you grope your way along narrow passages, and you enter the houses. You may then go from room to room, mostly small, low rooms; but not only will almost the whole floor-space be covered in with platforms or beds, but there will nearly always be a second tier—a light wooden framework supporting an upper set of beds, so that quite a small room may contain quarters for as many as sixteen or eighteen persons. These rooms generally have absolutely no ventilation, even what should come in by the various cracks round the doors and windows being kept out by paper pasted over the interstices. Yet nearly every man is smoking, either opium—which is against the law, but is almost impossible to prevent—or small quantities of tobacco. How, under such circumstances, these people can live is a mystery. It seems as if our ideas of ventilation and fresh air were absolutely erroneous.

Another anomaly that strikes one on visiting these densely-packed warrens is how they can exist for any time without being burnt down. They are mostly built of wood, with wooden fittings all about ; yet not only does every man have a lamp *in his bed* to light his pipe by, but in all sorts of places—such as under the lower beds, and in any available corner— are the 'joss-sticks' silently smouldering. With some of the houses—notably the actors' quarters in the theatre—it would take quite a long time for anyone to get out of a centre room to the outer air ; and when one imagines the crowded rooms, the many women and children, the very narrow passages and the extreme inflammability, not only of each building, but of the whole quarter, it seems as though an awful catastrophe must happen some day. Fires do occur, of course, occasionally, but somehow they manage to put them out. I suppose because there are always people ready at hand to extinguish the fire when first it begins.

There are two good large Chinese theatres, the

charge for entrance to which is cheap enough for the genuine Chinee, but much more expensive for the European, who is provided with a chair on .the stage. The reason for this difference is that if Europeans (of the lowest class) were to mix with the native Chinamen there would be sure to be a row sooner or later, and the hidden revolvers illegally carried by the one would have to contend against the formidable knives borne equally against the law by the other.

The plays are the usual long, tedious, incomprehensible pieces (often lasting from 4.30 p.m. till midnight), in which two or three characters are on the stage together, chanting to a fearful noise of gongs and various frightful instruments, which soon make the ears of an ordinary Christian mortal long for the solitude of the street outside. The scenery is very peculiar, but, though extremely simple, is not easily to be comprehended by the uneducated eye; thus, the chief object consists of a table, over the front of which hangs a red cloth. Presently the scene-shifter will come on—of course he is known, and no one takes any notice of his walking about the stage, and running against the actors—and he simply turns the table round. On the other side, however, hangs a grey cloth, which is now presented to view, and denotes an entire change of scene. Then they have a quaint method of expressing the act of leaving a house. This the actor does by lifting his feet as though he were stepping over a high threshold. It is very curious to see two or three of them do this in turn on a perfectly empty stage, and then you know that the scene is shifted, and that now it is out-of-doors. The representation of death is peculiar, too. The villain of the piece strikes his victim, who falls ; the scene-shifter walks on with a small paper full of gunpowder, which he lights, and the victim retires under cover of the puff of smoke, and a dummy is sometimes put in his stead.

These Chinese actors lead a curious life, I am told. They cannot, as a rule, even venture out into the street with safety to themselves, and all live in the building of the theatre.

There are, of course, numerous fine joss-houses, each one belonging to three or four families. Some of these are extremely well decorated, with most elaborate and beautiful carved woodwork. The josses are supposed to be life-like images of the heads of the families, and I may here mention a very curious fact I was told of, on good authority, whilst in one of these joss-houses. In China there are, of course, thousands and thousands of josses, but amongst all of them there is (not unnaturally) only one portrait of a white man. That one is said to represent Marco Polo, and is in a joss-house in Canton.

There are several remarkably good Chinese restaurants, in fine large buildings, kept scrupulously clean, and beautifully decorated with gilded carved wood. The food looked clean and well served, and outside the dining-rooms was arranged a row of metal basins, each with its napkin, for the customers to wipe their mouths and fingers.

It is interesting to go the round of the shops— all open and well lighted up to a very late hour of the night.

The druggist's shop is one of the most curious. Behind the counter is a large chest of small drawers, not unlike those usually seen in an English chemist's shop; but the peculiar thing is that none of them are labelled, and on opening any one it is seen to be divided into three or four divisions, in each of which is a different kind of drug. Now watch the apothecary compound. He takes the hieroglyphic-covered slip of paper which serves as a prescription, and lays it before him. He pulls open one drawer, and with peculiar little hand-scales he measures out the desired quantity of the drug, empties it into a mortar, and beats it up with the pestle. Then he goes to another drawer, and repeats the operation— and so on with perhaps a dozen different drugs— taking a given quantity of each, and always knowing exactly which drawer to go to, despite the absence of labels. These drugs are mostly roots of different sorts—some are nuts—but there are also many other more nasty things—beetles, for instance—and doubtless many more that they would not like to show us.

The jeweller's shop was not less interesting, and,

by the way, these tradesmen are all hard at work, even though it be past ten o'clock at night. What a lesson to the eight-hour advocates! Here sits a man with a piece of gold-foil before him. Carefully he weighs out some exact measure of it in his scales. He wishes for a solid bar of gold, so this foil must be melted. The lamp, or furnace, consists of a dish of oil, in which numerous wicks are lying. When a powerful fire is required, these wicks are gathered together and brought to one side of the bowl, where they burn with quite a large flame. When only required as a lamp, most of the wicks are knocked back into the oil and extinguished. But to melt the gold it is placed in a hollow piece of charcoal, with a smaller piece of charcoal laid on top, so as to enclose the gold in a sort of small chamber. The blowpipe is now brought into play, the operator drawing in his breath through his nose, and thus keeping up an almost continuous blast from his mouth. In this way in a very few minutes the gold is reduced to a red-hot liquid mass, and is then hammered down on an anvil, and beaten into the required shape. More wonderful still is it to watch the filigree worker cutting up minute pieces of gold-wire—so small you can hardly see them—and placing them together with delicate forceps, and soldering them in position.

The pawnshop is the next place to visit. And here one is struck with the very systematic order in which all the various articles are kept. The whole of

26

the small premises is crammed with shelves and drawers, filled up with knives, jewellery, clothing, pipes, musical instruments, and all sorts and conditions of things. Yet every article is carefully labelled and classified. On my expressing surprise at the very calm way in which our detective guide walked through the shop, opening drawers, unwrapping articles, and prying into everywhere, he explained that if the broker should attempt to object to his conduct, all that would be necessary would be for him to obtain a search-warrant, whereupon he could bring three or four men down, and they would force open every lock, upset all the drawers, etc., pull all the goods off their shelves, and leave the place to be put in order again. Very naturally, under these circumstances, the pawnbroker is only too pleased to let the detective quietly look into his stock-in-trade whenever he pleases. Whilst we were inside the shop behind the counter, an innocent Chinee came to pawn a huge knife, and laid it on the counter. Now, a Chinaman can be heavily fined for carrying a knife concealed about him. So our detective friend simply eyed him for a bit, remarking it would be mean to take advantage of the man that way— besides, he couldn't prove that he was carrying the knife *concealed;* but, nevertheless, he had 'spotted' his man, and had mentally marked him down as a suspicious character. We then visited some of the more respectable private houses — in fact, went visiting, and were formally introduced to the occupants, who offered cigars and other hospitalities. The rooms were generally very small, and the atmosphere stuffy, from joss-sticks and bad ventilation ; but, of course, they were a great improvement on the dens of the poorer classes.

Gambling is here strictly against the law, but it is, nevertheless, carried on extensively. The outer door of the place where this goes on presented the appearance of a portal of an old castle, being thickly studded with huge nails, and made of several thicknesses of hard wood ; inside were numerous bolts, as though it were the door of a prison. All this was done simply as a precaution against a police inroad. It seemed remarkable that they should own their guilt so far, and defy any sudden onslaught of their would-be discoverers. Generally in these places they play 'fan-tan' with such apparatus as can be immediately destroyed, or of innocent appearance. Almonds are used for coins, and eaten when necessary, a chop-stick to count out with, and an inflammable square of paper for placing the stakes upon.

After thus spending several hours in the midst of Chinese men, houses, and customs, with no signs of aught but Chinese, it is like waking from a dream suddenly to return to the well-lit streets of San Francisco, thronged with 'European' pedestrians.

After what has been said, it may easily be imagined that San Francisco is by no means an early closing place. At eleven o'clock at night the streets are full of people, the shops brilliantly illumin-

ated.   About 3 a.m. is the sort of time to stroll into
a restaurant for supper ; but you need not hurry—
they are open all night.   It is told of an innocent
clergyman who entered a restaurant at about eight
o'clock one morning to get some breakfast, that, in
reply to his question of 'What have you got to
eat ?' the blear-eyed waiter replied, 'Well, it's mighty
late, but p'raps I could get you a grilled bone !'

. I am told that it is somewhat risky to stroll about
the streets alone late at night, especially if not carrying a good stick, or pocketing a more far-reaching
weapon.   The town, as is well known, swarms with
ruffians of the deepest die.   The police 'officers'
are most peculiar-looking individuals, being dressed
in frock-coats and black 'pot' hats, with a small
gold cord round them ; but I am assured they are
highly respectable men, many of them being also
very well off.

The fire brigade is another well-known institution
of San Francisco.   The harness, with collars to open
on hinges, is hung over the 'place where the
horses ought to be,' ready fixed to the engine in
such a way that it can be dropped straight on to the
horses, and the men swarm down a pole from the
room above.

The Englishman in America feels much the same
as if in some foreign country where he knows the
language pretty well ; for, while speaking fluently,
he occasionally hears something said which he
may not quite understand, and often, too, though

he express himself in plain English, he finds himself misunderstood. Experience soon shows that it is not pure plain English spoken here. Such words as 'railway station,' 'trams,' 'legs' (human), 'lift,' don't exist. These are respectively translated by 'depot,' 'street cars,' 'limbs,' 'elevator.' Then there are other words which puzzle the novice. On asking the price of some article, one is often told, 'Two bits.' A 'bit,' there is some difficulty in discovering, is twelve and a half cents.

To follow out the regulation programme for sightseers, one has to take tram to see the Golden Gate Park (not that it is near the Golden Gate), which is a really beautifully laid-out park, with pretty hilly surroundings. It possesses all the usual appointments of such a place—large conservatories, bandstands, etc., and some pleasant drives, along which you see the inhabitants of the city being dashed along in their buggies by fast-trotting horses. On the grass lawns are numbers of semi-tame Californian quail, with their tufty crests.

The next event in the programme is to go by train to the Cliff House, a kind of restaurant hotel, situated on a small cliff overlooking the Pacific. A few hundred yards in front are several small rocky islands literally covered with seals of all sizes and colours. It is a most interesting sight to go there on a stormy day and watch the waves dash over the rocks in a snow-white mass, and to see the seals quietly swimming about in the broken water, continually barking just like so many dogs. Numbers of sea-birds also frequent the rocks.

After the seal rocks, you go up a hill behind to the Sutro Heights, and see the view from the tower, and then one can go on to the ' Presidio Reservation,' whence one may get a beautiful view of the Golden Gate and the hilly promontory on the opposite side.

The return journey is made by another line of trams, on the cable system. In this part of San Francisco there are some steep hills, and it is marvellous how easily these cars ascend and descend them.

Many of the villas in the outskirts of the town are very fine buildings, possessing great architectural effect. But in one of the streets we met a good-sized wooden house, with porches and balconies, out for a drive. It was being slowly rolled along, to change its ' location.'

Of course I had not been long in America before a mysterious stranger called to see me at the hotel, and announced himself to be connected with one of the leading journals of the place, and would like to know. my opinion on San Francisco, Imperial Federation, the present state of the British army, or any other views I might be willing to impart. I think it is Baron Hübner who relates how he interviewed an interviewer, the latter declaring he had no time to *read* up subjects ; all his knowledge was gathered from questioning other people. And *from* the mixed-up version of our conversation which appeared in next day's paper, I rather imagine that *my* friend was not very deeply read—at all events, on those subjects which we discussed.

A few hours by rail from San Francisco carries us down the shores of the harbour, or bay, to San José, a nice little town, with an excellent hotel, electric light, electric tram-lines, and all improvements. The surrounding country is laid out in fruit-trees, and is mostly level ; but some twenty miles to the east the hills rise into a regular range of mountains, some 4,000 feet high, and on one of them, Mount Hamilton, is perched the great Lick Observatory. It is extraordinary how misleading people often are in attempting to give you directions as to how to reach any place, especially when they have not been there themselves. Now, I asked a man who *ought* to know how I could get up to the observatory. I suggested riding. That would be impossible, he said, as the road was so steep that I should have to dismount and lead my horse all the way down. Now, after having been up, I will undertake to say that I would *canter* a horse not only all the way down, but all the way up too ! It is an excellent road, with a very gentle slope throughout. The drive (for I *drove*, after all) is a very pleasant one, first past the innumerable fruit-ranches, then over mountainous places, with bare hills and oak-trees, everywhere seeing numbers of ground squirrels or 'prairie dogs,' which live in holes like rabbits.

The Lick Observatory is a very fine building, or series of buildings, the principal part having a large entrance-hall and two wings. At the end of one is the large dome, containing the big telescope; at the other end is a smaller observatory. The great white dome forms a conspicuous landmark, and can even be seen from San José. The big telescope, thirty-six inches in diameter, is the largest refractor in the world. The origin of this great

THE LICK OBSERVATORY.

observatory was that a peculiar old man, James Lick, who had been a piano-maker, but had made a large fortune, thought one day that the United States, possessing most big things, ought to have the largest telescope in the world—not that he knew or cared anything about astronomy—so he left a large sum of money (700,000 dollars) to be devoted to this object.

I was unfortunate in the night when I visited the observatory. No planets were visible; nebulæ,

looking merely like small clouds, are not so interesting to an amateur, neither are double stars ; but
an ordinary star of the first magnitude, as seen
through the great telescope, surprised me greatly.
Not that I could see, of course, more than a mere
speck of light, but it was so intensely brilliant as to
be unpleasant to gaze at too long. It appeared
just like an electric arc-light, with a violet tinge.

Mr. Keeler, one of the assistants, showed me
some interesting drawings of Mars sketched through
the big telescope, and some of these showed a
peculiar projection from one side of the planet,
which, he said, had been discovered quite accidentally
by a sightseer, who, one Saturday night, was looking
through the great telescope, and asked what that
bump sticking out at the side of the 'star' was.
The astronomer naturally thought the man was
making some ignorant mistake, but, looking through,
to his surprise saw this most unaccountable pheno-
menon, which only lasted for a day or two.

Again we are in the train, rattling away through
the plains of California to Monterey. Small fruit-
trees extend on all sides, bare, of course, at this
time of year (February), planted in regular rows,
with ground kept beautifully clean between them.
The Americans are very boastful of their railway
travelling accommodation, but I was not greatly
taken with it. The carriages are generally over-
heated, and an open window would let in too violent
a cold air. The newsboys, who continually come

into the cars and shout out the list of papers they
have for sale, or describe some wonderful series of
'portraits of all the American Presidents' for half a
dollar, etc., or come in with fruit or peppermints,
are a perpetual nuisance ; and the conductor is much
too fond of asking for tickets. I was rather startled
when, having shown the guard my ticket, he began
to pull my hat about. I thought there must be
something wrong with it, but, all the same, I considered the man might have apologized. When he
had finished, I took my hat off to see what he had
been up to, and then thought he was trying to make
a fool of me by sticking a piece of red paper in the
brim. But finally I discovered that this was the
method of showing him at a glance that he had
taken my ticket.

They also have a neat way with some tickets of
inscribing indelibly the date, cost, etc., with a small
punch. In one place on the ticket is printed ' Jan.,
Feb., Mar.,' etc., and the punch is made through
the desired month. Then comes a row of numbers
from one to thirty-one, and another hole will then
show the day of the month, and so on with dollars
and cents, and other information.

It was at Monterey that the Americans first (1866)
took California, which till then had formed part of
Mexico, and two years later they made it a State.

Near Monterey is the splendid great hotel Del
Monte. It is a marvellous place, has a separate railway station of its own, and the grounds surrounding it

comprise 126 acres, and are said to require no less than fifty gardeners to keep them in the beautiful order in which they are. The house itself is perfectly huge, being nearly 400 feet long, and is not unpicturesque, all built in one quaint old style of architecture, with a great deal of woodwork. The rooms are large, clean, and well fitted. It is a sort of watering-place in itself. In the grounds all sorts of amusements are to be had ; swimming-baths, tennis-courts, archery ground, a large maze, and I don't know how many more attractions.

There is a splendid collection of cacti, and lots of big shady trees all round. Drives and walks may be taken out to the sea-coast, along which, wherever there are rocks, numerous seals are to be seen disporting themselves in the surf. There are many picturesque spots along this coast, and among other trees there are some fine old cedars. But beware of the poison oak, a small plant with a leaf not unlike a bramble, which causes nasty sores when it stings you, and not only to men, for even dogs get bad places on them from having merely rubbed up against the leaves of this objectionable plant.

If you want to be called in the morning at the hotel, a loud and powerful electric bell will sound in your room at the appointed hour. You then *have* to get up, in order to press the button which stops the bell and tells the porter you are awake and up. In the event of fire, every bell in the house can be rung at once.

From Monterey, the train may be taken up the coast to Santa Cruz, another thriving city, with numerous villas overlooking the Pacific breakers; and not far beyond this is the station of 'Big Trees.' Here are the great redwood trees, a kind of sequoia or pine. Near their bases are some wooden buildings and numerous seats, where, at certain seasons, the excursionist may gather comfort for the inner man, whilst the eye is feasting on the giants of the forest. All the largest of these trees— for there are a dozen or so of exceptional size—have names given to them, which are painted on a board nailed to the trunk. 'General Grant' is about the largest, and must measure perhaps sixty feet in circumference, and is said to be over three hundred feet high.

We walked on a few miles to a village near, and lunched at the inn, so as to see what an American out-of-the-way country place was like. One is so accustomed to look upon the States as consisting entirely of huge cities and prairies, that one never considers these little country places. There is very little difference between them and the typical English village.

We then returned to San Francisco by the line running up the other (inland) side of the bay. Here we pass over miles of flat country—most of it absolute marsh—and cross several wide rivers. Thus we get to the terminus at Oaklands, which is an important suburb of San Francisco, connected with it by large steam-ferries, on board of which complete trains can be run, and which are furnished with good waiting-rooms and every convenience.

The capital of California is Sacramento. This city is much smaller, and of less importance, than San Francisco ; and, indeed, it would probably now be a very insignificant place, were it not the seat of Government. The Capitol is a very fine building, a small edition of that at Washington, being built of white stone, with numerous columns and a large dome. The building is well situated, with neatly-kept grounds all round it. The right thing to do is to ascend to the top of the dome, so as to get a bird's-eye view of the city. Perhaps this is the best aspect of it ; I don't think much of any other. The building contains two chambers—for the Senate and the Assembly—and all the Government offices, including some fine large rooms for the Governor of California, a typical American gentleman, civil and courteous, with whom I had the honour of a conversation.

The Assembly is very different in many respects from our House of Commons. In the first place, anyone can walk straight into the strangers' gallery, or even on to the floor of the house, without so much as giving his name (and this is the case also even in Washington). Members can ask their friends right in, and sit and chat with them during the debates ! Some laughter was produced, whilst I was there, by a certain honourable member, who was so engrossed in conversation with a lady sitting beside him, that his attention had to be called to the fact that the House was waiting for him to make some statement. Each member has a chair and a writing-desk, all being placed facing the Speaker's chair, and newspapers and books are eagerly read during the more tedious harangues.

There is very little else to be seen in Sacramento. Long streets of dirty-looking shops and houses with wooden verandas, badly-paved roads with trams and wooden side-walks, numerous villas in the out-skirts, two or three small theatres, and several second-class hotels, are all that would strike a visitor.

To the north of Sacramento is the chief fruit and vine growing district. It is said that £13,000,000 is invested in the vineyards of California.

Once again we are on the move, and the great transcontinental journey is commenced in a train consisting of ten Pullman cars and three engines. For the first 130 miles from San Francisco the land is comparatively low, and after that a gradual ascent is made up into the Sierra Nevada. Up, up we go during the night, and when we wake early in the sleeping-car, and pull aside the blind to see what it is like outside, we realize our ascent by seeing everything covered in a deep mantle of white snow. We see the frost on the window-pane, and seem to feel cold at the very sight of the view before us, notwithstanding the stuffy warmth of the carriage (I beg pardon—car). Shortly before Truckee we have reached the highest point, some 7,000 feet above the sea. And then a gradual descent is made, passing numerous ice store-houses, where ice is collected from the frozen mountain - streams, dammed up for the purpose.

Soon after, the great desert with its numerous salt lakes, is passed through, and finally we see the Great Salt Lake of Utah (100 miles long), along the north shore of which the line runs for many miles, till Ogden is reached. The route by which I went here turned south, and goes through Salt Lake City. Of course, the great wonder of this place is its marvellous mushroom-like growth in the midst of a desert since 1847. But much of its former interest, from its associations with the Mormons, is now lessened, since Mormonism as a religion is much changed, many of the Mormons have migrated to Mexico, and numbers of ordinary mortals having taken up their abode in this thriving city of some 40,000 inhabitants. People talk of the marvellous garden in the midst of the wilderness to be seen here, but in winter-time it certainly looks a most dreary and desolate style of garden. The great attraction of the town is the Temple Square, where is a most ugly-looking turtle-backed edifice called the Tabernacle, said to be capable of *seating* 9,000 people, and supposed to be a marvel for acoustic properties. There is also the Temple, begun in 1853, and never yet finished. Salt Lake City boasts three daily papers.

Soon after leaving Salt Lake City the country

becomes more and more hilly and mountainous, and monotonous barren brown country stretches on all sides. The railway then enters a valley, and runs beside a mountain stream, interesting and picturesque at this time of the year, when half frozen over—in one place a sheet of rough ice, in another a raging torrent, carrying young icebergs along on its crest.

Then we arrive at the *pièce de resistance* of the

THE CASTLE GATE.

grand scenery of Utah. The Castle Gate is a most appropriate name given to two peculiar walls of rock jutting out from the sides of the valley, as if to completely dam it up, but leaving a gateway in the middle to allow the river and railway to pass through into the wilds of the Rockies.

Soon after, a colliery is passed, where the train coals up, and the journey across the Rockies is then continued at an altitude of 6,000 to 7,000 feet. But there is not much of mountain scenery in the ordinary sense of the word ; it is all bleak, barren, uninteresting country, the term Rocky being truly appropriate, for there is but little else than rocks to be seen.

On awaking in the morning, we found ourselves descending a narrow cañon, on each side steep rocky hills of red sandstone, with a few stunted firs (all looking very suggestive of bears), and an icy raging torrent running alongside the line. Soon we approached the Royal Gorge, where the hills close in till they are mere precipices on each side, narrowing in till at last there is no room for both stream and railway, so the latter has to be carried by a ' flying bridge '—that is, a bridge supported by huge girders fixed transversely across the gorge from cliff to cliff. One can stand outside on the platform of the rear car to see the marvellous view of this gorge, with its rocky precipices rising some 1,000 feet into the sky ; it is certainly the grandest scene I witnessed in America. On rattles the train, and one is very glad to get back into the car out of the cold. Soon Canyon City is reached, with its numerous oil - wells, made manifest by a huge erection of wooden scaffolding over each ; and at Pueblo our easterly course is suddenly changed to almost north. A grand view of Pike's Peak now presents itself, and for miles we travel along a flat and barren plain, with the lofty snow-capped mountains away on our left.

27

On the whole, then, I was much disappointed
with the scenery of the Rockies. I am told we
passed some of the best bits by night, but that is
not much comfort. We went through very few
snow-sheds, these consisting simply of long barn-
like wooden sheds, substantially built, and looking
from the inside not unlike a well-ventilated tunnel.
Continually after this we passed numerous snow-
screens, which have the appearance of large bar-
hurdles, made with supports so as to slope over and
catch the drifting snow. They are portable, and

SNOW-SCREENS.

merely placed along in the fields—say fifty yards
from the edge of any cutting.

The ice-collecting is done in an interesting way.
The artificially-made ponds have a large wooden
storehouse on one side. Work is then commenced,
at the side farthest from this, with an ice-plough
drawn by a horse. This is an apparatus very like
an ordinary plough, with the share replaced by a
large-toothed saw. Thus is the ice sawn in strips
perhaps two feet wide, these again being sawn into
lengths with hand-saws. First a 'canal' has to
be cut right across the pond from the store-shed

to the other side, wide enough to float the pieces along. The square pieces of ice thus cut out are moved by means of a spiked pole, and shoved along the 'canal' to the store-shed, so that the whole of the ice on the pond is thus floated right up to the store.

The typical wild Red Indian, in feathers and scalps, is conspicuous by his absence in this sort of journey; but a good many of his poorer brethren, with wide-brimmed hats, long black hair smoothed over their ears, wrapped in gay-coloured blankets, were to be seen hovering around the stations (I mean 'depots'), or standing beside their wigwams on the side of the railway.

Denver, the capital of Colorado, is a fine young city. Only twenty years ago it was a small village of 4,500 inhabitants. Now it is a flourishing city of 160,000. It is well laid out in the ordinary rectangular style, and possesses many well-built edifices.

I arrived one intensely cold night. Everything seemed hard frozen, even including the air itself, which was full of minute specks of ice crystals only visible when flashing under the electric lights. Sledges were going rapidly to and fro, and everyone, wrapped up to the eyes, looked intensely uncomfortable. The large hall of the Windsor Hotel was crowded with people. It is usual in all American hotels to make the entrance-hall a place of public resort, where everyone can meet and discuss business, and on a very cold night like this it would seem almost a public necessity to have some large well-warmed place where people from outside could assemble. But it hardly adds to the comfort of those using the hotel for its more legitimate purpose.

Denver appears like a model of a city of the future, and recalls to one's mind such books as 'Looking Backwards.' The straight well-built streets are nothing so very peculiar, nor are the well-regulated cable-trams or electric lights; but where else is hot and cold air laid on to all the houses, so that in winter you can turn on a tap and get your room warmed, while in the stifling days of midsummer a current of cold, refreshing air can be generated without a punkah?

Why does not some enterprising individual lay on to London houses some of the pure country air from Hampstead or the Surrey Hills, warmed or cooled as required?

The old-fashioned scaffolding has quite gone out in Denver in building. Huge cranes are all that can be seen above the walls of the growing mansions.

I know not whether it is a sign of the times, but here are to be found an uncommon number of pawn-shops. It seems as if every other shop was one.

There is a grand opera house, a city hall, several fine churches, and a large State capitol is rapidly rising.

After leaving Denver the country is again flat and uninteresting, and now mostly under snow. The usual train life is continued. At intervals the 'conductor' looks at your ticket, and the newsboy brings new books, and the inevitable baby begins crying, which, by the way, was an event which came off in almost every car I travelled in in America.

Later on the country gets prettier, and is almost suggestive of English scenery. Various villages are passed—muddy, dirty-looking places for the most part, a sort of cross between a typical Australian and a typical Russian village. We arrive in time at the great town of Oxford, which apparently consists of about three or four good-sized houses.

The Missouri is crossed on a large iron bridge shortly before getting to St. Joseph, and after a few hours more the mighty Mississippi is also crossed. We passed by a newly laid-out town, or, rather, the site where a town is intended to come. The roads are all there, laid out in rectangles; trees are planted along the boulevards; wooden pavements, carefully made, enable one to stroll around the would-be city without getting one's feet wet in the damp grass (at least, I can see no other object in these neat-looking paths). Even shrubs are planted about to adorn the gardens of the future homes. But of buildings there are none.

I found Chicago just exactly what I had expected

to find it—a vast mass of huge buildings without any interest. Lake Michigan looks peculiar, being a fresh-water lake, yet stretching away to the horizon, and looking for all the world just like the familiar old sea, especially when you see the shipping of all kinds floating on its waters. The hotel I went to was huger than ever, but very dismal and badly lighted, the hall crowded and containing the book-stalls, telegraph-offices, barber's shop, etc., which are always set around the halls of American hotels.

The streets, as usual, were dirty and cabs expensive, though I *did* have the honour of an introduction to the gentleman who was about to possess himself of all the cabs in Chicago—a large order. Anxious to see how their great business buildings are 'worked,' I visited one. Streams of people going in and out remind one very much of a beehive, but having got safely through the ever-swinging glass-doors without getting your fingers crushed. the thing to do is to make straight for the elevator. There are two, one going up while the other comes down. As soon as one is down and the door opened, everybody—that is, as many as can do so—get in, and up it goes at a great pace, stopping at the various floors like a train does at a railway station. Arrived at the desired floor, you step out and take a walk around the passages, full of business offices of all kinds, and when you have had enough of that, you again make for the elevator and descend, no fare, of course, being collected.

Again we are in the train, passing docks, wharves, huge warehouses, and those parts of Chicago devoted to receiving and despatching its large trade. And soon we have passed the lake and all its belongings, and are speeding across Indiana on our way to the eastern coast.

Ohio is passed through, and Pennsylvania reached, and we find ourselves in the industrious, if dirty, town of Pittsburg. We now pass town after town, all so close together as to almost form one long city extending for many miles. Next an oil region is passed, with numerous oil-wells dotted about among the hills, with their pumping-engines— some, oddly enough, on the tops of hills, others in the bottoms of the valleys. In places we even see flames of gas coming straight out of the ground! From this we get to more picturesque parts : a fine swollen river dashes along the winding valley, which is enclosed with steep fir-clad hills. And we really have glimpses of scenery as fine in their way as anything we saw in the Rockies.

At length Harrisburg is reached, and here is the junction whence one can go to Washington or Philadelphia and New York.

The Pullman 'vestibule' train, known as the Pennsylvania Limited, which runs daily between Chicago and New York, professes to be the most perfectly fitted-up train in the world. Not only does it contain sleeping 'berths of spotless linen' (as the advertisement has it) and dining cars, but also 'a plunge bath for men, and a bath-room for women, daintily equipped' (which reads as though there was a bath for men without a place to have it in, and a room for 'women' without a bath!). There is also a barber's shop and 'a smoking-car with sofas and a cabinet, on which stand nargilis and vases of Doulton and Sèvres.' Besides libraries, there are 'writing-desks with linen paper that is free for the use of passengers.' And in addition to the usual attendants are a ladies'-maid, and 'stenographers and type-writers for the free use of passengers in conducting their correspondence. The stock quotations and financial news of the day is received and posted several times each day.' It all sounds well, but I think on the whole I prefer an ordinary English first-class carriage; at all events, for day travelling.

Washington is very unlike other American towns. It is cleaner, handsomer, and more picturesque than most others. Many of the streets are paved with asphalte, and planted with trees. The White House, the various Government offices, and, above all, the Capitol, are fine handsome buildings, well situated, and giving to the whole town an air of refinement so wanting in everything else in America. Then, again, the members of Congress and of the Senate, as well as of the various embassies and legations, impart quite an aristocratic air to the place. There is an excellent club, where I was entertained to a typical American dinner, with such luxuries as clam

chowder, a thick white soup of shell-fish ; terrapin, a
kind of small turtle cut in bits and stewed ; oyster
crabs, small crabs the size of peas, said to be found
inside the oyster-shells ; and several other peculiar
dishes.   I am very much afraid I did not give due
praise to any of these excellent dishes.   I believe
they fulfil the summit of ambition of an experienced
gourmet, but I am not a gourmet.

The Capitol is, as all the world knows, a splendid
building.   As a rustic critic designated one of
Millais's paintings ' an enlarged copy of that picture
in the *Graphic*,' so it may be said that the Capitol
at Washington is an enlargement of the one at
Sacramento.   I think, setting aside all associations,
and taking into consideration the situation, design,
and general effect, it is the finest building I have
seen (always excepting Windsor Castle).   The interior is, however, slightly disappointing.   The
chambers are large and well arranged, but low and
not imposing.   There is a huge central hall under
the dome, and numbers of corridors decorated with
numerous large oil-paintings of American historical
subjects.

The arrangements are much the same as at
Sacramento.   The galleries are open to the public
to hear the debates, and the members each have
their own desks, while pages run messages, and sit
and play between whiles on the Speaker's daïs.

Philadelphia is another not very exciting place.
It has a grand new city hall, but otherwise is very

like any other large town. In the smaller streets, as in many towns of the eastern States, the pavements are of red brick, giving almost a Dutch appearance to the older parts. I had the pleasure of dining with one of the leading men of the place in a most comfortable and luxurious style, not different in any very appreciable way from a good English dinner, and therefore very unlike the ordinary American hotel meal.

I also stayed in a country-house some miles out of Philadelphia. The arrangements and manner of living were the perfection of comfort, the house being fitted with all the latest improvements. Very good stabling was attached, and a large coach-house containing no less than eight carriages; but these consisted of a brougham, small kind of waggonette, hooded buggy, a 'buckboard,' dog-cart, chaise, another kind of buggy, and a sleigh.

Of New York I shall not say much—one might as well try to describe London. My first impressions were that it was very like parts of London. The good old gas-lamps of just the same pattern, and the older back-streets, are very like those at home. I went to the Fifth Avenue Hotel, but could not have been more uncomfortable in every way, so soon changed my quarters to a humbler, quieter, less railway-station-like place where I was better looked after.

There are several capital clubs, and the Knickerbocker, of which I was kindly made honorary member, is said to be the best.

Everybody has heard of New York's theatres. In the Madison Square Theatre they have a novel plan of scene-shifting ; the whole stage rises bodily, and beneath it is another stage with the next scene ready set, the original one being rearranged during the scene.

There are several 'armouries' belonging to the different regiments of National Guards—large buildings containing barrack-rooms and offices, many of which have a subterranean rifle-range of about 100 yards long, a capital idea for our volunteers, if not regulars, to imitate, as the man who can make himself thoroughly proficient at 100 yards requires very little practice to become a good shot at long range.

I returned home in the White Star steamer *Teutonic*, which I hear universally pronounced to be the finest ship afloat. It would indeed be hard to beat her in every way. She is said to have done her twenty-two knots, and is certainly the fastest of American liners, as well as one of the biggest. But it is in every detail of decoration and fitting that she is so perfect. No scamped work is there visible. Everything is clean, comfortable, and of the very best make. Artistic decorations meet the eye on every hand, and yet as a mechanical leviathan she is not to be beaten. But so great is the competition that probably ten years hence she may be eclipsed, superseded, and out of date!

Arrived at Queenstown, we were delayed some hours whilst our 900 bags of mails were lifted, each by one man, and carried to the edge to be lowered into the tender. I presume when these bags got ashore at Queenstown, each had again to be lifted up and taken to the train. The train on arrival at Kingstown would again require great labour to disgorge its 900 bags on to the mail steamer, and the same tedious process would have to be gone through at Holyhead. Does it not seem as if it would be quicker if the big steamer did not lose this time at Queenstown, but rushed on at her train-like speed straight to Liverpool, there to disgorge her precious cargo, much of which, I expect, is to remain in Liverpool or its neighbourhood? But I had a startling lesson of one reason why this would not always do. On arriving off the Mersey we came into a thick sea-fog; so thick did it become that we had to anchor. It was no mere delay of a few hours. Four-and-twenty hours did we wait, and for at least the greater part of that time an impatient crowd of seafaring passengers was to be seen restlessly pacing the deck in tall hats and black coats, with umbrellas and wraps in their hands, ready to land at any moment.

My journey is done! After an absence of just over three years I return to find but few changes.

I am delighted with the old country, and after all the brag of Australians, Americans, and others, after the magnificence of the East, the glories of the Indies, the wonders of the Antipodes, the curiosities of Savagedom, and the marvels of the great States, all I can do is to reiterate the very well-worn quotation, 'Be it ever so humble, there's no place like home.'

MILEAGE OF JOURNEY

———•◦•———

		English Statute Miles.
London to Constantinople	1,814	
Constantinople to Alexandria (*vid* Smyrna and Athens)	1,100	
Alexandria to Suez (*vid* Cairo)	240	
Suez to Colombo (sea)	3,412	
In Ceylon and India	850	
Colombo to Albany (sea)	3,390	
Albany to Adelaide (sea)	1,072	
Adelaide to Melbourne (sea)	570	
Melbourne to Sydney (sea)	658	
Sydney to Brisbane (sea)	520	
Journey to Australia	——	13,626
Brisbane to Sydney (sea)	520	
Sydney to Melbourne (land)	576	
Melbourne to Brisbane (land)	1,298	
Brisbane to Warwick and back (land)	466	
„ Toowoomba and back (land)	206	
„ Maryborough and back (sea)	320	
„ Bundaberg and back (sea)	415	
„ Cairns and back (sea)	2,012	
Townville to Hughenden and back (land)	450	
In Queensland	500	
Brisbane to Sydney and back (land)	1,444	
„ Sydney (sea)	520	
In New South Wales	220	
Brisbane to Cooktown (sea)	1,062	
Thursday Island to Brisbane (sea)	1,300	
In Australia	——	11,309
Carried forward ...		24,935

			English Statute Miles.
Brought forward ...			24,935
Cooktown to Samarai (sea)			492
Samarai to Chad's Bay and back (sea)			140
„ Port Moresby (sea)			262
Port Moresby to Motumotu (sea)			122
Motumotu to Murray Island (sea)			331
Murray Island to Thursday Island (sea)			152
In New Guinea ... ... ——			1,499
Thursday Island to Batavia (sea)			2,566
Batavia to Singapore (sea)			570
Singapore to Sarawak (sea)			432
In Sarawak			140
Sarawak to Batavia and Thursday Island (sea) ...			3,708
In Malaysia ... ... ——			7,416
Sydney to Auckland (sea)			1,315
In New Zealand			362
Auckland to Tonga (sea)			1,434
Tonga to Samoa (sea)			587
Apia to Tutuila and back (sea)			160
Samoa to Honolulu (sea)			2,659
Honolulu to San Francisco (sea)			2,450
In Polynesia ... ... ——			8,967
San Francisco to New York (land)			3,350
In California			295
New York to London			3,550
——			7,195
Grand total			50,012

(N.B.—As authorities vary, the above distances are not guaranteed absolutely correct.)

INDEX

———◦◦———

A.

ACHEEN, 230
Adelaide, 57
Aden, 30
Ægean Sea, 17, 19
Air, Hot or cold, 420
Albany, 53-56
Alexandria, 20
Alum, 304
Aloes, 18, 46, 313
Americanisms, 405
Ancell, Captain, Murder of, 148
Ancient remains, 21, 283, 333
Annexation, New Guinea, 129
    South Sea Isles, 339
Antimony, 257
Apia, 345, etc.
Argus pheasants, 251, 285
Armed forces: South Australia, 58
    Queensland, 90
    Dutch East Indies, 222
    Sarawak, 245
    Hawaii, 385
Athens, 18
Auckland, 288
Australia, Western, 51, etc.
    South, 56, etc.
Australians, Typical, 55, 58
    Aboriginal, 115-120, 147

B.

Baker, Rev. S , 322, 369, 372
Bamboo houses, 224, 228
    for water, 158
    -plant, 92
Banyan-trees, 45, 368
Barrier reef, 132, 196
Barron Falls, 124

Batavia, 210, etc.
Bear, Australian native, 81
'Bêche de mer,' 181
'Betel-nut,' 145, 252
Big trees, California, 412
Billiard-tables, 381
Birds of paradise, 144
Bird-nest caves, 261
Bird-nests for soup, 233
    weaver, 46
Blacks, Australian, 115, 120
Blue Mountains, 66
Boars, Wild, 163, 171, 285
Bones, Weak, 59
Boomerangs, 118, 119
Borneo, 243, etc.
Bosphorus, 12
Botany Bay, 63
Bottle-tree, 95
Bread-fruit, 143, 163, 369
Bridges, 228, 263
Brisbane, 85, etc.
British New Guinea, 129, etc.
Brooke, Sir J., 243
    Rajah, 244
Bucharest, 7
Buck-jumpers, 83
Buda-Pesth, 6
Buddha, 41
Buitenzorg, 223
Bulgaria, 10
Butterflies, 192

C.

Cairns, 132
Cairo, 21
Caltura, 35
Calliope, H.M.S., 345

28

Camels, 28
Cannibalism, 146, 186
Canoes, 32, 153, 164, 182, 206, 347
Capitol, Sacramento, 413
　　　Denver, 420
　　　Washington, 424
Carrington, Lord, 65
Cassowary, 80
Catamarans, 153, 172, 182
Caterpillars, Vegetable, 305
Cathedrals : Vienna, 3
　　　Singapore, 236
　　　Brisbane, 86
　　　Melbourne, 68
　　　Honolulu, 381
Cava, 334, 357, 364
Caves : Jenolan, 68
　　　Borneo, 261
　　　Tonga, 338
Cedercrantz, Baron, 352
Ceylon, 32, etc.
Chad's Bay, 148, 154
Chalmers, Mr., 202
Chameleons, 28, 263
Charters Towers, 113
Chicago, 421
Chief Justice of Samoa, 352
Chinatown, San Francisco, 396
Chinese in Australia, 95
　　　Borneo, 244
　　　Java, 213, 214, 224
　　　Johore, 239
　　　Singapore, 233
　　　San Francisco, 396
Chinese houses, 215, 396
Christmas, 193, 344
Churches, 55, 86, 198, 248, 330, 350, 377
Cinchona, 254, 285
Coal, 97, 266
Cockatoo, 193
Cocoanuts, 162, 163, 368
Coffee, 42, 239, 253, 283
Colombo, 32, 35
Constantinople, 13
Consulates, 329, 351
Convicts, 63, 92
Copra, 47, 331, 337
Cook, Captain 124, 320, 345
Cooktown, 124
Coral, 132, 180, 195
Corroboree, 120

Cotton-plant, 21, 47, 369
Crabs, Tree-climbing, 156
　　　Land-, 138
　　　King-, 239
Crocodiles, 196, 206, 246
Cuscus, 139, 152, 161, 192

D.

Damien, Father, 388
Danube, 6, 7, 9
Defence force, 58, 90
Defence of Australia, 52, 91
Denver, 419
'Dives' in San Francisco, 393
Dogs : Constantinople, 15
　　　Egypt, 24, 25
　　　New Guinea, 187
　　　Australian, 88
Druggist, Chinese, 400
Duck, 11, 80
Dugong, 121, 156
Dutch East Indies, 210, etc.
Dyaks, 243, 254, 268, 271, 274

E.

Egypt, 20, etc.
Elephantiasis, 145, 349
Elephants, White, 47
Emigrants, Hints to, 47

F.

'Fantan,' 240
Fever, 195, 207, 218, 225
Fight with natives, 177, 185
Fire, Watch-, 179
　　　-brigade, 404
　　　-escapes, 288
　　　-flies, 40, 274
Flags Sarawak, 250
　　　Samoan, 350, 356
　　　Hawaiian, 379
Flax, New Zealand, 293
Flying foxes, 38, 82
　　　squirrels, 193
Fortification, Maori, 290
　　　by Taboo, 162
Friendly Isles, 314
Frozen meat, 106
Fruit : Californian, 407
　　　Java, 220
　　　Queensland, 94
　　　Tonga, 331

G.

Gambling, 240, 403
Gems, 34, 37
Germans in Australia, 98
Geysers, 296, 301, 308, 310
Gold, 98-100, 108-110, 258
'Golden Gate,' 392
'Golden Horn,' 13
Gongs, Wooden, 340
    Chinese, 214
    Malay, 254
Government House, Brisbane, 87
    Auckland, 288
    Melbourne, 61
    Port Moresby, 197
    Singapore, 237
    Sydney, 64
    Ceylon, 41, 43
Governors, 61, 65, 127, 152, 236
Grandchester, 97
Grass-trees, 95
Greece, 18
Grey, Sir G., 289
Guards, Samoan, 354

H.

Haapai, 320, 336
Hailstones, 94
Hair-dye, 145
Harrier yacht, 202
Hawaii, 378
Holland, 2
Honolulu, 378, etc.
Hornbills, 143, 285
Horse-racing, 61, 89, 367
Horses, Wild, 311
    Australian, 55, 83
    Tonga, 333
Hotels, American, 393, 419, 422
    Ceylon, 34
    Del Monte, 410
    New Zealand, 288
Hot lakes, 296, 303
    springs, 296, 299
    baths, 297
Houses, Dyak, 268
    Australian, 54
    Hawaiian, 386
    Javanese, 224
    New Guinea, 141, 142
    Samoan, 349
    Tongan, 329, 337

Hughenden, 114
Hunting, 88
Hurricane in Samoa, 345
Hygeia, New Guinea yacht, 150

I.

Ice collecting, 418
Iguana, 80
India, 44, etc.
Interviews, 406
Iroquois, U.S.S., 370, 374

J.

Jackson, Peter, 287
Java, 210, etc.
    sparrows, 238
Javanese, 211, 226
Jewellers, Chinese, 401
Johore, 239
Joss-houses, 399

K.

Kanakas, 102, 105
Kangaroo, 81
Kauri gum, 290-292
Kea, 312
King George's Sound, 52
King of Hawaii, 382
    Samoa, 352
    Tonga, 341
Kiwi, 312
Krakatoa, 231
Kuching, 245

L.

Ladies on horseback, 382
Lakatoi, 199
Language, Chinese, 235
    New Guinea, 147, 180
    Samoan, 349
'Lava-lava,' 318, 348
Leprosy, 371, 388
Lick Observatory, 408
Lizards, 80, 263, 344, 368

M.

MacGregor, Sir W., 150, 152, 155, 190
Madura, 47
Malays, 211, 239
Malietoa, King, 352

Mangosteens, 37, 220
Mangroves, 169, 203, 246, 283
Maoris, 296, 298
Mariner, W., 320
Mars, 409
Maryborough, 100
Matang, 282
Melbourne, 60
' Mias,' 270, 278
Milne Bay, 188
Mines, Gold, 99, 113, 260
    Coal, 97, 267
    Antimony, 257
Missionaries, 188, 198, 202, 322,
    377
Mitylene, 17
Molokai, 388
Monkeys, 250, 274, 276
    Wanderoo, 38
    Wou-wou, 263
    Proboscis, 277
    Orang-utan, 278, 280, 284
Monte, Hotel del, 410
Monterey, 409
Moreton Bay, 85, 91
Mormons, 415
Mosquitoes, 281
Motumotu, 202
Mount Hamilton, 407
    Morgan, 108, 109
Murder of Captain Ancell, 148
Murray Island, 207, 208
Musgrave, Sir A., 127
    Mr. A., 196

N.

Naval officers, American, 376
    English, 379
    German, 361
Navigators' Isles, 345, etc.
Navy, Queensland, 91
Neptune, 50
Neutrality, Tongan, 322
New Guinea, 129, etc.
    houses, 142
    natives, 144, 165, 199, 203
New South Wales, 63, etc.
New York, 426
New Zealand, 287, etc.
Nile, 26-28
Norman, Sir H., 65, 127
Nukualofa, 316
Nuwara Eliya, 41, 43

O.

Oahu, 378
Oil-wells, 423
Oranges, 94, 331, 343
Orang-utan, 270, 274, 278
Orchids, 260, 264, 273
Owyhee, 378

P.

Paddy, 37, 223, 228
Pademelon, 81
Pago Pago, 377
Palms : Areca, 252
    Betel-nut, 143, 252
    Cocoanut, 143, 162, 163, 196,
        316, 331, 368
    Date, 21, 368
    Nipa, 246
    Palmyra, 45
    Talipot, 40
    Sago, 143, 254
Pandanus, 143
Papua, 132
Papuans, 144, 165, 199
Parkes, Sir H., 66
Parliament Houses :
    Honolulu, 384
    New Guinea native, 161
    New South Wales, 65
    Queensland, 86
    Sacramento, 413
    Samoa, 350, 356
    Victoria, 61
    Washington, 425
Parrots, 82, 145, 192-194
Pearls, 126
Pearl-shell, 125, 195
Pepper, 253
Performances : Chinese, 398
    Dyak, 254
    Java, 214, 222
    Samoa, 366
Philadelphia, 425
Pigeon-English, 105, 158
Pike's Peak, 417
Pitcher-plant, 269
Platypus, 82
Police : American, 395, 404
    Egyptian, 22
    New Guinea, 155, 173
    Queensland, 91
    Samoan, 361
    Sarawak, 261

CPSIA information can be obtained at www.ICGtesting.com
Printed in the USA

240165LV00008B/23/P